M000251985

# The Rise and Fall
# of the Christian Coalition

# The Rise and Fall
# of the Christian Coalition

*The Inside Story*

JOEL D. VAUGHAN

RESOURCE *Publications* · Eugene, Oregon

THE RISE AND FALL OF THE CHRISTIAN COALITION
The Inside Story

Copyright © 2009 Joel D. Vaughan. All rights reserved. Except for brief quotations in critical publications or reviews, no part of this book may be reproduced in any manner without prior written permission from the publisher. Write: Permissions, Wipf and Stock Publishers, 199 W. 8th Ave., Suite 3, Eugene, OR 97401.

Resource Publications
A division of Wipf and Stock Publishers
199 W. 8th Ave., Suite 3
Eugene, OR 97401

www.wipfandstock.com

ISBN 13: 978-1-60608-580-6

Manufactured in the U.S.A.

Scripture taken from the New King James Version, © 1979, 1980, 1982 by Thomas Nelson, Inc. Used by permission. All rights reserved.

*Dedication*

*To the state directors, chapter chairmen,*
*and local activists of the Christian Coalition 1989–1999.*
*It was an honor to serve you.*

# Contents

# Introduction

"JOEL, YOU SHOULD WRITE a book," they would often say after I had finished telling an anecdote about a particular Christian Coalition event or about my experiences with its founders, Pat Robertson and Ralph Reed. My standard reply was, "No, I would never do that." My opinion was that only the characteristic "kiss-and-tell" book would be mass-marketable and get the attention of Beltway politicians and pundits. I was not interested in being involved with such a book. God would not honor the effort.

I do not approve of "tell-all" books, many of which are nothing more than a series of quotes taken out of context and strung together in order to detract from a public figure. As a rule, people who are fortunate enough to be included in the inner circle of a leader, whatever the arena, should not divulge privileged information they learn while there. In fact, in a meeting over coffee, a representative from a well-known publisher told me he had serious interest in this book until he began reading and realized it was *not* going to be a negative exposé on Pat Robertson.

From a historical point of view, I was in a position to detail the inner workings of the Christian Coalition. Having been there at the inception in 1989 and leaving just under ten years later, I witnessed more than anyone and played a role in much that occurred. Beginning as a volunteer during the organization's infancy, I became a full-time staff member in 1991, serving over six years as assistant to the national field director and then deputy field director. In 1998, I was promoted to the dual positions of assistant to the president and director of administration.

No other individual was on the inside, both as often and as long. A few were of higher position at times and, therefore, might know more inside details from the time in which they were there, but none of those were with the Coalition long enough to accumulate a true historical perspective. Likewise, a few were with the organization slightly longer than I, but they worked in clerical positions, without having the opportunity to go into the field and work on political projects and events. This meant, most notably, that they had not worked closely with Executive Director Ralph Reed.

When Ralph autographed my copy of his first book, *Politically Incorrect,* he began the inscription, "To Joel—To think that you were present at creation!" I had first met Ralph in 1989 on the very first day he arrived in Virginia to start Christian Coalition. He even slept on the couch in my apartment for a couple of nights as he looked for permanent housing for his family who were still in Georgia. And Ralph never forgot those early days. In mid 1998, upon visiting the Coalition's headquarters approximately one year after departing as its executive director, Ralph was overheard to say jokingly, "Joel was here when I came. He was here when I left. And he'll be here when I'm dead."[1]

"But would anyone buy a book containing a *favorable* view of Christian Coalition?" I kept asking myself. Nonetheless, in 1999, as I read George Stephanopoulos's book, *All Too Human,* which chronicled his years of working for candidate and President Bill Clinton, I could not help thinking, "I could do that."

Another benefit from reading Stephanopoulos's book was that it provided me with a review of many political happenings during the time he worked in the Clinton White House, which coincided with most of my time at Christian Coalition. He detailed many of the programs and issues supported by the Clinton Administration, which refreshed my memory about Christian Coalition's activities due to the fact that, whatever they were fighting for, we were fighting against, and whatever they were fighting against . . . well, you get the point.

With the unfortunate and tumultuous downfall in the Coalition's fortunes that began in early 1999 due to leadership changes, staff departures, and declining revenue, it became apparent that a positive, yet frank, account of the group's history was called for. I even received input from the academic community that I had a *duty* to write about the Christian Coalition so that its activities would not be forgotten.

It was important that I begin while the details were still fresh in my mind. So, later that year, I began scribbling down notes on a yellow legal pad that I kept beside my bed, and dictating into a micro-cassette recorder that soon replaced the legal pad on my nightstand.

## Introduction

My two-fold purpose in writing is, first, to give an accurate history* of the organization that can be useful to other non-profit groups, and utilized by professors and students seeking to study the pro-family movement. Second, I want the reader to perceive what it was like to be at the Christian Coalition during each year in question; therefore much of the narrative of the early and middle years will be quite sanguine, while other portions, the late years, will portray a sense of regret and misfortune.

Christian Coalition's fall was not the result of the decisions, actions, or mistakes of any one person, just as its ascent was due to the work and talents of many. These pages neither cast blame nor laud praise. Further, I attempt to editorialize as little as possible, only reporting events as they happened and words as they were spoken, in order to showcase the true spirit of Christian Coalition, highlight the personalities of the main characters, and explain the factors that contributed to the organization's downfall.

My view of the participants, particularly of Pat Robertson and Ralph Reed, is written out of the perspective and emotion I felt at the time when the events of each respective chapter actually occurred. The reader may notice, therefore, somewhat of a maturation in my perspective as the material progresses. I was only twenty-four when I first began my association with Pat Robertson as a Regent University student and almost thirty-nine when I left the Coalition.

Just as Christian Coalition was both a political and a religious organization—I often called it a political organization made up of religious people—this book will be both a political and a religious book; one man's observance of the rise and fall of what was arguably the most effective and fastest-growing American political organization of the late twentieth century. I hope you enjoy this account of the Christian Coalition, living its motto of *giving Christians a voice in their government again*—written by one who was *present at creation*.

Joel D. Vaughan
Colorado Springs, Colorado

---

* I have become weary of articles and books written by—and quoting—"experts" on the Christian Coalition, including grossly inaccurate "facts," such as that there once were as many as fourteen lobbyists in the Capitol Hill office, while in reality, the most lobbyists ever employed in the D.C. office at one time was four or five.

# A Presidential Campaign Story

## *Bush vs. McCain vs. Robertson\**

THE FIELD FOR THE Republican Party's nomination for president in 2000 was crowded to say the least. Texas Governor George W. Bush and publisher Steve Forbes fought closely for the early spending battle, and were joined by a host of others, including former Vice President Dan Quayle, former Cabinet secretary Elizabeth Dole, television commentator Pat Buchanan, former Tennessee Governor Lamar Alexander, U.S. Senator Orrin Hatch of Utah, former UN ambassador Alan Keyes, and former Family Research Council head Gary Bauer. These candidates competed in the attention-getting Ames (Iowa) Straw Poll in August, 1999, before the primaries and caucuses were to begin the following January. Bush won the straw poll by garnering 31 percent of the votes, defeating Forbes by ten percentage points and Dole by seventeen, with the also-rans scoring in single digits.

One candidate who decided to skip the Iowa straw poll was Arizona U.S. Senator and Viet Nam war hero John McCain, who lay low early on, foregoing campaigning for the official Iowa caucuses the following January, which were won by Bush, followed by Forbes, Keyes, Bauer, McCain, and Hatch in that order, with the rest having dropped out by the time the caucuses rolled around.

McCain, however, roared back to a resounding win in the next big contest, the New Hampshire primary, picking up the most of that state's

---

* This chapter takes no account of the eventual nomination of Sen. John McCain as the 2008 Republican Party nominee. Similarly, the chapter was written prior to the 2007 death of the Rev. Jerry Falwell. Other individuals mentioned in this book have since died as well. Likewise, several events and pieces of legislation referenced in the past tense in may have returned to the political stage.

delegates to the July 31–August 3 Republican National Convention in Philadelphia. Bush came in second in New Hampshire, and within a few weeks, only he and McCain were left as viable candidates, the others dropping out. From the time the modern primary process began until the 2000 primaries, no Republican, and only one Democrat, Bill Clinton, had been elected president without winning the first-in-the-nation New Hampshire primary. Therefore, McCain's win made him quite formidable.

Bush bounced back strong from New Hampshire, winning the South Carolina primary on February 18. South Carolina, in the Bible belt with its conservative voting patterns, had promised to be a "firewall" for Bush after losing New Hampshire. Four years earlier, strong support from Christian voters in general—and alleged support by the Christian Coalition in particular—had provided similar fortification for the eventual 1996 GOP nominee, Senator Bob Dole of Kansas, over Pat Buchanan.

Conventional wisdom said that if Bush won South Carolina in 2000, he would likely win the rest of the Southern states two weeks later, putting a virtual end to McCain's candidacy. But McCain pulled off an upset win in Michigan only three days after losing in South Carolina, which made it an entirely new ballgame, toppling Bush's momentum and leaving him struggling to hold on to the title of frontrunner. McCain's post-Michigan euphoria was short-lived, however, as on March 9 he announced the suspension of his campaign, admitting that Bush had won the battle for the nomination.

Why did it all fall apart for McCain so quickly in 2000? For the answer, we must look to the Commonwealth of Virginia, Tuesday, February 29, where just one week after his victory in Michigan, McCain's campaign was dealt a death knell, with the candidate himself inflicting the fatal blow. With McCain grabbing the momentum by winning New Hampshire and Michigan, the outcome of the Virginia primary would have a much weightier effect on the entire process than could have been imagined when Republican leaders in the Commonwealth voted to abandon their customary practice of voting for a presidential nominee through a caucus system. A speech by Senator McCain on the eve of the vote in Virginia provided added drama and proved to be the turning point in the entire Republican presidential nomination, when he traveled to the resort city of Virginia Beach for a rally at a local high school. There he chose to make a very personal attack on a particular and prominent Virginia Beach resident, Christian broadcaster and Christian Coalition founder

Pat Robertson, as well as on the Reverend Jerry Falwell, whose base was just a few hours up U.S. Highway 460 in Lynchburg.

Just as Virginia had been the birthplace of the land that would become the United States almost 400 years earlier, it also was the birthplace of the modern Christian conservative political movement. Falwell, founder of the Moral Majority, had been the most prominent leader nationally of religious conservative voters in the decade of the 1980s, and Robertson, with his own presidential campaign in 1988 and his founding of the Christian Coalition the following year, had been his successor. Before the Virginia primary, Greg Mueller, a spokesman for numerous conservative candidates and causes, told the *Chicago Tribune*, "The Christian conservative movement is one that Pat Robertson has built by and large."[1]

Mueller's statement discounted somewhat the enormous contributions of other Christian leaders, men such as Falwell, Dr. James Dobson, and Florida pastor Dr. D. James Kennedy, along with women like Phyllis Schlafly and Beverly LaHaye, each founding a grassroots organization of their own. But whereas Falwell got Christians off their couches and into the voting booths in the early to mid 1980s, and Dobson, to the halls of Congress through his calls for activism on his *Focus on the Family* daily radio broadcast, it was Robertson who, with his 1988 presidential candidacy and, later, the Christian Coalition, transformed them into precinct workers and party leaders, and trained them to run for office themselves, many of whom did so to great success.

McCain's 2000 diatribe against Falwell and, particularly, against Robertson was a shot heard round the political world and was trumpeted in Robertson's hometown newspaper, *The Virginian-Pilot*, the next day: "Neither party should be defined by pandering to the outer reaches of American politics and the agents of intolerance, whether they be Louis Farrakhan or Al Sharpton on the left, or Pat Robertson and Jerry Falwell on the right," McCain said, adding that he represented "the Republican Party of Ronald Reagan, not Pat Robertson."[2] As McCain spoke, he smiled like the cat about to swallow the canary and gave an oddly timed "thumbs-up" signal that he seemed to think the crowd was waiting for. Even after suspending his campaign, he was unrepentant, telling CNN's Larry King, "I would not change a word."[3]

McCain's tactics in Virginia were very surprising to most—although if headlines were his goal, he certainly got them. Pundits felt McCain's words were targeted for an impact beyond Virginia; that his strategy was to forfeit to some extent the votes of conservative Christians in Virginia in order to court moderate voters in upcoming primary states like New York. And some were almost giddy. *Boston Globe* writer David Nyhan wrote that McCain's speech in Virginia Beach possibly set the stage for bigger things: "It was the highest stakes speech of the campaign to date, and with it John McCain carved out a slot in our nation's political history, never mind what happens with election results."[4]

Robertson had done his part, to say the least, in provoking McCain's ire in primary states leading up to Virginia, having authorized thousands of automated calls featuring a recorded message from him to his own supporters in Michigan, and making personal phone calls into South Carolina to Christian Coalition supporters and others across the state. The Michigan calls raised the most dust, becoming the topic of political talk shows before and after the vote was held, due to the fact that Robertson severely criticized McCain campaign chairman and former U.S. Senator Warren Rudman, who had made what Robertson felt were degrading and bigoted remarks about religious conservative voters.

Two days before the Virginia primary, the *Chicago Tribune* reported, "[T]he most visible figure of the Christian [R]ight made his presence felt in the South Carolina and Michigan primaries on behalf of Bush."[5] On a Sunday news program a few weeks earlier, Robertson said that if McCain won the GOP nomination, the Christian Coalition might refrain from distributing its voter guides in November. Although, McCain likely would not have cared if the voter guides had not gone out, considering that a campaign finance reform bill he cosponsored at the time, along with Democrat Senator Russ Feingold of Wisconsin, would inhibit citizen groups from representing their members in the public square. The "McCain-Feingold" bill—later passed and signed into law as the *Bipartisan Campaign Reform Act of 2002*†—was an assault on the First Amendment guarantee of freedom of speech, in this case, political speech. If *Senator* McCain endangered Christian Coalition's voter education programs, would *nominee* McCain be any friendlier? And what about *President* McCain?

Conservative pundit Tucker Carlson, who rode on McCain's campaign bus, the Straight Talk Express, wrote an article for *The Weekly Standard* stating that on the campaign trail in 2000 McCain used

---

† BCRA has seen many of its tenets challenged and overturned in Federal court.

Democrat jargon in referring to the Christian Right as the "extreme right" and to a particular group of Christians in South Carolina as the "bunch of idiots."[6] Not incidentally, McCain was the only Republican candidate who turned down the invitation to address Christian Coalition's annual Road to Victory conference the year prior to the primaries. Carlson also offered an explanation of McCain's attack on Falwell and Robertson. Evidently, McCain blamed Christian activists with spreading rumors of his wife's alleged drug addiction.

As for the Virginia Beach speech, McCain's willingness to pick a fight with a lion in his own part of the jungle may have resulted because he believed his support among Christians to be stronger than it was. Just days before the South Carolina primary he had landed the endorsement of another prominent leader of Christian conservatives, recent drop-out candidate Gary Bauer, which sent strong signals that McCain was making an all-out attempt at swiping away the votes of religious conservatives from Bush, who had been endorsed by Robertson and had hired former Christian Coalition Executive Director Ralph Reed as one of his consultants.

Bauer's motives possibly were more personal, as he may have sought to distance himself from Robertson and Reed. Earlier, Robertson had been somewhat critical of Bauer's candidacy, even saying that Bauer, when asked by Robertson in a private meeting, could not state his reasons for running.[7] And there was a history of a sibling-like rivalry between Bauer and Reed, at a time leaders of the two most prominent religious conservative political organizations, who often competed for media attention.

During CNN's *Inside Politics'* coverage of Bauer's endorsement of McCain, Tucker Carlson said that Bauer had been telling people that he thought both Robertson and Reed had been too critical of McCain's record.[8] The same evening, Bauer appeared on two successive MSNBC television talk shows, and on each he warned that his endorsement of McCain would not necessarily bring Christians into the camp. "People don't care who Gary Bauer supports. They don't care who Pat Robertson or Ralph Reed support,"[9] he said, in what seemed to be a veiled instruction to Christian voters that the endorsements of Robertson and Reed did not mean that they, likewise, should go with Bush.

Grassroots activists were quite displeased with Bauer's endorsement of McCain. According to a receptionist at Christian Coalition, on the day Bauer endorsed McCain phones at the Coalition's Chesapeake, Virginia, headquarters rang off the hook, with more than 180 calls, mostly from outraged Christians who mistakenly thought Bauer represented Christian Coalition,[10] making it the busiest day in months for the virtually dormant organization.

February 29, a day that comes around only once in four years, seems ripe for phenomenal occurrences, and the political year 2000 was no exception. When voters in Virginia began going to the polls at six o'clock in the morning until the polls closed at seven that night, thousands upon thousands voted for George W. Bush. CNN exit polls showed that 83 percent of self-identified religious conservative voters in Virginia voted for the future president.

And the impact was felt beyond the Old Dominion, as just one week later, Bush won the large majority of the Super Tuesday primaries, including the two states with the most delegates to offer, California and New York, where John McCain had been given a more than legitimate chance to win, leaving his campaign—not bruised, not wounded, but dead. The response by religious conservatives in states with primaries held after McCain's Virginia Beach attack on Robertson and Falwell had been a huge determining factor. CNN's Bill Schneider reported that on Super Tuesday Bush won each and every state where religious conservatives composed at least 15 percent of the Republican vote.[11] On the same program, Jeff Greenfield concluded, "McCain's attack energized the core of faith-based conservatives."[12] Beginning in Virginia and continuing through Super Tuesday, the McCain campaign suffered a death of unmistakable proportions and it came at the hands of Christian voters.

McCain's strategy had backfired, with his attack on Robertson and Falwell being taken personally by their supporters, motivating them to vote against McCain, and giving many other conservative voters a very negative impression of the senator. He not only lost Christian voters in droves, but the harshness with which he criticized Robertson and Falwell, even referring to them the day after his Virginia Beach speech as "forces of evil,"[13]‡ cost him the votes of many, including many women, who otherwise might have supported his message. He exhibited "a strident tone that turned off a number of women voters," said CNN reporter Candy Crowley.[14]

‡ *World* magazine added that McCain later called the "forces of evil" remark "an attempt at humor."

Reagan education secretary William Bennett, who had said earlier that McCain was more viable than Bush, wrote in *The Wall Street Journal* that McCain's remarks against Robertson and Falwell were "highly intemperate and wildly misdirected."[15] He continued: "The blast against Messrs. Robertson and Falwell is the worst manifestation of an emerging pattern with Mr. McCain . . . He is attempting, quite literally, in the most recent case, to demonize his opponents. That has no place in American political discourse."[16]

McCain's strategy baffled many in the media as well, many of whom had previously been on his bandwagon unlike any Republican candidate in recent memory, as exemplified by Carlson's assertion in his *Weekly Standard* article that employees of major news organizations often "slipp[ed] into the habit of referring to the McCain campaign as 'we'—as in, 'I hope we kill Bush.'"[17] *The Washington Post's* Charles Krauthammer wondered:

> Why did McCain commit hara-kiri, gratuitously throwing away a quarter of the Republican electorate with his attack on the Christian [R]ight? It was not tactical—he forfeited the support of social conservatives while gaining nothing in the center. (In Ohio and California, those who found McCain's views of the religious right important voted 8 to 1 against him.) It was personal. McCain made the cardinal mistake of any presidential candidate. In politics as in the Mafia, there is business and there is personal. McCain could not make the distinction. The one essential quality of winning candidates is discipline. [18]

As I watched television clips of a beaming Pat Robertson answering reporters' questions on the night of Super Tuesday, I knew that he was delighted that Christian voters had played such a pivotal role in the primaries. "I think [McCain has] energized the religious base in a way that George Bush couldn't possibly have done,"[19] Robertson said on CNN's Super Tuesday election night coverage. "I was just frankly astounded when I heard about what the senator had said,"[20] he continued.

Robertson then countered McCain's criticism of him and his place in the GOP by pointing out that, beginning in 1997, for the first time since Reconstruction, Republicans controlled both houses of the Virginia legislature as well as the governorship, indicating that he personally had spent over $500,000 of his own resources to bring that about. "We've worked like beavers for the last few years here in Virginia and in other states," he continued, and then credited Christian Coalition and its pro-family allies with the 1994 GOP takeover of Congress. "There wouldn't have been a Chairman McCain of the (U.S. Senate) Commerce Committee if it hadn't been for us," he added.[21]

Robertson's calls into Michigan and comments naming Rudman had been quite strident,[22] and the Bush campaign—even Bush, himself—quickly scrambled to say they had nothing to do with the calls. Robertson's criticisms of the Bauer candidacy had been strong, and even he admitted that he had gone too far in his criticisms of McCain's qualifications to be president. "I basically said a few harsh things . . . and I later regretted it,"[23] he told CNN's Robert Novak and Al Hunt on their Saturday program. Months later, just prior to the Republican National Convention in Philadelphia, Pat Robertson wrote to McCain expressing regret for their mutual contempt, asking McCain's forgiveness for any "hard words" that he, Robertson, had spoken about him. "He blasted me hard and I forgive him . . . And I hope that he will do the same thing,"[24] Robertson told the CNN duo.

President Harry Truman said, "If you can't stand the heat, get out of the kitchen." Pat Robertson likes the heat just fine, which brings him even more opposition. John McCain, however, crossed the line, and he paid the price. To make matters even worse for McCain, the Christian broadcaster was on a charitable medical mission in Mexico on the day McCain was in Virginia Beach attacking him.[25] The timing of the mission was poetic.

Christian Coalition, Robertson's grassroots political organization, at the time was twelve months into the process of abdicating its heavyweight role in conservative politics that it had enjoyed for almost a decade. Due to leadership changes, financial difficulties, and staff departures, the previous year had seen a steep decline in the group's political power. Yet, Pat Robertson was determined to do whatever he personally could do. As far as the primaries were concerned, he played a far greater personal role in 2000 than in 1996 or 1992, motivating the activists directly, relying on his own voice coming over the phone in states like Michigan, South Carolina, and Virginia.

During the fallout of his exchange of salvos with McCain, CNN's Judy Woodruff called Pat Robertson "The man who has become a *big* factor in the Republican race for president this year."[26] William Neikirk of the *Chicago Tribune* wrote: "Members of Congress, political experts and academics . . . said that despite the Christian Coalition's financial and staff troubles, they expect Robertson will seek to use the force of his personality to turn out religious conservatives for Bush in the primaries and the general election."[27] But that was Pat Robertson acting personally for the most part, rather than through an organized Christian Coalition apparatus of local chapters as had been the practice in 1992 and 1996.

The beleaguered Coalition's efforts during the 2000 South Carolina primary consisted mainly of the already stated personal phone calls made to activists in the state by Robertson, as well as by South Carolina Christian Coalition State Chairman (and national executive vice president) Roberta Combs, and by Ralph Reed. *The Arizona Republic* quoted Bill Dal Col, Steve Forbes's former presidential campaign manager, as saying that South Carolina Forbes supporters received calls from one of the three in days leading up to the primary, encouraging support for Bush over McCain.[28] Forbes dropped out of the race well before the campaign calendar reached South Carolina, but a Christian Coalition state board member had been Forbes's volunteer coordinator in the state and may have had access to the list.

South Carolina previously had been a cauldron of contention among Republican voters, especially in presidential primaries, with 2000 being no exception. And each time, right in the center of the controversy were Robertson and his top lieutenant in the state, Combs, whom he also gave control of his national organization in early 1999.

For example, in the 1996 primary season South Carolinians witnessed a separate contest within the actual presidential primary between camps led by the two conservative Pats, Robertson and Buchanan, which was the latest round in a feud going back to 1992 when the commentator made a primary challenge to sitting President George H. W. Bush much to Robertson's displeasure. In 1996, Buchanan blamed Christian Coalition for unfairly rigging a Columbia, South Carolina, rally for his opponent, Senator Bob Dole, a complaint that cost the Coalition national grassroots support and goodwill among Buchanan supporters. According to Nina Easton in her 2000 book, *Gang of Five*, Dole's handlers accepted the Coalition's invitation to speak at the rally only after his supporters were allowed in the hall early so they could take the best seats.[§] Dole won

---

§ In fact, it was the only rally put on by one of the Coalition's state affiliates that year at which the senator accepted the invitation to appear. He was invited to all, yet went only to South Carolina.

the primary while Pat Robertson, the media, and Buchanan's camp, gave credit to Christian Coalition.[29]

In late 1999, a *St. Petersburg (FL) Times* article about Christian Coalition included an account of the decline of its national profile, along with examples of Combs's political activities in her home state. "[W]ithin South Carolina political circles, her flamboyance is legendary,"[30] the *Times* reported. According to the article, Combs had broken ranks with Republican leaders across the board, from others in the pro-family camp, to former Governor Carroll Campbell, in order to accomplish her own objectives—and Pat Robertson's—in the Palmetto State.[31] Of course, the national Christian Coalition had never been afraid of hardball politics; and much of the criticism against Combs and the group's efforts in South Carolina came from adversaries of her political activities. Combs, an effective motivator when on the phone with precinct activists, definitely had an impact. Nevertheless, her organization, both nationally and locally, was running on fumes by the time of the presidential primaries in 2000. Furman University political scientist James Guth told *The Washington Post* that by the arrival of the 2000 primary the South Carolina Christian Coalition was "moribund."[32]

What brought the Christian Coalition to this point? The answers lie ahead.

2

# A New Face in Town

W E'RE GOING TO HAVE to wear ties next week," I told Fred Shafer, treasurer of what remained of Americans for Robertson (AFR), Pat Robertson's presidential campaign committee, one late summer day in 1989. Fred, one computer operator, and I were the final three employees of the campaign that had taken American politics by storm in 1988. "Joel, I haven't worn *socks* since May," Fred answered. Our casual office attire, consisting of polo shirts, khakis, and Top Siders boat shoes, was a by-product of spending lonely days at 2127 Smith Avenue, a suburban Chesapeake, Virginia, warehouse/office building, as we worked toward the retirement of the remaining campaign debt.

The reason for our change in dress code the coming week was that we were expecting the arrival of an additional person to share our corner office in the cement structure. A few days earlier, someone from Pat's* office at CBN had phoned to say that "Ralph Reed" would be arriving soon to start the new organization. Neither Fred nor I were familiar with that name as we waited to meet our new office mate.

To describe Fred's and my first impressions of Ralph Eugene Reed, Jr., I'll rely on an introduction once given by Tom Scott, founding chairman of the Coalition's Florida state affiliate. In 1992, Tom was asked to introduce Pat Robertson to a banquet audience at the group's second annual Road to Victory national conference, but he began with the story of his first meeting with Ralph, which happened at the Orlando airport. Tom said he waited at the gate as one by one several men in business

---

* Students and professors at Regent University most often call Pat Robertson, "Dr. Robertson," as an indication of his status as the school's chancellor. He has a juris doctorate from Yale and an honorary doctorate in theology from Oral Roberts University. But due to the familiarity of television and the fact that his co-hosts have always called him "Pat" on the air, to virtually everyone else he is just "Pat."

suits walked down the jet-way; but there was no one who appeared to be Ralph. "People are coming off . . . I don't see Ralph Reed. There *is* this *child* standing off to the side . . ."[1] Tom said, as the crowd erupted in laughter.

Suffice it to say that Ralph's youthful appearance belied the shrewd political mind that lay beneath. In those early days, in both attitude and in philosophy, Ralph was not unlike the teenage character Alex P. Keaton as portrayed by actor Michael J. Fox on the popular 1980s NBC sitcom *Family Ties*. He knew what he wanted to do and how to get it done. And he had a decisive game plan from day one. In fact, his mother, when asked by a reporter from the *London Guardian* what Ralph always wanted to be when he grew up, answered, "In charge."[2]

I knew that Pat was planning to start a new organization to provide a vehicle for him and for the hundreds of thousands of new voters his campaign had brought to the political arena. The new venture would be a "501(c)(4)" organization, the Internal Revenue Service's designation for tax-exempt (meaning revenues are not taxed) groups called "social welfare" organizations, which may spend a majority of resources on non-partisan "lobbying" activities: educating voters on issues and encouraging those voters to contact their representatives in government, as well as a somewhat less amount of organizational direct contact with the legislators themselves. To contrast, "501(c)(3)" classification denotes "charities" that are educational, religious, fraternal, or service-based in nature and designated by the IRS as "tax deductible" (meaning donors may receive income tax deductions for their contributions).

After the call from Pat's office, I phoned Allan Sutherlin, the final campaign manager for AFR, who was working out of his business office in Indianapolis, to let him know that Ralph Reed was coming to start the new group. "Who is Ralph Reed?" he asked. Allan and I had discussed the fact that Pat was planning to start a new organization; but in his own inimitable way, Pat had gone outside the likely choices to find someone in whom to entrust leadership.

As I often heard Ralph tell the story, the two had met when they sat beside each other at a dinner in honor of President George H. W. Bush's inauguration in 1989. They discussed the political landscape and what should happen next to keep the conservative movement alive and growing. Pat told Ralph about the new 501(c)(4) organization he was planning to start and was so impressed with Ralph's political acumen that, after dinner, he suggested they step back through the curtain into the kitchen, at which time he offered Ralph the job of getting it off the ground. Years later, Ralph joked to a CBN chapel audience that he had since learned "that's how everyone at CBN got their job."[3] My experience was that Pat placed high value on first impressions, as he did with Ralph. Sometimes he was wrong, but in Ralph's case, his intuition and what he surely felt as God's leading, was right on.

Ralph turned Pat down that night, as his immediate plans were to complete his PhD and begin a teaching career. Pat asked if he, at least, would compose a memo for him, outlining what such a grassroots organization would look like and how it would operate. Ralph went back home to Atlanta and soon mailed or faxed the memo to Pat. Then, he heard absolutely nothing for several months, until later that summer when Pat called to again offer him the job of starting Christian Coalition. His PhD in hand, this time, Ralph accepted.

Ralph's doctorate in American history would provide invaluable facts and information that would help make him such a formidable debater and interviewee during his political career. I remember an article about him years later, which lauded his knowledge of facts and trivia. The writer pointed out that Ralph often made jokes during his speeches that were so esoteric in nature they were understood only by the reporters in the room.

A few days after Ralph arrived, I realized that he would soon be in charge of disposing of the presidential campaign files and warned him about a small, two-drawer, white filing cabinet, which contained the confidential correspondence held by Pat's personal secretary, Glenda Yon.[†] I encouraged Ralph to always keep that cabinet in the utmost confidence and security. True to his historian's education, he countered that for history's sake papers like that should be preserved for posterity, not hidden away in secrecy.[‡] And in keeping with the same spirit, he took very few, if any, papers with him when he left Christian Coalition in 1997.

I had little interest in working for the new organization, for several reasons. First, I felt that the new "lobby group," as Ralph referred to the Coalition, needed fresh blood, not campaign holdovers. Second, the new organization showed little promise of succeeding. A significant part of the

† Pat's secretary at Americans for Robertson, not to be confused with his long-time executive assistant at CBN, Barbara Johnson.

‡ This statement by Ralph helped embolden me to write this book about the Coalition.

remaining campaign debt was owed to former campaign workers across the country, the very individuals who would be needed to organize the new venture. There was no money to pay them, much less start a new group. Ralph encountered that sentiment when he began holding informational meetings around the country. Further, Pat had made an unsuccessful attempt to start a political action committee after dropping out of the presidential race, and I did not see how the Coalition could fare any better. Finally, to one who had worked on the presidential campaign, the yet unnamed group held little luster.

But I did not understand then what I was to experience with emphasis over the next eight years: the determination and resolve of Ralph Reed. He simply did not know the meaning of the word "failure." Like biblical Joshua and Caleb over 3,000 years earlier,[§] Ralph looked at the land that lay before him, dismissed the giants, and only saw victory. He would not only take the territory, he would thoroughly inhabit the land—with help from God, and from Pat's leadership and enormous fund-raising ability— making sport of his critics in the process. And I am quite sure Ralph felt that, one day, the giants would be working for him.

Immediately, Ralph began to accomplish the impossible. First, he sold the campaign's IBM 38 mainframe computer, a room-size dinosaur in comparison to the new micro models that had become available and could house the amount of information on a PC that had taken up an entire room before. When I learned that Ralph had convinced someone to buy that obsolete hunk of metal and circuitry, I became more of a believer in his chances of success at starting the new organization.

Initially, Ralph did not even have money to pay *himself*, much less support a staff. Thankfully, with the aid of Pat's son Gordon, a local lawyer who was chairman of the local Republican Party,[¶] I accepted a congressional appointment as field director for the 1990 Decennial Census in Virginia's 4th Congressional District. Until the new job began I spent my last few days at AFR helping Ralph and making a few early fund-raising phone calls to a list of high donors to the presidential campaign.

Ralph's practice was to call people who had supported Pat's campaign for president, pitch the vision for the new "lobby group" and ask for seed money to get the effort started. He always ended the explanation by

§ See Numbers 13–14.

¶ Later named co-host of *The 700 Club* and succeeding his father as CEO of CBN.

confidently asking the donor, "How's that sound?" If they responded affirmatively, Ralph would follow with a request for $500, $250 or whatever they could give. Then, the next day, we would mail each prospective donor from the night before a letter from Pat with a return envelope in which to send their donation.

In those early days, Ralph worked very closely with Pat, checking in with him for every significant decision. The first fund-raising letter for the Christian Coalition was signed by Pat and focused on the Federal government's funding of pornographic and other objectionable "art" through the National Endowment for the Arts. The NEA had made grants to support artists such as Andres Serrano and his photograph of a crucifix submerged in a jar of urine. Others included an exhibit of photographs with strong homosexual themes, some including nudity, by Robert Mapplethorpe. The letter was mailed to the list of donors to Pat's presidential campaign and Pat loaned the Coalition $20,000 to pay the costs of the postage. Soon, the responses started coming in. The Coalition's repeated renting of the campaign mailing list provided funds to AFR that were used for further reduction of the campaign debt.

In 1990, the Coalition continued its assault against the NEA, purchasing a full-page ad in *USA Today* for an open letter to Congress from Pat Robertson calling for a halt to taxpayer funding of the organization. In 1991, the Coalition sent videotapes of a homosexual film, *Tongues Untied*, which had received an NEA grant, to each member of the House of Representatives, along with a letter against congressional backing of such "art." Finally, in 1992 President George Bush called for the resignation of the organization's president, John Frohnmayer. His removal became a huge victory for the Coalition and was like a trophy, his head metaphorically mounted on the office wall.

Working for Pat Robertson had been a desire of mine since reading his bestseller *The Secret Kingdom* shortly after I graduated from college in 1983. I enrolled in the masters program for biblical studies at the graduate school he founded, then called CBN University,\*\* in the fall of 1985 and, much to my delight, became casually acquainted with Pat as he frequented the Shoney's restaurant where I worked nights during school. After graduation in June, 1987, I began volunteering at his campaign in the afternoons.

\*\* Later renamed Regent University.

The first months at AFR were beyond compare. The electricity in the air was unlike any I had experienced and as I remember those days while writing these words, I can still feel it. There is just something about a presidential campaign that stirs one's bones. The height in excitement was Pat's second-place showing in the Iowa caucuses on February 8, 1988, soundly beating Vice President George Bush.

A close second was Pat's astounding win in the attention-getting Ames (Iowa) Straw Poll on September 12, 1987. The following Monday, he came to AFR's fifth-floor suite of offices in the Armada-Hoffler Tower,[††] which was located in nearby Chesapeake. As Pat came through the office he stopped to talk with a small group of employees and exclaimed, "Well, we did it!" as everyone cheered and offered congratulations. Only a volunteer at the time, I stood by and watched, thoroughly excited and soaking in all that I could. All the while, I yearned to become a full-time employee, and was officially hired in October as a scheduling assistant, working there (off and on) until Ralph Reed arrived to launch Christian Coalition, almost to the day, two years later.[‡‡]

The presidential campaign effectively ended only six months after I was hired, with Bush's landslide win on March 8, 1988, in the Super Tuesday, Southern primaries. Pat did not officially withdraw his name from nomination, however, until two months later, and during that interval, I became his personal driver after he relinquished his Secret Service protection.

Before I could begin, Randy Estes, Pat's personal aide at the time, phoned him one afternoon to get approval for my hiring. Pat said that he did not know me, leading Randy to explain that I had worked on the campaign for about a year. Of course, Pat had been out on the campaign trail, rather than around the office every day, so that did not help his memory where I was concerned. Next, Randy mentioned that I had graduated from CBN University; but so had hundreds of other people, therefore it did not help Pat recall me, either. Finally, as Randy told me later, he said, "Well, sir, he said you might remember him from Shoney's," to which Pat replied, "Oh yes, he's a delightful young man,"[4] indicating that I would be

††  From the window of what ultimately became my final office at Christian Coalition headquarters, I could look across our parking lot and see the Tower, where my political life had begun over ten years earlier.

‡‡  Presidential campaigns usually maintain a skeleton staff after the election is over.

acceptable. I remained through June and then worked as an advance man[§§] for him at the Republican National Convention in New Orleans later that August, where he had been invited by the Bush campaign to make a major evening address.

With Pat Robertson, the gospel of Jesus Christ comes first. For instance, late one evening in 1996, when flying home with him on a chartered Learjet from Houston to Norfolk, I looked out the window and noticed the lights of a large city off to the south. The pilot identified the city as New Orleans, which reminded Pat of a time when CBN had held a telethon at a station there that had resulted in many instances of healings and other miracles. He was delighted to relate the stories of God's power to those of us in the plane as we passed by.

Once, during the final days of his presidential campaign, we were planning a trip for Pat to New Hampshire. I called the hotel in Manchester to reserve his hotel room—as well as one for myself, as I was supposed to fly up the day before Pat arrived, in order to advance the trip. In talking with the hotel's reservations clerk, she began asking questions about Pat and about the Christian faith. I gladly shared my beliefs with her and promised to continue in person when I got to the hotel. Unfortunately, my trip was later cancelled, although Pat still went.

When Pat returned to the Norfolk airport I was there to pick him up, and as we walked through the terminal on our way to the car, he said, "Well, Joel, I don't know what you said to that girl in the hotel up there, but she sure was sorry you weren't with me." Somewhat embarrassed at how exuberantly she must have approached him in the hotel, I replied that we had been "talking about the Lord," to which Pat emphatically exhorted, "Well then, call her back!" While, unfortunately, I do not remember the results of the later phone call, I fondly recall the desires of the recent presidential candidate who had his priorities well in order.

After the 1988 GOP convention in New Orleans, my next job was on a campaign for Virginia's junior U.S. Senate seat, after which I returned to AFR to work on liquidating the leftover debt from the campaign, remaining until October when I left for the Census Bureau. Just few weeks earlier, however, Ralph Reed arrived, and those extra few weeks proved to be instrumental in my future.

---

§§  One who arrives early and arranges logistics.

Even after leaving my job at Americans for Robertson it seemed that I was destined to work with Ralph. We both attended Kempsville Presbyterian Church in Virginia Beach and as I was leaving the service one Sunday I bumped into Ralph. "Hey, Joel," he said, "How'd you like to come over and have hot dogs with Jo Anne and me this afternoon? We'll watch football. And, would you help us stuff some envelopes?" Of course I said, "Yes." I learned early on that you cannot tell Ralph Reed, "No," when he asks for your help. He is so persuasive that you really cannot think of a valid reason to decline, so you might as well just agree and go on.

Ralph's debating and reasoning skills are just as effective. I remember once discussing this with D. J. Gribbin, the Coalition's national field director from 1994 until 1997, who lamented the futility of getting into an argument with Ralph because, "Ralph is so much smarter than everyone else that he will just intellectually beat you to a pulp."

After going home to change clothes, I arrived at the Reeds' rented, one-story, brick house in the College Park area of Virginia Beach, where Ralph and I had moved in their furniture a few weeks earlier, to see that they already had eaten and that two hot dogs remained in a pan of tepid water on the stove. I ate, and we stuffed envelopes. Christian Coalition was well served.

When Ralph arrived in Virginia, the Commonwealth was in the midst of a gubernatorial election between its then lieutenant governor, Democrat L. Douglas Wilder, and a former Republican attorney general, Marshall Coleman. Wilder won the election by about seven thousand votes out of two million cast, or an average of just over two votes per precinct. Ralph later proclaimed that if Christian Coalition had an up and working state chapter in Virginia at the time, educating Christian voters, the more conservative candidate, Coleman, would have won. And in proof of his prediction, in each of the next two gubernatorial elections, conservatives won by landslide margins. In fact, the GOP won eight of the next ten statewide contests in Virginia, including a sweep of the top three state offices in 1997. But in what might be called a post-Christian Coalition Virginia, Democrats reclaimed the governor's mansion in 2001, repeating in 2005, and also captured both U.S. Senate seats, winning two years in a row, the last being Pat Robertson's father's former seat, in 2008.

Ralph did not give up easily in 1989, however. In the final weeks of the campaign, he ghost-wrote a letter from Pat, endorsing Coleman, that we mailed to a list of several African-American pastors from the U.S.

Senate race I had worked on the previous year, that candidate being the first ever African-American candidate for statewide office in Virginia.¶¶ Wilder, who also was black, was strongly supported by abortion advocates because of his pro-abortion stance, which should not have carried weight with the pastors, and Ralph hoped to use it against Wilder.

I still remember Ralph's punch line. His goal was to appeal to the pastors on behalf of the unborn, hoping that they would find the pro-life cause to be the paramount issue in the race. He listed several pro-abortion groups that supported Wilder, and then came the punch line: "Doug Wilder is carrying their blood-soaked banner."[5] When I read that, I saw that Ralph Reed knew how to play hardball. But that was only an inkling of his true potential.

After the election, other than helping Ralph move the old Robertson campaign furniture and fixtures, which the Coalition would soon purchase from the campaign, into a new, smaller suite of offices a few blocks away, I was not involved with Christian Coalition for the next year and, actually, had no expectations of ever being involved in the future.

---

¶¶ AFR paid for the mailing, amounting to no more than $25, therefore the Coalition made no expenditure in the election.

3

# Never Say Never

I HAD LITTLE OCCASION to speak with Ralph Reed during my twelve months working for the United States Bureau of the Census. As the assignment was drawing to a close, however, I called to let him know that I would soon be seeking employment. Admittedly, I still did not want to work for Christian Coalition specifically, but Ralph knew lots of people and chief among them was Pat Robertson, who I was certain needed a guy like me on staff at CBN. Ralph was solicitous to my situation and as we ended the conversation, he suggested that I send him a résumé.

In late February, 1991, after one job possibility at CBN had fallen through and my bank account slowly evaporated, I found a message on my answering machine from a man named Guy Rodgers, who identified himself as the national field director with Christian Coalition and said he wanted to talk to me about a job in the field department, having come across my résumé in the files. I remembered Guy from the Robertson campaign's Iowa staff, but until his call I did not know that Guy had been working with Ralph for the past month or so.

Upon arriving at 805 Greenbrier Circle, Suite 202, for the first interview with Guy, I was impressed at how the Coalition had grown since I helped Ralph move over a year earlier. The organization had taken off like gangbusters. Ralph had really worked hard, and God's blessings were evident. The Coalition's budget had grown to $2.8 million in 1990 and was projected at just under $5 million for 1991. There were nine incorporated state affiliates* and a few dozen county chapters in those and other states.

---

* California, Colorado, Florida, Georgia, Illinois, New York, North Carolina, South Carolina, and Texas.

The chosen motto was *Giving Christians a Voice in Their Government Again* shown on a flashy membership brochure featuring a soiled Christian flag on the cover under a headline that read, "Christian Americans Are Tired of Getting Stepped On." The brochure encouraged people to become dues-paying members and highlighted the Coalition's five main objectives:

- Represent Christians before local councils, state legislatures, and Congress
- Speak out in the public arena and in the media
- Train Christians for effective social and political action
- Inform Christians about timely issues and pending legislation
- Protest anti-Christian bigotry and defend the legal rights of Christians.

The brochure included the endorsements, along with photographs, of five leaders in the Christian community: Southern Baptist luminary Dr. Charles Stanley, Concerned Women for America President Beverly LaHaye, Florida Presbyterian pastor Dr. D. James Kennedy, Catholic leader Fr. Michael Scanlan and, of course, Pat Robertson. Protestants and Catholics, men and women, charismatics and Baptists, Ralph had covered all the bases.[†]

Before being redesigned in 1998, no fewer than one million of the membership brochures were printed and distributed hand-to-hand in meetings and conferences across America. We had to reorder them time after time. It just seemed there were never any around, with our supply constantly being depleted by requests from chapter leaders and state directors[‡] to pass out to prospective members.

Guy gave me several manuals, handbooks, and videotapes to bring me up to date on the Coalition's objectives and strategies, including the *Christian Coalition Ten Year Plan*. Page one gave the group's mission statement: "[T]o mobilize and train Christians for effective political action, and to organize an exemplary grassroots field and training program far above

---

† Mrs. LaHaye may not have imagined that this new organization to which she had lent her name would soon be the foremost of all pro-family groups, eclipsing her own, although ultimately lacking its longevity.

‡ Our generic term applying equally to the state chairman and to the executive director of a state affiliate.

industry standards to accomplish this mission."[1] Goals to be achieved by the year 2000 included several that we eventually achieved: an activist and donor data base of two million persons, voter guide distribution to at least 30 million pro-family voters, 50,000 training graduates, establishment of a Washington, D.C. lobbying office, and a fax or computer in all 435 congressional districts. Many goals were not reached: annual national revenues of $36 million, trained precinct captains in each of America's 175,000 voting precincts, and local chapters in each of America's 3,000 counties. Ralph later said that when Pat first laid out these objectives for him, each seemed tantamount to swallowing a watermelon, whole.[2]

The *Ten Year Plan* listed four national factors that in 1989 comprised the need for such an organization as Christian Coalition. First was the end of the Robertson presidential campaign, which had laid the foundation for a new wave of Christian involvement in public policy and politics. Second, the Moral Majority had recently closed its doors, leaving a vacuum at the grassroots and creating the impression that Christian political involvement was waning. Third, the end of the Reagan Administration meant that Christians could no longer look to the White House to set the agenda for restoring the moral strength of the nation. Fourth, the United States Supreme Court's 1989 *Webster* decision returned the abortion issue to the state level, placing the battle for the future of the pro-family agenda with the grassroots.

Christian Coalition's operating plan was quite different than the strategy implemented by the Moral Majority in the 1980s. Primarily, the Coalition wanted to build solid and functioning state affiliates and county chapters across America. In *Blinded by Might*, a 1999 treatise *against* Christian involvement in politics, former Moral Majority Vice President Cal Thomas wrote: "Most of our state chapters were little more than a separate telephone line in a pastor's office."[3]

In contrast, by the 1994 congressional elections, Christian Coalition had affiliated organizations in forty-nine states and over 1,500 local chapters. Some were far better organized than others, but all were incorporated, with state chairmen and boards of directors. With only a handful of exceptions, each year the Coalition's national conference found each state represented by a state director or board member, in addition to activists and other supporters.

The Coalition never had an affiliated state chapter in Utah because Christians in that state felt the environment set by the Mormon religion sufficiently influenced politics to the conservative point of view. Therefore we found no one willing to head up a Christian Coalition state affiliate. We, nonetheless, worked hard to distribute our voter guides in Christian churches across the state each election year, and likely, voter guides ended up in Mormon facilities as well.

I did not know exactly why Pat chose "Christian Coalition" as the name for the organization, but I had an idea. At a 1989 chapel service at CBN,§ I listened to Pat describe a recent experience at a dinner hosted by a statewide Republican candidate from Virginia. Before dinner was served, someone in charge of the program asked Pat if he would say grace before the meal. He responded that he would prefer they allow someone else the privilege. The person, however, awkwardly explained that they *already* had listed Pat in the program as doing the prayer. So, of course, he complied, ending his prayer with the customary, "In Jesus name." Afterwards, Pat was approached by another attendee who was outraged at his use of the Lord's name rather than offering a non-sectarian prayer. This did not sit well with Pat, who replied that he was not ashamed of Jesus Christ, who had died for his sins. Pat said that he had run for the Republican Party's nomination for president, not to be its chaplain. Further, he said that he had not requested to pray at the dinner but did so to oblige the program. After all that, if he wanted to end a prayer by using the Name above all names, and that was not acceptable, then, *too bad.*[4] I always had a feeling that Pat chose the name of the Coalition with that experience in mind. As anyone could understand, being stereotyped was a sore subject with Pat at the time, having often been ridiculed by the media as just a "televangelist" running for president.

Another early goal stated in the *Ten Year Plan* as well as articulated by Pat Robertson in an accompanying promotional video called *America at a Crossroads* was "effective control of at least one major political party."[5] Throughout my time at the Coalition our critics made much of this "goal" but I don't recall that we ever mentioned it publicly again. "They're trying to take over" was the cry, mostly from pro-abortion and moderate Republicans. We simply encouraged our supporters to become active. If pro-family voters were the majority at a political party meeting, they would control the outcome. It was that simple. Our desire, whether it was a local committee meeting or the Republican National Convention, was

§ As an alumnus of Regent University I often attended events at CBN.

simply to have the most people present who would then vote their conscience. This goal was reached in 1996 when the Republican presidential nominee, Senator Bob Dole, was faced with so many of our like-minded activists who had been elected delegates to the convention that he had to choose a pro-life running mate or he would have faced seeing his choice voted down by the delegates on the convention floor.

From the outset, Christian Coalition was accused by its critics in the media, in government, and in the more liberal churches as being too closely aligned with the Republican Party. While it was true that most of our supporters were Republicans, as were almost all of our employees and state directors, Christian Coalition officially was a nonpartisan organization. Of course the Republican Party was a more willing vehicle for our supporters, programs, and activities, than were the Democrats. In August, 1997, C-SPAN *Washington Journal* host Steve Scully asked then Christian Coalition President Don Hodel if the Coalition would be more active at the 2000 Republican National Convention than at the Democrat alternative, to which Hodel responded, "And probably a great deal more welcome . . . "[6] The Democrats had exhibited quite an inhospitable attitude to pro-life voters. As an example, at its 1992 national convention in New York, pro-life Governor Robert Casey of Pennsylvania, the country's fourth-largest state, was denied the opportunity to speak.

Of course, many moderate Republicans were less than pleased with Christian Coalition and its supporters, and resented our insistence that the Party maintain the strong pro-life plank in its platform. As Hodel concluded, ". . . although, not *totally* welcome even *there.*"[7]

I accepted Guy's offer of a job, thankful to have employment, but still under whelmed by Christian Coalition. I comforted myself with the idea that I would stay there only long enough to find another job, hopefully at CBN. But as is always the case with God's interventions in our lives, He has our long-range benefit in mind, although the timing and the "need to know" are His alone.

Ralph was quite frugal in those early days. In fact, I had to begin by working only twenty hours a week while waiting for a student intern from Regent University to complete his time there and graduate, thus opening room in the budget to pay me a full salary. During my first months at Christian Coalition each employee had to take a weekly rotation emptying all the garbage cans in the office each day, which saved money that, otherwise, would have been paid to a custodial crew.

Few of the early employees at headquarters had much, if any, experience in politics prior to coming to the Coalition. They were a group of about ten wonderful Christian people, who would have felt less out of place at a church social than at a political convention. Data processors Dianna Forrester and Diane Goodall, along with remittance clerk Linda Jimerson, remained with the Coalition until late 1999 when the organization made plans to close its Chesapeake office and moved to Washington, D.C. And receptionist Ann Ballard served the grassroots activists who called the national office until retiring in 2007, a full sixteen years after she began working there, making her by far the longest serving employee in the Coalition's history.

The small size of the staff necessitated that the Coalition rely on volunteer help, including one couple, Alonzo and Lottie Kight, both around 90, whose daughter had been volunteer coordinator for the 1988 Robertson campaign. They sat in their den watching Christian television programs, while folding and inserting our Thank You letters into envelopes. Almost every day, someone from the staff loaded trays of letters and empty envelopes into their automobile and drove over to the Kights where several minutes of conversation and, usually, cookies and soft drinks followed.

In my job as assistant to the field director, I was the hands-on person for most projects, and the first of note was to begin a local chapter of Christian Coalition right there in our Hampton Roads area.[¶] Nascent local Christian Coalition chapters were encouraged first to recruit "leaders" from the religious, business, and civic communities. We began in the same way, with a small meeting of leaders at Guy's home, followed by a larger, public meeting at the CBN-owned Founders Inn and Conference Center in Virginia Beach, featuring Pat Robertson as the speaker. The larger event provided me my first lessons in politics Ralph Reed style.[**] They were very valuable lessons, indeed, and they were put into practice in virtually every future event the Coalition put on.

We began by mailing invitations to the people on our mailing list in the area (about 1,200 at the time) and received about sixty RSVPs. Lesson number one: *call everyone back on the day of the meeting and remind them*

¶ The urban portion of Virginia's Tidewater region.

** These were unofficial, widely-used principles, but Ralph stamped them with his own flair.

*to come.* Otherwise, they might forget. As Guy Rodgers often said, "You can *expect* only what you *inspect.*"

I arrived early at the Patrick Henry Room of the hotel[††] and ensured that the staging crew had put out the right number of chairs—sixty. Perfect. I then set up a table outside the room, along with sign-in sheets and ballpoint pens. Lesson number two: *get a list of all who come.* You'll want to contact them again. Even if they do not come back, they might give money later.

Ralph was among the first ten or so people who arrived at the event. As Pat was going to be the speaker, Ralph's attendance was essential, for both Pat and himself. Lesson three: *if your boss is speaking at the meeting, be there, and be there early.* If something goes wrong, he will come to *you* first.

The first thing Ralph did was to begin removing chairs from the room, saying that you want only half enough chairs in the room at first. Then, afterwards, people will remember that you had to bring in extra chairs. Lesson number four: *make it easy to exceed expectations.* A subsequent start-up meeting in a neighboring city was held in an auditorium and, though it had an even larger turnout, the otherwise successful event appeared to be a flop simply because of the high number of empty seats— that were bolted to the floor and could not be removed.

That first meeting at the Founders Inn successfully kicked off a chapter that proceeded to distribute about 100,000 Christian Coalition voter guides each election year under a succession of chapter chairmen, including retiree and church deacon Lou Williams, and homemaker Betty Hansel, who personally delivered multiple tens of thousands of voter guides each election year all by herself.

The death of U.S. Supreme Court Justice Thurgood Marshall brought the first significant national grassroots mobilization project to our organization. President George H. W. Bush's appointment of Appeals Court Judge Clarence Thomas to replace the revered Marshall sent shock waves across America. Thomas was an African American, as of course was Marshall, an American icon, especially among civil rights activists. He had been the attorney in the landmark *Brown v. Board of Education* U.S. Supreme Court case in the 1950s. Critics of Bush felt that Marshall's replacement should mirror not just his race, but also his philosophy. On most matters,

---

†† Political meetings almost always are held in hotels.

Marshall was very liberal while Clarence Thomas was a conservative. And the Democrats in the Senate were determined to derail the Thomas appointment during the confirmation process.

Conservatives loved the choice of Thomas, and Christian Coalition was no exception. Among other activities, Christian Coalition designed and distributed a petition promoting Thomas's nomination, and collected approximately 50,000 signatures in support. At that point in our organization's development that was a tremendous number of signatures, with photocopiers humming for days so that the names and addresses could be copied, and then entered into our computer after the original petitions were sent on to Congress.

Future petitions garnered hundreds of thousands, if not millions, of signatures on projects such as fighting the Fairness in Broadcasting Act, which conservatives referred to as "Hush Rush" due to the fact that it would have forced stations to give liberal counterpoint time to Rush Limbaugh's hugely popular radio show; Bill and Hillary Clinton's national health care program in 1994; and supporting the impeachment of President Clinton in 1998.

On the day of the U.S. Senate's final confirmation vote for Judge Thomas, we all crowded around the television in Ralph's office to watch the roll call vote. It was fifty-two to forty-eight with eleven Democrats[‡‡] voting in favor of Thomas's confirmation.[8] We had won the first significant battle of the Coalition's existence.

Projects like this usually encompassed the entire staff in one way or another. For a given lobbying campaign, the Capitol Hill office, opened in 1993, worked with Congressional insiders to establish a list of targeted legislators. These were members of Congress whose votes and influence were considered to be essential on the issue at hand. Legislators who were definitely against our position on an issue were left alone. No need spending resources on someone whose mind was made up. Those in favor of our position were thanked for their support and encouraged to stand strong. (Ralph often said that politics is the opposite of evangelism: "In evangelism, you leave the ninety-nine to look for the one lost sheep. But in politics, you forget the lost and guard the ninety-nine so that no one takes

---

‡‡ Boren (OK), Breaux (LA), DeConcini (AZ), Dixon (IL), Exon (NE), Fowler (GA), Hollings (SC), Johnston (LA), Nunn (GA), Robb (VA) and Shelby (AL). Shelby became a Republican after the 2004 elections.

any more.") The major push was saved for the "swing votes," members who had not yet made up their minds.

We made phone calls, mailed letters and post cards, and, as Ralph often said, used "high-speed fax machines," to alert supporters in every Congressional District in America, so those communications could be forwarded around the district, alerting even more voters and activists to call or write their respective members of Congress. There were multiple versions of the alerts for each project depending on how many legislators were being targeted. For example, when we were lobbying for passage of the Religious Freedom Amendment in 1998 we targeted over thirty House members. We also encouraged our chapter leaders to schedule face-to-face meetings with members of Congress back home during Congressional recess or on holidays. Each time Ralph Reed—or his 1997 successor as executive director, Randy Tate—was on television hammering away at an issue, or verbally battling with a Democrat, at least fifty people were back at headquarters, cheering him on, realizing that their efforts were aiding in his protest and making the Coalition's lobbying activities possible.

"The board thinks we should have a national conference,"[9] Ralph announced after returning from a spring meeting of the Coalition's directors. The original, four-person board consisted of Pat and his son Gordon, along with two close Robertson confidants, Dr. Billy McCormack, a Baptist pastor from Louisiana, and Texas businessman Richard Weinhold, both of whom had held significant positions in the Robertson presidential campaign. In fact, it had been Billy's urging that prompted Pat to create the Christian Coalition in order to give his supporters a way to stay involved in politics. And now they wanted a conference.

A small "Founding Conference" had been held in Washington, D.C. in May, 1990, but this "Road to Victory Conference and Strategy Briefing" would be the group's first "national convention." The decision turned out to be a master-stroke for Christian Coalition, as well as a fortuitous event for me, influencing my desire to be a part of the organization on a long-term basis, for it was during the production and excitement of that first Road to Victory that, after six long months, I finally felt as if I "belonged" with Christian Coalition.

In later years, we would see future state directors and county chapter chairmen who initially became Coalition "believers" at Road to Victory. The attendance of state and local leaders was essential at each and every Road to Victory, as the conference provided them an annual opportunity to energize and invigorate them for the next year's organizing activity. In addition, they could meet new people from their respective states who had come to the conference, share success stories, and agree to pray for each other during the coming year.

The dates November 15 and 16 were chosen for the event, which was to be held at the Founders Inn and Conference Center. Soon, we began mailing out invitations to those on our nationwide mailing list. The list was made up of only about 100,000 donors at that time, far below the eventual high of 2.1 million members and supporters. But registrations poured in, reaching over 1,100, which virtually filled the hotel's Virginia Ballroom.

Before Road to Victory came elections for the Virginia General Assembly.[§§] Each member of the state house and state senate was up for reelection in 1991.

In Virginia Beach that year, all but one of the incumbents were Democrats. Challengers were at the ready for every seat, however, with the focus race being the 8th Senatorial District, featuring liberal incumbent Democrat Moody Stallings and his Republican challenger, former Virginia Beach policeman Ken Stolle. Stallings had made headlines since his razor-thin victory four years earlier by leading the fight for gun control legislation in the Commonwealth. He was a pro-abortion, well-known local attorney who got lots of television news coverage. We felt that Stallings would not stop at the state senate; he wanted to be attorney general. And of course there was only one thing to run for after attorney general—governor. He must be derailed. This would be a perfect opportunity to put our grassroots organizing program of voter identification and education to the test. If it would not work in our own back yard, how could we expect it to work elsewhere? The 1991 elections would be the first opportunity to engage a strategic voter identification and mobilization effort.

Christian Coalition had distributed nonpartisan voter guides in several U.S. Senate races in 1990, including 750,000 in a nail-biter in North Carolina between conservative Republican stalwart Senator Jesse Helms and a former Charlotte mayor, Democrat Harvey Gantt. As Ralph told the 1991 Road to Victory audience:

---

[§§] Virginia's bicameral legislature. School students in the Commonwealth know that Virginia's House of Delegates is the longest continual democratic legislative body in the world.

I had access to internal tracking, and I knew Senator Helms was down by eight points. So Pat called me up and said, quote, "We have got to kick into action." Bottom line is, five days later we put three quarters of a million voter guides in churches across the state of North Carolina, and Jesse Helms was reelected by 100,000 votes out of 2.2 million cast.[10]

The voter guides did not advocate Helms's re-election, only portraying his positions on the issues, along with stating that Gantt chose not to return an issue survey sent to him by the Coalition. Nonetheless, the senator felt the voter guides had helped pull him through.

From the beginning, Pat's strategy for Christian Coalition centered on precinct organization, which was the key to narrow victories and losses. Unlike many other religious leaders who speak out on political issues, Pat Robertson, even before running for president, had a life-long background in politics. His late father, Senator A. Willis Robertson, was a long-time Democrat from Virginia, who served over thirty-five years in the House and Senate. Pat often joked that the first word he learned after "Mommy" and "Daddy" was "constituent."

In the 1960 presidential election, John F. Kennedy defeated Richard Nixon by only about 175,000 votes nationwide, which amounted to an average of about one vote per precinct. While this average margin made no difference in terms of the presidential Electoral College—with each state allotted a number of electoral votes as we know all too well from the 2000 George W. Bush vs. Al Gore presidential election—in other elections, which are decided by winning a majority of the popular vote, winning an average of one extra vote per precinct could be the margin of victory.

Pat's original goal was for Christian Coalition to identify at least ten pro-life voters in every one of America's 175,000 precincts, creating a virtual army of activists across the nation. The plan was to concentrate on grassroots activism, leaving flashy television campaign tactics to the political parties. We would train these activists in the nuts and bolts of politics, as well as how to reproduce their numbers every year.

In 1991, during that first state senate race, Christian Coalition knew what had to be done and did it well, beginning by employing Abraham Lincoln's four rules for winning elections.¶¶ First, get a list of voters; second, find out where they stand on the issues or candidates; third, persuade

¶¶ Often espoused by conservative guru Morton Blackwell.

the undecided with someone in whom they have confidence; and fourth, contact those in agreement with you and get them to the polls. We made thousands of phone calls to voters in Virginia Beach in order to identify their positions in the race based on issues as well as doing door-to-door voter canvassing. They later were contacted by phone and mail, and encouraged to go vote based on those issues. Phone banks were in place and phones throughout the city began ringing. And of course, nonpartisan voter guides were distributed in churches throughout the region on the Sunday before Election Day.

On Monday evening, before the polls opened at six o'clock the next morning, Ralph came in with an assignment from his boss. "Pat wants us to do exit polls," he said. By standing at predetermined polling places around the city and asking voters whom they voted for we hopefully could ascertain which candidate would win the election.

The race of the most interest was for the high-profile 8th District senate seat. The November weather had turned particularly brisk but *very* early the next morning, Ralph (even the boss goes out when *his* boss calls) and I, along with two other staffers, arrived at our chosen locations. We knew the voting history for each precinct in the city and chose four precincts that always went heavily in favor of the GOP candidate. If Republican Stolle were doing well or even better than average in these, we would be far more comfortable until polls closed at seven in the evening. As voters exited the polls, we stood, wrapped in overcoats, scarves, and gloves, with our requisite clip boards and asked, "May I ask whom you voted for?"

At my precinct Stolle was well ahead, but when I went to a pay phone at the pre-appointed time to call Ralph on his cell phone, he said we were well behind there, and that the Democrat, himself, was campaigning at the site. At the time, Ralph was fairly unknown publicly and could stand outside a polling place and not be recognized, even by one of the candidates. That anonymity would not last long at all.

Stolle ended up winning the state senate seat, in what Pat Robertson called "a hard fought victory" to the Road to Victory crowd two weeks later. In fact, Republicans won six of eight races in Virginia Beach, including Regent University alumnus Bob McDonnell's defeat of a twenty-year incumbent state delegate.

This early success precipitated a quote that would haunt Ralph throughout the remainder of his Coalition tenure. In a post-election interview with a reporter from Norfolk's *Virginian-Pilot* newspaper, under a front page headline entitled "Robertson's phone corps boosted GOP—Local Democrats claim network ambushed them,"*** Ralph uttered the following words about our activities in the election: "I want to be invisible. I do guerrilla warfare. I paint my face and travel at night. You don't know it's over until you're in a body bag. You don't know until election night."[11]

As future Christian Coalition staffer Chuck Cunningham once reminded me, the quote did not make waves at first, but a few months later, one of our state affiliates included it on a flier at a conference where Ralph spoke. After that event the quote took on a life of its own, constantly being included in articles about Ralph and the Coalition, as well as in speeches by Democrats seeking to paint us as extremists. It would not go away. Like President Ronald Reagan's "evil empire" statement in referring to the Soviet Union—a quote that conservatives loved, of course, and still point to as the pivotal moment in the decline of Communism in Europe—Ralph's "body bag" quote provided the media with a target to shoot at throughout the rest of his political career. Ralph later explained the oft-mentioned quote as his inarticulate attempt to show the differences in Christian Coalition's grassroots techniques in contrast to the traditional methods of campaigning only by television and through the mail.[12]

Ralph was widely acclaimed as an extremely good communicator. In fact, few were better. He spoke eloquently about political or religious topics and was at his best before a television camera. He could be serious and he could be funny, and each in a manner that left others speechless. It seemed that no Democrats or moderate Republicans could hold their own in debate with him, and that no reporter could stump him. Videotapes of his best media interviews were copied and distributed by headquarters to Coalition state directors, chapter chairmen and training seminar attendees around the country to show them how to respond to reporters' questions.

Ralph had a way of expressing himself that often was colorful and to the point. Once, a group of Florida local school board members came under fire for passing a decree that students must be instructed that, in a multi-cultural environment, the predominant "American" culture was "the best." Because at least one of the board members had close ties to Christian Coalition, we were drawn into the controversy and Ralph went

*** *The Virginian-Pilot* (and a few other papers referenced here) prefers headlines written in sentence case.

on CNN's *Crossfire* to defend our organization, although not necessarily the decree. During the program, Ralph confidently gave an example that our culture must be pretty desirable among people from other countries, otherwise, "Why would they cross oceans, riding on ironing boards with lawnmower motors strapped to them, just to get here?"[13] How could any opponent cope with logic like that?

Once, during a very heated interview with CNN's Judy Woodruff, Ralph was confronted with a quite accusatory "fact" about his post-Coalition business dealings that Woodruff had gotten from someone who refused to be identified. "Well, Judy, it's not my job to comment on a blind quote from an anonymous source,"[14] Ralph shot back, blunting her dart.

Around the office, Ralph could be very funny, as well as, on occasion, quite irreverent and caustic. Whether in a meeting or when a few people just talked in the hallway, over the years Ralph uttered some of the most humorous comments I have heard. With a phrase he could make you double over in laughter or recoil in personal embarrassment. And no member of the staff was safe. A prime example was his off-handed reaction to a potential health problem once encountered by a senior staff member, who had noticed a mole on his body that looked as if there was cause for concern as a possible skin cancer. Several employees learned of his anxiety and we had likely prayed for him during our staff prayer meeting.

Ralph was on a trip at the time, but after he returned to the office, the executive, not knowing that someone already had informed Ralph of his potential health issue, approached him right in front of my desk and began to explain the situation in somewhat circumspect terms, only to have Ralph interrupt and ask off-handedly, "Oh, is this the mole thing?" causing Ralph's secretary and me to make eye contact across the room while suppressing spurts of laughter.[†††]

And Ralph was quite adept at reducing an entire argument to one sentence. He once agreed for the national office to subsidize part of the salary of an executive director of one of our state affiliates. The executive director was a hard worker but to our dismay spent most of his time organizing a "Life Chain," an exercise where people stand hand-in-hand to show their support for the pro-life cause, rather than building local chapters of the Coalition. We did not encourage our state affiliates to partici-

†††  Fortunately, the mole was found to be benign and, therefore, was nothing more than "a mole thing."

pate in these symbolic activities, which were prevalent across the country at the time, preferring that they concentrate on more effective ways of stopping abortion, such as through the legislative process. The man had organized a Life Chain the previous year as well, *before* headquarters began helping pay his salary. Unfortunately, other tasks had not received as much of his attention as had the Life Chain, and his state chapter was not growing. Finally, it was obvious that he was not cut out to organize effective county chapters, so the leadership of the state affiliate replaced him, but only after the national Coalition had kicked-in about $10,000 over several months. In retrospect, an exasperated Ralph told Guy and me one day in a self-deprecating manner, "Basically, we paid [him] $10,000 to put together a Life Chain that he had done the previous year for free."

Just as Christian Coalition had an early plan for *mobilizing* its activists, it likewise had a plan for *educating* them. We needed a broader and more in depth plan of training the activists than just the voter guides at election time, which were for the purpose of educating the masses of Christian voters.[‡‡‡] First known as "Leadership Schools," and later as "Christian Coalition Training Seminars," the two-day political action seminars were held in cities across the nation with Ralph as the primary teacher. He was replaced in 1991 by Guy Rodgers. By 1994 a succession of field operatives—including myself—went on the road for state affiliates holding seminars every couple of weeks in cities such as Asheville (North Carolina), Topeka (Kansas), and Omaha (Nebraska).

Approximately eight weeks prior to the date of a school, letters were mailed over Pat's name to Coalition supporters within a two-hour commute of the event's location. Enclosed with each letter was a red-colored, tri-fold brochure with the headline "Think Like Jesus, Lead Like Moses, Fight Like David, Run Like Lincoln." In addition, fliers were placed in churches, and in Christian schools and bookstores. Public service announcements were run on Christian and talk-radio stations, as well.

The Leadership Schools also featured local conservative leaders and elected officials as faculty, along with sessions on videotape that were sent from headquarters. Inviting local personalities to teach at the schools brought a measure of legitimacy, considering that the name of Christian Coalition was not exactly a household word at the time. The schools actually helped to publicize the Coalition early on, whereas in later years,

[‡‡‡] To be discussed in depth in the next chapter.

the reverse was true; the well-known name, Christian Coalition, attracted prospective students to the schools.

The curriculum was revised every few years in order to keep the seminars from getting stale, but it was difficult to improve on the quality of the content in the original manual and videotapes. They were the best. One such lesson was by Paul Weyrich, president of the Free Congress Foundation, who had been a founder of the "New Right" in the early 1980s and had also coined the term, "Moral Majority."§§§

Weyrich's videotaped session for our Leadership Schools, entitled *Victories and Defeats of the Religious Right*, discussed mistakes made by conservative activists during the Reagan and (first) Bush Administrations. He concluded that our movement lost its focus during these two friendly presidencies and was more concerned with being invited to breakfast at the White House than with a continued focus on grassroots organization. This was our most popular and most widely distributed videotape in the training series, and contained an important warning to our movement. Sadly, as we will see in later chapters, Christian Coalition failed to heed Weyrich's warnings, succumbing to an event and media strategy, and abandoning its focus on precincts.

"We need a flier!"[15] Ralph exclaimed one day as Road to Victory was approaching. It is virtually impossible to promote a political event without a flier showing the pictures of the invited speakers. We listed Pat, of course, along with several other pro-family and congressional leaders, including Senator Jesse Helms, who, at the time was the most prominent conservative in the Congress.

Still, we felt the need for a huge-name speaker to add to the list in order to erase any doubt in the minds of our supporters as to whether they should travel to Virginia Beach to attend. "What about Quayle?" someone said, during one evening planning meeting in Ralph's office. Everyone agreed that it was a good idea and that Vice President Dan Quayle might actually come. So, the next day, Ralph's secretary prepared a letter of invitation, but mistakenly addressed it to "Daniel J. Quayle" rather than "J. Danforth Quayle." Nonetheless, the vice president accepted our invitation and our phone lines soon began buzzing with calls from the Secret Service and White House aides. Christian Coalition had hit the big time.

§§§ A well-known fact in conservative circles.

All was well on Friday morning, November 15, 1991, as the boom-ing voice of a back-stage announcer introduced Ralph, and the enthralled crowd of 1,000 excited activists¶¶¶ leaped to their feet in applause. Ralph opened the conference by proudly telling our audience, just minutes prior to Quayle's entrance, "If I may paraphrase Mark Twain, the reports of the death of the religious right have been greatly exaggerated." The announcer then introduced the vice president, who strode to the podium, followed by Senator Helms and a very proud Pat Robertson. The front row of the audience was occupied by recently elected Republican state legislators who had been featured on our voter guides. Christian Coalition was on the map, and the giants already were starting to work on Ralph's behalf.

¶¶¶ Including scores of CBN employees we had invited.

# 4

# Who Do You Trust?

As the calendar turned to 1992, Christian Coalition was preparing to move into a new office building. Actually, it was just across the parking lot from our old building, the one I had helped Ralph move into three years earlier, but it provided much more room. We were a fairly laid-back operation in those early days. None of the individual office doors had locks, and when Ralph was out of town other staff members occasionally could be seen working at his desk due to a lack of space. It occurs to me that he may never have known that others used his office.

Our new suite, 1801 Sara Drive, was tastefully painted in the familiar Colonial Virginia colors of Williamsburg blue and gray. We all were thrilled to have the much-needed space, although, due to the organization's growth it became too small almost from the outset. By 1997, we had more than doubled the size of our space in the new building by acquiring additional square footage whenever an adjacent neighbor, including the phone center for the QVC home shopping network, moved out. The landlord just kept knocking out walls for us. Our most uncommon neighbor, however, had to be the medical research facility immediately to our right, which was a front for a condom factory. One day just after we moved in I saw a box of their product in our mailroom, which they evidently had dropped by as a joke. "We gotta get these out of here," I said to someone on our mailroom staff, imagining a condom accidentally falling into an envelope with a letter destined to be opened by one of our best contributors.

Early in 1992 Pat Robertson became interested in the race for chairmanship of Virginia's Republican Party. Virginia did not have stringent laws governing political campaigning, and Federal Election Commission laws did not govern politics at the state or local levels; therefore, our nonpartisan status was not threatened by such activities. Having a pro-life state party chairman is instrumental in assuring that candidates for local and statewide offices reflect those same values.

One day in late February, as Ralph walked out of his office and introduced me to his guest, I had no idea that Mike Rothfeld and I would have many phone conversations over the next three months as the statewide nominating process swung into action. Mike, a statewide grassroots organizer, supplied me with the dates and filing forms for the local city or county meetings, and I prepared letters for Pat's signature that would be mailed to our supporters across Virginia, encouraging them to attend their respective citywide or county "mass meetings," the Virginia term for local political conventions. Without endorsing any candidates, we gave them brief instructions in how to become delegates to their mass meeting, as well as their Congressional District convention and the state convention. And they did!

Several hundred of our supporters attended the state convention at the Civic Center in Salem, Virginia, on the outskirts of Roanoke where the central Virginian Piedmont region blends with the Blue Ridge Mountains. There, "our guy" Richmond lawyer Pat McSweeney was elected the new state Republican Party chairman. After McSweeney's victory was announced, an excited Ralph approached me on the convention floor. "Joel, few people in this room had more to do with this victory today than you," he said. I enjoyed receiving such a hearty compliment.

A few weeks prior to the convention, Pat Robertson hosted a fundraising reception for McSweeney at his stately home on the Regent University campus. Almost all institutions of higher education have a home for the chancellor or president on campus, and Regent's, a Georgian structure made from red, aged brick, with four chimneys pointing toward the sky, looked as if it had been built 200 years earlier, and was on a par with any, although lacking such lavish accoutrements as a tennis court or a swimming pool. When the house was under construction, critics in the local press objected; so much so, that Pat almost chose not to move in upon completion. Instead, he used the royalties from his best-seller *The Secret Kingdom* to pay for the house himself, and then donated it back to the university.[1]

Several people associated with the Coalition sold $35 tickets to the McSweeney reception. The goal was to have 200 people gathered in Pat's backyard on that warm Saturday afternoon in May. Ralph always seemed to know just the right number of attendees to make an event successful.

To the dismay of the staff, however, the "right" number usually increased with each succeeding event. A few days before the reception, Guy, Ralph, and I were in Ralph's office strategizing when Ralph called Dave Hummel, a board member of the Virginia state affiliate of Christian Coalition, to see how his ticket sales were coming. After Ralph grilled him about his production, an exasperated Hummel (I visualized his head in his hands) just stopped and said, "Ralph, I wish I had your drive."

"Driven" is possibly the best word to describe Ralph Reed. Among those who have known him for many years, stories abound of his relentless pursuit of goals and his meticulous attention to detail. Ralph had a knack for inspiring the staff to achieve far more than they would have thought was possible. He had an innate ability to see into the future and visualize the outcome of a project. After seeing one of those outcomes become reality, staff members were more easily inspired to undertake them in the future.

Personally, I accomplished many feats that were beyond what I could have imagined due to how high he had "set the bar." And I never wanted to tell Ralph that a task could not be accomplished. First, "cannot" usually is a copout that really means, "I don't want to work that hard to make it happen," or "I really don't agree with you that it is necessary." But second, and more importantly, anyone telling Ralph that something could not be done would most likely have to live through the embarrassment of watching Ralph do it anyway, himself.

A major legislative battle of 1992 was a pro-abortion initiative that had been introduced in Congress, called the Freedom of Choice Act (FOCA). Pro-choice liberals who still controlled Congress at the time promised the radical feminist groups they would pass this bill in order to stop further judicial encroachments against abortion, like 1989's *Webster* decision and 1992's *Casey* ruling by Reagan-Bush appointed Supreme Court justices. Further, Democrat presidential candidate Bill Clinton promised, in an August fund-raising letter for the Democratic National Committee, to "make passage of the Freedom of Choice Act one of [his] top priorities."[2]

Christian Coalition encouraged its chapters and activists to fight FOCA like no battle before. Ralph called the troops to action with a March 3 *ACTION GRAM*, a memo on bright-yellow paper with a red-lettered banner across the top, informing them that FOCA "would essentially bypass the Supreme Court's jurisdiction on abortion by statutory fiat, imposing on (the) fifty states an abortion-on-demand standard that would prevent states from protecting the lives of the unborn."[3] In the end the "pro-aborts"* gave up and allowed the measure to die without a vote.

The prime electoral event of 1992, of course, was the presidential election. Incumbent President George H. W. Bush was a shoo-in for the Republican nomination even though he was faced with opposition from commentator and columnist Pat Buchanan, who almost beat Bush in the bellwether New Hampshire primary. Buchanan built on his 1992 success to actually win in New Hampshire versus eventual nominee Bob Dole in 1996. Challenging the sitting president was anathema to Bush supporters, as it weakened his campaign by forcing him to absorb negative criticism, which would be used by his Democrat opponent in November, as well as making him spend valuable campaign resources in the primary, rather than saving them for the general election. Those outraged at Buchanan included Pat Robertson, who wrote a sharp letter endorsing Bush that was mailed to our supporters in Georgia before that state's primary. Keeping our strict adherence to Federal election laws, the Bush campaign paid for the mailing.

A few of our hard-core activists in Georgia, however, were offended by the action and promptly resigned from the Coalition. This struggle between the national office and many of our most purist supporters would rise up several times over the years, including a similar struggle with Buchanan loyalists when he ran for president again in 1996, and more notably, during the impeachment of President Clinton in 1999, the fallout of which began to dismantle the entire Christian Coalition.

We were hoping to have President Bush speak at our national conference that year, which we had dubbed Road to Victory II. There was much other work to do first, however. This election year would be our first nationwide voter guide distribution operation and we were planning a rally for pro-family delegates in conjunction with the Republican National Convention in Houston. Looking back on those days, I never cease to be amazed at the amount of work accomplished that summer by our field staff, which consisted of Guy Rodgers and me, along with new hire Steve Jordan, and two successive interns.

Guy Rodgers was a dedicated worker, both for the Coalition and for the cause. That summer and fall, Guy personally oversaw the produc-

---

* Our common name for those who supported abortion.

tion and distribution of 40 million voter guides in scores of thousands of churches, a 3,000-person rally in Houston, and the minute details of Road to Victory.

From the 1990 mid-term congressional elections and throughout the remainder of the decade, Christian Coalition's primary vehicle for affecting American politics was the voter guide operation. Voter guides, a brief and to-the-point look at the issue positions taken by two or more opposing candidates in an election, were the main asset—along with the personalities of Pat Robertson and Ralph Reed—that average Christian voters identified with the Coalition. With a Christian Coalition voter guide in hand, a previously uninformed voter could quickly assess which candidate best reflected his or her own views. This was the case whether the voter in question was a liberal or a conservative, since each candidate's views were accurately shown. In the 1992 presidential election, a pro-life voter would see that George Bush was the pro-life candidate. Likewise, a pro-abortion voter would clearly see that Bill Clinton mirrored his or her position.

We started voter guide production in April by compiling a list of all candidates seeking election to Congress or as governor of a state that year. This meant phoning the board of elections or secretary of state's office in each of the respective fifty states, and then waiting for a fax to arrive. The names many candidates chose to use on the ballots were hilarious. One candidate for Congress ran under the name "God Almighty," while another called himself "Love 22." A candidate seeking to solidify the anti-abortion vote had even legally changed his middle name to "Pro-Life," as in "Andy Pro-Life Jones."

The next step was to mail issues surveys to each of the candidates. They received a cover letter explaining our project as well as a request to furnish us with a picture for our voter guides. If you think the names are strange, you should have seen some of the photographs, which ranged from professionally done portfolios to homemade versions alongside a family pet.

At the top of the seven-page survey candidates were asked to complete and return, Guy had included a blank for the candidates to print their names, followed by another to list the particular race in which they were running. Imagine our surprise—and laughter—when one candidate filled in the blank labeled "Candidate Race" with only one word: "White."

Ralph personally proofed each and every Federal race voter guide that year, which added an extra set of eyes after Guy had scrutinized each himself during production and after they came back from layout. As I recall, Ralph found only one or two errors, with the one I remember best being a candidate's position on an important issue being reversed; "Support" rather than "Oppose" or vice versa. "That's why I had to look at them," he said afterward. "I'd know if something just did not seem right."[4] Ralph knew that particular candidate's position on the issue in question and when it was incorrect on the voter guide proof it leapt out at him.

Monday of Republican convention week was to be the day for our "God & Country Rally" for pro-family delegates. The term grew to be used often by the national Christian Coalition, as well as state affiliates in their own events. We secured the Sam Houston Ballroom at the Sheraton Astrodome Hotel just across the street from America's first indoor baseball arena, where the Republican National Convention was being held. Speakers included Vice President Dan Quayle, Eagle Forum President Phyllis Schlafly, and U.S. Senator Don Nickles of Oklahoma, who had been chairman of the platform committee hearings held earlier in Salt Lake City. Entertainer Pat Boone emceed and Pat Robertson introduced Dan Quayle. This would be a wonderful media boost for the Coalition as well as an activist recruitment tool for the Texas state affiliate.

We were expecting protests at the rally, some possibly being violent in nature, but we had only volunteer security personnel, in addition to Quayle's Secret Service detail and Pat's CBN security staff. The decision was made that any protesters who made their way into the rally and attempted any disruption would be surrounded by our Christian volunteers and guided to the nearest door. The intention was to have so many men surrounding the protesters that physical force would be unnecessary. This strategy actually worked like a charm when needed during Vice President Quayle's speech, as a protester began to shout from the back of the crowd.

Marlene Elwell, a prodigious organizer, who had orchestrated Pat's upset win in the 1987 Ames (Iowa) Straw Poll, had come to Houston to script our event, and local volunteers had put in many long hours toward the event's success. The Coalition did not yet have a full-time press spokesman, so we retained the services of the former Robertson campaign director for the state of Washington, Bruce Hawkins, to handle press relations.

In order to boost attendance at the rally, during the late-night hours on the eve of the event, Ralph had Bruce and me, along with one volunteer, go throughout the hotel, sliding promotional fliers under each door—which amounted to several hundred rooms spaced throughout three or four buildings. In addition, thousands of letters and post cards with Quayle's picture on the back had been mailed from our national office to Christians in Texas in order to publicize the event. Also, the Coalition's Texas state affiliate had a small, portable, automated telephone dialer up and running for several days, making calls to their list of activists in the Houston metro area.

The result was a room so filled with people that if anyone had fallen, his or her body would have taken a long time to hit the floor. In fact, the crowd of over 3,000 pro-family activists stood for nearly three hours after many came early to get a good "seat." We began with a Dixie-Land band playing the popular song *The Yellow Rose of Texas*, after which a choir from a local church sang praise to God. The room was so jam-packed with people that the band's trombone player had to point his instrument at the floor, rather than in the customary horizontal direction.

The choir was still singing, and the audience impatient, when Pat and Quayle were ready to take the stage, but Ralph found himself in very hot water with the pastor from the choir's church as he stood right in front of him to give him the hand-under-chin "cut it" sign. It seemed that the pastor had dealt only with Marlene and Guy, and did not know that the young man† insisting that his choir stop singing actually was their boss.

Quayle's appearance provided me with a story to include in speeches and lectures for years to come. As the Vice President addressed this excited and packed rally, which was covered by no fewer than sixty television cameras on two elevated press risers at the back of the room, he attempted to lead the audience in a chant for George Bush. I was standing on one of the risers with a sea of people before me as I listened to Quayle rev-up his cadence. "The Democrats want you to trust Bill Clinton and Al Gore for your future," shouted Quayle, to loud groans from the audience. "But you don't trust Bill Clinton and Al Gore, do you?" "No!" came the thunderous response. "Who do you trust?" asked Quayle. "JEEE-sus!" they shouted, as Quayle adjusted. He learned the hard way that Christian Coalition activ-

† Ralph was thirty-one at the time.

ists kept their perspectives in order. Of course, Quayle is a Christian, but his speechwriter that day certainly did not expect *that* response.

As Guy and I flew back to Virginia the morning after the rally, he worked on a letter in opposition to an upcoming Equal Rights Amendment ballot initiative in Iowa. Christian Coalition was about to get in the fray. Marlene Elwell had been contracted by a coalition of anti-ERA groups in Iowa to lead the fight under the title, the Iowa Committee to Stop ERA, and we were sending a fund-raising letter from Pat to support their efforts. The ensuing letter, which, I believe, was "punched-up" by Ralph's addition of language politicos call "red meat" before being mailed to thousands of Iowa activists, brought a firestorm like we had never seen. The text of the letter contained some quite explosive rhetoric: "The feminist agenda is not about equal rights for women. It is about a socialist, anti-family political movement that encourages women to leave their husbands, kill their children, practice witchcraft, destroy capitalism, and become lesbians."[5]

Regardless of the fact that quotes and lifestyles of feminist leaders backed up the statement, Pat began being attacked in newspaper columns, on television talk shows and almost anywhere else people were discussing politics. It all peaked one evening months later when he appeared on *Larry King Live,* and confirmed rumors that he had not actually written the letter, but that it had been authored by a staff member.[6] For years, the letter rivaled Ralph's "body bag" quote in terms of being blown out of proportion by our critics.

Ralph, Pat, and the board felt that in order to maximize our effectiveness in gearing up the grassroots activists for the elections, Road to Victory II should be on September 11 and 12. This date was comfortably after the summer vacation season and allowed plenty of time for our activists to put what they learned into practice before the November election.

Unfortunately, in the spring when we called to reserve the space, the Founders Inn had already booked a Regent University conference for those dates. This evidently was a very popular conference, which guaranteed a sell-out of the almost-new hotel facility. The problem was, however, that *we* needed the hotel. The Founders Inn staff refused to budge in order to keep their commitment to Regent as well as to capitalize on the capacity weekend. The fact that our conference would likely feature the President of the United States did not sway their stance.

So, Ralph brought Pat into the picture. As chief executive officer of CBN, which owned the Founders Inn,‡ and as chancellor of Regent, hopefully he could shed some light on the situation—which, evidently, he did. Our contact at the Founders Inn soon called to say that they had been informed that *Christian Coalition* would be hosting a conference in their hotel on the weekend in question, and conference planners at Regent were notified that their event would have to be postponed.

"I don't think that's what they were supposed to do,"⁷ said a quizzical Ralph, upon learning that Regent, instead, had moved their event to a competing hotel for the same weekend, thus taking much-needed revenue away from its sister organization, the Founders Inn. "Whoever made that decision might have some explaining to do," I thought. We were delighted, as the November election was getting closer by the day. It sure makes a difference when you own the hotel.

As mentioned in the previous chapter, Ralph exhibited a masterful usage of the English language, was quick on his feet, and never seemed to be stumped by a reporter's question. Perhaps my favorite example of Ralph's verbal skills came as he once highlighted the hypocrisy of those in opposition to educational choice. Increasing numbers of parents exhibited support for school choice, in which they would receive a voucher or tax credit to take their children out of grossly unproductive and often dangerous public schools. Specifically, African American parents, the majority voting block in Washington, D.C., voted overwhelmingly for school choice in the District, only to be countered by Democrats in power. Ralph pointed out that in the 1960s, Alabama Governor George Wallace and the Democrats stood in front of the schoolhouse door trying to keep black children *out*. But in the 1990s, Democrats and the National Education Association stood at the schoolhouse door forcing them to stay *in*.⁸

It might have put even Ralph Reed to the test for words to describe his dismay, however, if we had lost President Bush as a speaker at that year's lavish Road to Victory Friday evening "Presidential Banquet." And for a few hours, it seemed that we might. Someone in the campaign hierarchy wondered if cozying up to Christian Coalition was the best thing for Bush's re-election effort. Speculation in *The Washington Post* was that it had been campaign chairman Jim Baker, who learned the event was on the president's schedule after he left his post as secretary of state in

‡ Ironically, CBN transferred ownership to Regent years later.

order to take over the campaign.[9] Fortunately, the Bush campaign kept its promise and he spoke to a packed house, each of whom had been filtered through Secret Service check-points and intimidating metal detectors, a necessary security measure for such occasions.

In the days leading up to the conference, Ralph told *The Virginian-Pilot* that the Bush campaign had given him assurances that Bush's speech at Road to Victory would be "the central campaign speech by the president on family values."[10] The front-page headline in the same newspaper on the day after the speech, however, read, "Bush talks jobs, not values."[11] With a sluggish economy and the Clinton campaign making "It's the economy, stupid!" its mantra, Bush had an uphill battle from the start, despite his record approval ratings after the 1991 Gulf War. For those reasons, as well as what may have been a reaction to left-wing criticism of his appearance at our event—remember, even some among his own staff did not want him to come—Bush spoke mostly about economic issues in Virginia Beach that night.

While President Bush was the most prestigious speaker that year, first-time speaker Oliver North was the most popular, with our attendees lining up for what seemed like hours throughout the hotel to receive an autographed copy of his recently released autobiography, *Under Fire*. The next week, a *Virginian-Pilot* headline proclaimed, "A 'God-solid' Ollie preaches to the choir,"[12] referencing a characterization of North by one of his dedicated fans in attendance. Pro-family activists already greatly admired him, and anticipated his promising political career. However, we did not know then how closely North's name would be linked with the Coalition in the future.§

Voter guide distribution was handled as meticulously as production. We mailed a letter from Pat, co-signed by a list of Christian luminaries, including Bill Bright, founder of Campus Crusade for Christ, Dr. D. James Kennedy, and Houston Baptist pastor Ed Young, Sr., a recent president of the Southern Baptist Convention, to a rented list of over 100,000 churches across the nation,⸲ asking how many voter guides each church would like. Based on the responses, Guy suggested to each state director the total number of voter guides they should receive per Congressional District.

§ See Chapter 6.

⸲ You can rent mailing lists for most anything, including several varieties of Baptist churches, contributors to various organizations and causes, people who own guns, and consumers who buy religious products out of magazines.

Basically, he just "eyeballed it." The state affiliates and county chapters then distributed the guides to the churches out of the bulk supplies they received.

Many thousands of pastors who wanted to receive our voter guides returned blue response forms, which were entered into our database—which, by the next presidential election cycle reached 125,000 churches, having been augmented by similar mailings in 1994 and 1996. The names and addresses of these churches were mailed to our state directors in time for distribution.

A few churches always fell through the cracks, however, including that year, the huge First Baptist Church of Atlanta. I remember being passed a phone call from our receptionist approximately one week before Election Day. "It's Pastor Charles Stanley, looking for his voter guides," she said, as I cleared my throat and took a deep breath before taking the call. Dr. Stanley, whose voice sounds even much deeper on the phone than on television, patiently listened as I assured him the voter guides would be there that day, after which, I made an urgent call to Pat Gartland, the new chairman of our Georgia state affiliate. Pat had not been slacking off; he was just very busy getting out the guides around his state. It took him longer because he personally drove a van around the state delivering the guides to each of his county chapters. In 1994, Alabama state chairmen Bob and June Russell worked in conjunction with a pharmaceutical company to distribute the guides around that state as its delivery vans made their rounds. And a Georgia chapter chairman and his wife, both retirees, used a golf cart to deliver voter guides throughout their community.

Christian Coalition voter guide distribution was always targeted for the Sunday prior to Election Day. This one-day distribution gave the voter guides the maximum effectiveness by not allowing time for liberals or the media to detract from their effectiveness by spreading false allegations. Pastors were encouraged to insert the guides into the bulletins, or to have ushers pass them down the aisle. Failing that, handing them out as parishioners entered or left the church was the next best choice. Finally, as a fallback position, making them available on a table in the foyer** was requested. The level of distribution depended on the preference of each respective pastor. Most were eager to participate, with an occasional pastor taking a voter guide into the pulpit and holding it up during the ser-

---

** Church lobby.

vice, encouraging the congregation to vote. Pastors then and now must be careful not to endorse any particular candidate or party, however.[††]

We again planned to take exit polls on Election Day. Having an early indication of the outcome had been comforting in the Virginia Beach state senate election the previous year, and it seemed like a good idea to try and do so in 1992, as well. Our state directors were asked to find one precinct in their state from the 1988 George Bush-Michael Dukakis election that had the same results as the statewide percentage, and then either to stand at that precinct or recruit a volunteer to do so. If Bush were doing well in those same precincts in 1992 his re-election would be likely, and vice versa. The state directors were supposed to call in their results at noon in their respective time zones.

It all became moot, however, as according to news network exit polls, Clinton's lead was so commanding in the eastern time zone that, by the time noon arrived in the others, our exit poll operation already had crumbled due to the disheartenment of our state leaders—and our staff. While pro-family candidates made significant pick-ups in the House that day, it was hardly enough to compensate our sorrows. The inclusion of third-party candidate Ross Perot on the ballot would actually have thrown us off kilter, had any results even been phoned in. His percentage of the total vote ensured that a majority was not required to win in a state—Clinton was elected with only 43 percent nationally—thus rendering meaningless the comparison to the 1988 results.

According to the media and to moderate Republicans, the prominence of religious conservatives at the Houston convention, along with Bush's staunch pro-life position on the abortion issue were major factors in his loss. Christian Coalition, of course, did not agree, feeling, among other factors, his campaign message was confused, as evidenced by his economic speech to an ardently pro-life crowd at Road to Victory. And certainly, reneging on his 1988 campaign pledge not to raise taxes was a large nail in his coffin. The responsibility for the loss belonged to the president, himself, as well as to his campaign handlers and strategists.

As Ralph Reed told *The Virginian-Pilot*, "[T]he pro-family message carried out of (the Republican convention in) Houston closed the gap for Bush from being 20 to 30 points behind to 10. The problem is the Bush campaign can't make up the other 10."[13] Ralph was even more colorful

---

†† This book should not be seen as a legal guide to such activities—the laws change often.

when he spoke with E. J. Doinne of *The Washington Post*: "Blaming the evangelicals for this defeat is like blaming the sinking of the Titanic on a waiter who dropped some dishes."[14]

Pat Robertson also resented being blamed with the loss. *The Virginian-Pilot* quoted him telling a news conference outside CBN head-quarters the morning after the election that, "If the other elements of the Republican Party did what evangelicals did (in getting out the vote)" Bush would have won.[15] And on *The 700 Club*, Pat was quite critical of those Christian voters who deserted Bush for Clinton's promises of a better economy, saying: "Evangelicals put money ahead of principle. They put money ahead of abortion. They put money ahead of homosexuality. They said, 'We want money. We want a better economy. We're not concerned about family values.'"[16]

Pundits wondered how Christian Coalition would recover from the loss. Would we take a step back from being so prominent? Or would we now have more control over the GOP? On election night, Pat Robertson sat in CBN's studios doing several remote television interviews for net-work news programs. As he readied himself for NBC's Tom Brokaw, Pat clearly was frustrated beyond compare. Just before the camera rolled, Ralph warned that Brokaw would ask Pat if he planned to take over the Republican Party. "What's left to take over?" Pat responded.[17]

Ralph put his own detailed spin on the election in a detailed four-page *Memo to Grassroots Leaders*, in which he critiqued conservative movement efforts in 1992 and made poignant suggestions for future ac-tivity. Receptivity to the memo was one of the first indications of Ralph's growing persona among religious conservative leaders and activists. *The Virginian-Pilot* printed Ralph's key principles as an Op-Ed, highlighting his five keys to a Republican comeback:

- Back to the grassroots: emphasize local organizing
- First things first: concentrate on the present and worry about 1996 later
- Remain pro-life and pro-family
- Appeal to the Perot voters
- Offer a positive vision: i.e., remember the conservative basics.[18]

The year ended with a state directors meeting at the Founders Inn on the first weekend in December where we recapped the year and made plans for 1993, and where Pat Robertson gave an inspiring Saturday evening message from Sun Tzu's *The Art of War*, after which we distributed copies of the book to the state directors. Following the weekend we buckled down for what promised to be four *long* years, having no idea, however, of how dramatically the Coalition's fortunes would change under the Clinton Administration or of how different the prospects of the GOP would appear just two years later.

# 5

## 10,000 New Members a Week

IN 1997, IN A retrospect on his tenure as Christian Coalition executive director, Ralph Reed wrote in his final "Priorities" column in our
*Christian American* publication: "It is never as bad as you think it is when
you lose and never as good as you think it is when you win."[1] As he wrote
the "when you lose" part, he was reflecting on the effect the 1992 presidential election had on the country, considering that, in Ralph's words, "Two
short years after his incredible victory, Bill Clinton presided over one of
the worst defeats in the history of his party, and the Republicans regained
control of Congress."[2] The Clinton presidency had a similarly explosive
effect on the fortunes of Christian Coalition.

Politically speaking, Wednesday, January 20, 1993, was the most
dreaded day in the Coalition's short existence. After twelve consecutive
years of a Republican in the White House, including the often-euphoric
eight years of the Reagan Administration, the United States was about to
inaugurate a liberal Democrat who sometimes masqueraded in moderate
clothing. On most issues, he was everything we—and most Americans—
were not: pro-abortion, pro-homosexual agenda, pro-taxes, pro-socialized
medicine. I could not even bring myself to watch the ceremonies, but I
remember that Ralph did so, on the television in his office. He knew he
would be asked to comment on Clinton's Inaugural address and had to
know what had been said.

Late in 1992, Ralph and our new fund-raising consultant, Ben Hart,
devised a program that revolved around the creation of our *Congressional
Scorecard*, which portrayed votes in Congress on pro-family issues over
the last congressional term. What originated in magazine form gave way
to a tri-fold brochure version in 1993, copies of which were included in
prospecting direct mail letters and in monthly mailings to current and
prospective supporters. "Prospecting" mailings were designed to reach

people who were not supporters, while the "house file" was the name given a list of our most reliable, core donors.

In conjunction with the Democrats' sweep into the Executive Branch of government and their retention of control of Congress, we began mailing millions of *Scorecards* to rented lists of Christian activists across America. The result was a previously unheard of number of new donors for the Coalition, reaching a high of 10,000 per week. People were coming out of the woodwork in opposition to the liberal, out-of-the-mainstream agenda of the Clinton-Gore Administration. This not only resulted in an increased rate of new donor acquisition, which continued steadily throughout the next two years, but it also helped the Newt Gingrich-led Republican takeover of Congress in the 1994 mid-term congressional elections.

The Coalition's incoming mail to P. O. Box 1990, Chesapeake, Virginia, progressed so heavily over the years that we eventually purchased a van to use to pick it up at the post office. At the height of our activity before the 1994 elections, it was not uncommon for the "tray count"* to reach as high as eighty trays in a given day, with the largest ever being a day with a tray count of ninety-six, in 1996, prior to the presidential elections. Of course not each envelope had a check enclosed, but most did.

We began running second and third shifts in our data processing department in order to enter the names and donations into the database. During the busiest months, the departments that processed the mail and handled data processing commonly worked from seven o'clock one morning until two o'clock the next, and often came in on Saturday. We hired additional workers, which spilled over into the conference room each day in order to process the checks.

An armed guard was brought in to escort the various persons who took the checks to the bank each day and, with the additional shifts worked by the remittance staff, we secured another guard to remain in the building while they were there late. Remittance Manager Jerry Ike and his daytime staff of clerks worked until after dark on many occasions in order to process the checks that came in from our loyal donors and new acquisitions. Director of Finance Judy Liebert once said the bank balance never went below $2 million at a given time.[3]

---

* Number of trays of mail, each containing as many as 500 letters.

Interestingly, we learned that donors often give much more money to fight something they disagree with than to support programs that they like. Christian Coalition's income went up dramatically—from $8 million in 1992 to $12 million in 1993—when Clinton came into office, and exploded—to about $22 million—in 1994 with the mid-term congressional elections, but fell slightly in 1995—to about $18 million—after Gingrich and the Republicans took control of Congress. This fluctuation is just one major reason that organizations must be good stewards of the money their supporters entrust them with. Just because money is pouring in one year does not mean it will the next.

Income reached an all-time high of just under $27 million in the 1996 presidential election year. And receipts in the months of August, September, and October in even numbered years† were an enormous percentage of each respective year's total. I must point out here that dollars raised by direct mail, while high in terms of "gross revenues" are much lower after expenses are taken out. Overhead costs for fund-raising can range from thirty to well over 50 percent of total revenues. Therefore, since direct mail was the primary source of our income, along with telemarketing, which is also quite costly, sometimes even more so, our net revenue was far less than the above description implies.

On Monday, February 1, 1993, a headline in *The Washington Post* entitled "Energized by Pulpit or Passion, the Public is Calling" appeared over an article about the grassroots lobbying techniques of the religious right in opposing President Clinton's proposal to lift the ban on homosexuals in the military. In the article, reporter Michael Weisskopf included a characterization of the followers of Jerry Falwell and Pat Robertson as "largely poor, uneducated and easy to command."[4] This set off a firestorm in our office and provided us with a sound bite with which to characterize the liberal media for years to come. Ralph asked me to write and fax a memo to our Washington, D.C. metro area supporters encouraging them to contact the *Post* and express their outrage. For years afterward, Ralph would be able to boast about the time the *Post*'s managing editor called to ask him to have our people stop mailing and faxing copies of their college and graduate diplomas to him. It seemed that Weisskopf had been wrong, at least, about the "uneducated" part.

† Those with Federal elections.

February also saw the opening of a Capitol Hill office in Washington, D.C. Conventional wisdom said that no successful political operation could be based outside Washington. But Christian Coalition gained a sense of independence by being located in suburban Chesapeake. Regardless, in order to be a real player‡ we had to have a lobbying presence on "the Hill." A fine location was found, 227 Massachusetts Avenue, N.E., on what is commonly known as "the Senate side," just across the street from our conservative ally, the Heritage Foundation. By 1996, the office had increased from one to three floors, housing thirteen personnel from four divisions of the organization: lobbying, development, field, and our African American affiliate, the Samaritan Project.

Ralph chose Marshall Wittmann, formerly with the U.S. Department of Health and Human Services in the Bush Administration, and Heidi Scanlon, who had been with accounting firm Price-Waterhouse, to head up the D.C. office. Heidi remained with the Coalition until late 1995 when her husband's law firm transferred him to its London office, and Marshall left about the same time to take a fellowship at Heritage.

There was one twist with their selections, however: Marshall was Jewish—and not a Messianic Jew, those Jews who embrace the reality that Jesus Christ is the Messiah. Ralph's rationale was that, politically, Marshall agreed with us on our issues, and second, he was the best person available to do the job. All the staff liked Marshall very much and welcomed him to the organization. He became a valuable asset to Christian Coalition, even though working with us most assuredly brought strains in his personal and family life. After leaving the Coalition, and then Heritage, however, Marshall began to move to the left politically. In 2001 he joined the staff of socially moderate Senator John McCain, in 2004 he began working for the Democratic Leadership Council, and later joined the U.S. senatorial staff of 2000 Democrat vice presidential candidate Joe Lieberman.§ Regardless of politics, I pray that Marshall saw true Christianity in those of us with whom he worked during his time at the Coalition.

Even though we were a public-policy-oriented organization that was made up of Christians, we also coordinated with politically like-minded members of other faiths. Christians and conservative Jews, for example,

‡ In politics, every person and organization strives to be a "player."

§ Lieberman faced primary opposition in 2006 when Democrat leaders objected to his support of the war in Iraq. He lost the primary but was re-elected in November as an Independent.

have much in common, politically and otherwise, and throughout the years Christian Coalition worked very closely with our Jewish friends. Rabbi Daniel Lapin, president of Toward Tradition, was a perennial speaker at our Road to Victory conference, always rating near the top of a poll of the attendees' favorite speaker. Also, Rabbi Yechiel Eckstein, president of the International Fellowship of Christians and Jews, worked with us on projects, and spoke at Road to Victory in 1995. As Ralph Reed often said, "Not all who share our politics share our faith, and not all who share our faith share our politics," the former alluding to our working with Jews, and with Mormons on occasion, and the latter explaining our differences with liberal Christians, both Protestant and Catholic alike.

Many of Christian Coalition's most dedicated supporters were offended by our attempts to educate voters who were not Christians, or even Christians who did not agree on one or more tenets of the faith. Some even left our ranks when we began openly working with Catholics in 1994, as Pat Robertson joined Chuck Colson and other well-known Protestants in signing *Evangelicals and Catholics Together*, a document that encouraged cooperation between the two main segments of Christendom. Even more left in 1995 when Christian Coalition launched a sister organization, the Catholic Alliance.

That always baffled me. Why would anyone refuse to work alongside someone who agreed on the public policy issues of the day? Even though Protestants and Catholics differ on many theological tenets, Christian Coalition was not established to further a particular sectarian dogma but rather to see religious conservatives elected to office, and to encourage governments to pass legislation that strengthens families and protects religious freedom.

In addition to Marshall Wittmann being Jewish—and later, Camille Mitzner, who served as grassroots legislative liaison—the Coalition staff was also composed of many varieties of Christians. There were Baptists, Presbyterians, and Methodists, as well as Pentecostals/charismatics— those who trace their beginnings to the biblical Day of Pentecost[§] and embrace manifestations referred to by the Apostle Paul as the gifts of the Holy Spirit.[**] We also had Catholics in senior leadership positions; and

---

[§] See Acts Chapter 2.

[**] See I Corinthians Chapter 12.

the staff included at least one member of the Greek Orthodox Church, Mike Russell.

Mike joined the Coalition in early 1993 as director of communications. He had been program director at a local radio station and had no political background. But he had the endorsement of Pat's media director at CBN, Gene Kapp, who had known him from earlier local radio and television work, and that meant a lot. Mike learned politics quickly working alongside Ralph and became able to anticipate and predict what our media strategy should be. And in traveling often with Ralph, he regularly entertained us with amusing stories from the trail. Mike actually was quite funny, and bore a resemblance in both appearance and in mannerisms to comedian Jerry Seinfeld.

The Coalition staff was diverse in terms of gender and race, as well. A fairly equal number of women and men worked at the Coalition, although there were more men than women among the senior staff. However, over the years nine division directors were women, as were six department heads. The senior staff also included one African American, while our department heads included four others, along with several assistant managers.

Our state directors were an eclectic group also. While most were established church, business, and political leaders, with many being former elected officials or former state leaders for the 1988 Robertson presidential campaign, others were from a more varied background, including small business owners, retirees, millionaires, PhDs, and homemakers. Over the years, our state directors included a few out-of-the-ordinary examples, as well, including a past Miss America contestant, a former homosexual activist who was delivered from that lifestyle after accepting Jesus, and two who had close ties to the abortion industry prior to accepting Christ. On the other hand, the state chairman and executive director of one state affiliate met while serving time in jail after being arrested for protesting abortion. And we had one bona fide American hero, one-time Missouri state chairman John Testrake, the famed TWA pilot and hostage, who passed away after suffering with cancer only a year or so after coming to the Coalition.

Of course there was turnover, with only a few states having the same state director for more than three or four years. And occasionally state directors had to be asked to step aside, due to personal or political problems they presented for the state and/or national organization. Since the states each had their own incorporation status and boards of directors, we were not at liberty simply to release a state director, instead having to negotiate their being voted off of their own board or, if not, breaking the affiliation agreement between national and that state board.

Unfortunately, at least two such replacements were mishandled by the national office over the years. In the mid-1990s we ended up paying $20,000 to one of our northeastern state boards—that had broken its affiliation with national—in order to regain the legal rights to the name Christian Coalition and, therefore, be able to organize a new state affiliate.†† Later, in a mid-western state, an outright war of words and legal maneuvering occurred when the state director was bunglingly "fired" by national. This instance happened in 1999 after the national office began to self-destruct, with at least one former national employee actually advising the state affiliate on how to battle headquarters with legal maneuvers.

Our county chapter chairmen included an even greater variety, with lawyers, doctors, pastors, and housewives heading up local organizations. The Spotsylvania County, Virginia, chapter chairman, Bill Murray, was the son of America's most notorious atheist, Madeline Murray O'Hair. A well-known Christian activist prior to joining Christian Coalition, Bill added a special flair to our ranks. And the national office once had an intern, a Regent University student, who spent his weekends working for Warner Bros. Studios as a *Batman* impersonator.

The county chapters were even more volunteer-based than the states and, with a few exceptions, did not focus a great deal on raising money. Growing from just sixty in number when I began with the Coalition in 1991, our total number of chapter chairmen reached 750 during the first year of the Clinton Administration. By 1996, the total had grown to just under 2000. The chapters varied in depth and in focus. Some were full-fledged organizations, having monthly meetings and several working committees, while other chairmen served as our solitary representative in their local area, focusing mainly on distributing voter guides at election time. Many knew their congressman on a first-name basis, while others were less experienced.

Finally, our donors represented a cross section of the economic spectrum. They included laborers, business owners, retirees, professional athletes, heads of other Christian ministries, television personalities, and at

†† They originally wanted $50,000.

least one member of the *Forbes* list of the 400 richest people in America.[‡‡] Some gave only to the national organization, while others supported both their state office and their county chapter.

While after several years of activity many states raised money well into the high six figures, most maintained small budgets, working out of donated offices or in their homes. These people certainly were not in it for the money, as many had to hold other jobs while also running the state Christian Coalition.

Until 1997, when the Coalition's indebtedness became out of control, the national office provided matching grants to the state affiliates. National matched fifty cents on every dollar they raised, up to $1,000 per month. They simply had to provide us with copies of deposit slips showing how much money they had raised. This provided a comical event in 1994 when we realized that the amount we gave the states in one month was (obviously) included in their next month's deposit slip photocopies. Our accounting staff had not been subtracting that amount, therefore we were matching dollars that *we* had given them.

In addition, we paid for the mailing of our *Christian American* publication complete with a state insert to our national donors in each state, as well as to the respective state's own donor lists. Also, when each new state affiliate came on board, we mailed a start-up letter from Pat Robertson to our donors in that state, requesting money for the state affiliate.

The first weekend in June, 1993, saw the Virginia Republican Party hold its annual convention in the Richmond Coliseum. Approximately 13,000 activists came to support their respective candidates for the Commonwealth's top three offices: governor, lieutenant governor, and attorney general. We had repeated our mailings and phone banks into the various localities just as we had done the year before. Pat's (and, therefore, the Coalition's) hopes for nomination were former Congressman George Allen as governor, home school pioneer Mike Farris as lieutenant governor and Commonwealth's Attorney Jim Gilmore for attorney general.[§§] In keeping with our non-profit tax status, of course, Christian Coalition was careful not to instruct our activists to support any particular candidate(s), but simply to show up—in large numbers—and vote their preferences.

---

[‡‡] Christian Coalition, as a 501(c)(4) organization, was not legally required to reveal the names of its donors, therefore I will omit the name here.

[§§] Farris had more Christian home school supporters present than we could have turned out by our efforts alone.

Friday evening was taken up with receptions hosted by the various candidates, as well as the Party's annual Road to Victory Dinner.¶¶ Ralph and I had dinner on our own, along with John Wheeler, editor of our *Christian American* newspaper, who also was in Richmond for the convention.

Conversation drifted until something came up about Christians and the use of alcoholic beverages. I recalled a story about a conflict between a Regent University bridegroom and the father of the bride over whether to serve wine at the wedding reception. My friend the groom was a teetotaler and did not want any alcohol at his wedding. Ralph agreed with the groom until I said that I had counseled my friend to stand his ground on the biblical principle that couples must leave their respective parents and—using King James English—*cleave* to their spouse.*** If she would not side with her soon-to-be husband in this instance it might portend larger problems of parental conflict later on. I was pleased to share the anecdote, in part because it put me firmly in agreement with Ralph, or so I thought. Ever the debater, after my convictions had been stated clearly, Ralph saw an opening and immediately changed his position, taking sides with the father. "Well if *I* [had been] that father, I'd say, 'Listen Mr. Cleaver, *I'm paying for this wedding . . .*'" he said, leaving me astounded at his swift reversal of sides, although impressed with his ability to do so.

Former Congressman George Allen won the gubernatorial nomination, which was a delight to most of our activists. He had a tooth-and-nail battle for delegates with a wealthy northern Virginia businessman, and, just as in 1992, our efforts to turn out supporters played a pivotal role.

At some point that afternoon, Ralph concluded that it was a good opportunity to get media attention for Christian Coalition out of this convention. In the year after a presidential election, politics is fairly quiet nationally, with the gubernatorial elections in Virginia and New Jersey providing the only notable opportunity for the media to cover electoral politics, so any interview he gave could become national news.

Even though Ralph had not yet reached the celebrity status he later achieved, he hardly could approach reporters at the convention asking if they wanted to interview him. But someone had to do so. Our first effort was for me to speak with an executive of the Richmond NBC affiliate.

---

¶¶ Not to be confused with the Coalition's annual event by the same name.
*** Paraphrasing Genesis 2:24.

I waited outside their makeshift production booth for a message to be delivered to him and saw him look under the blinds shielding the booth's activities from the convention crowd. He saw no one he recognized, so he never came out. However, I still had a job to do.

I had met several of the Richmond reporters when I worked on the 1988 U.S. Senate race in Virginia. I saw Jim Babb, lead political reporter for the same NBC station we were hoping to talk with, on the floor of the convention interviewing delegates, and I approached him with these words, "Would you like to talk to Ralph Reed?" Unlike the news executive, Babb readily recognized the opportunity I was offering and enthusiastically answered, "Yes!" I told him to wait there and went to get Ralph. The result was Ralph commenting on the convention directly from the hoopla of the convention floor—the same scenario as is commonly seen at the national parties' political conventions—as notice went out to Richmond viewers that Christian Coalition had made an impact.

At the 1992 Republican National Convention in Houston, former Congressman and Bush HUD Secretary Jack Kemp had won a poll as the attending delegates' top choice for president in 1996. Kemp had run in 1988, coming in fourth behind Bush, Senator Bob Dole, and Pat Robertson in that order. That campaign had ended with the Robertson and Kemp forces in quite a rift over a broken deal to pool delegates in Michigan in order to shut out Bush.

In order to run in 1996 Kemp would have to patch things up with Pat, which he apparently hoped to do, beginning with a breakfast meeting one Saturday in June, 1993, at the Founders Inn. After the meeting, Kemp needed to be driven to Petersburg, Virginia, where he would join his wife, Joanne, who was en route from Washington, D.C., on their way to Wake Forest University—just down Interstate 85 in North Carolina—to watch their son play football. Ralph's deputy, Judy Haynes, who by appearance could be the younger sister of Texas U.S. Senator Kay Bailey Hutchison, and I escorted Kemp.

After their breakfast, the two men exited the hotel's Swan Terrace restaurant and walked toward Judy and me as we waited in the lobby. I noticed that Pat was wearing his red-striped dress shirt with the contrasting white collar—the same shirt I had seen him wear on *The 700 Club* the day before—over which he wore a casual jacket and no tie. Kemp, on the other hand, was complete with a dark suit and his trademark tab-collar white shirt.

The meeting evidently had gone well. They parted very cordially, and Judy, Kemp, and I walked to Judy's waiting baby-blue Cadillac. I drove and Kemp sat in the front with me, while Judy rode in back, as we began the two-hour drive on U.S. Hwy. 460 to Petersburg.

The conversation was quite enjoyable, and Kemp was very pleasant. It isn't every day that you meet someone of his political stature, as well as his personal charm. He did most of the talking, taking great pains to be sure that Judy and I were entertained. I particularly remember him crediting his recent weight loss to a diet of coffee and Slim Fast, and the gain that necessitated the diet to his affinity for his wife's freshly baked cookies.

During the trip Secretary Kemp regretted that he would be unable to accept our invitation to address our upcoming Road to Victory conference, saying that after over a decade in public service, first as congressman and later as Cabinet secretary, he had to maximize his first opportunity to acquire speaking fees and accumulate a substantial degree of income. Upon returning to the office on Monday I reported to Ralph on the trip, conveying Kemp's apologies for having to miss Road to Victory. "He'll be there," Ralph said confidently, "He just doesn't know it yet." And as usual, Ralph's confidence was proven true. Although I had no idea how he made it happen, on Saturday evening, September 11, 1993, at the Road to Victory gala banquet, after the Coalition's Oregon executive director, Darrell Fuller, offered the pledge of allegiance and Dr. Billy McCormack gave the invocation, the first speaker was none other than Jack Kemp.

As Virginia and New Jersey were the only states holding statewide races in 1993, producing voter guides was much less work than the 40 million nationwide we had done in 1992. The year held another challenge, though. For the first time we were holding the Road to Victory conference in Washington, D.C. The size of the Founders Inn ballroom did not allow for further growth in the conference and, as with the reason we had opened the Capitol Hill office earlier that year, to be most effective, Road to Victory also had to be in Washington.

On September 10 and 11, over 2,000 activists from around the country came to the Washington Hilton and Towers on Connecticut Avenue in northwest D.C.††† It had the largest ballroom in Washington, and Ralph had introduced the hotel to our staff as "where Reagan was shot." Just

††† Later renamed the Hilton Washington.

outside the stone walled entrance to the hotel's Terrace Level, President Reagan had taken an attempted assassin's bullet in 1981. I remember trying to picture the scene when I later stood near the very spot where the president had been shot. By this time, the Hilton had constructed a bulletproof parking place for future presidential visits. Seven subsequent Road to Victory conferences were held at the Hilton, a hotel which soon felt like "home away from home" to many of our staff.

Persuading the most important conservative personalities to address the Road to Victory conference each year was fairly easy.[‡‡‡] By making a serious run for president and by founding a powerful organization like Christian Coalition, Pat Robertson had cemented his name on the list of people that most Republican presidential hopefuls felt they had to win over if they wanted any chance of winning the Party's nomination. Part of courting Pat Robertson included speaking at Christian Coalition's annual conference.

Along with the usual conservative leaders from Congress, Road to Victory '93 had at least one other particularly memorable speaker. In an effort to show nonpartisanship we invited Democratic National Committee Chairman David Wilhelm to speak on Friday morning. Ralph opened the conference, to be followed by Wilhelm and his Republican counterpart, Haley Barbour.[§§§]

As Wilhelm took the microphone I was one floor above the ballroom, checking on the various details of the conference. Soon, however, I heard Ralph's voice coming over the walkie-talkie instructing Guy Rodgers, staff member Steve Jordan, and me to, "Get in here!" I bounded down the escalator to the Hilton's Concourse Level and stepped into the back of the ballroom to a scene I had not witnessed before or have I seen since at a Christian event. Many if not most in the crowd were booing as Wilhelm spoke. It seemed that he had chosen to cast aside all courtesy and use his speech as an opportunity to chastise Christian Coalition and its members for opposing the "noble" programs of President Bill Clinton. He even went so far as to contend that the "Christian" position should be to support Clinton and his agenda, one that our members knew was pro-abortion and anti almost everything they believed in. So our people reacted in a very natural manner.

---

[‡‡‡] Although we never could entice Rush Limbaugh to appear.

[§§§] Later elected governor of Mississippi.

Ralph, however, realized that this was the very reaction Wilhelm had hoped to provoke. Television viewers seeing this portrayed every thirty minutes on CNN's *Headline News* would only think that the Christian Coalition reacted "hatefully" to someone invited to address their convention. Therefore, Ralph wanted Guy, Steve, and me to go throughout the audience "shushing" the people. This was one of my more difficult-to-accomplish assignments, however, as the more we shushed, the more Wilhelm taunted, and the more they booed.

Christian Coalition engaged in numerous outreaches to Democrats over the years, including a pro-life rally at the 1996 Democratic National Convention in Chicago. We often hosted Democratic speakers at our annual Road to Victory conference, including one of our favorites, pro-life Pennsylvania Governor Robert Casey. Democrat Congressman Mike Parker of Mississippi was included among the speakers for a 1995 state directors meeting in Washington, D.C., and at a 1993 State Legislative Policy and Campaign Institute, we not only had Democrats but also a representative from a heavily Democrat labor union, the United Mine Workers, who discussed how to win the labor vote. The seminar produced three winning candidates for the Virginia General Assembly that year, one future Virginia state senator, and a Cincinnati, Ohio, city councilman.

As for Democrats and voter education, Christian Coalition distributed voter guides in a 1993 special congressional election in Texas, featuring pro-life African American Democrat Beverly Clark, a Houston city councilwoman. We sent thousands of voter guides via Fed Ex directly to churches in Houston.

Most notably, we distributed voter guides in a Democrat primary in Oklahoma in 1994, where a pro-life challenger, retired school teacher Virgil Cooper, defeated incumbent Congressman Mike Synar, who went on to be named to the Clinton Cabinet. In that fall's general election both the Democrat who had defeated Synar, and his Republican opponent and the eventual winner, physician Tom Coburn, believed (and said) they enjoyed Christian Coalition's support. In his 2003 book, *Breach of Trust*, a scathing critique on career politicians, particularly those in the Republican Party, Coburn wrote that Cooper's defeat of Synar was the hint of smoke that signaled the GOP's inferno-like takeover of Congress that November.[¶¶¶]

¶¶¶ Coburn left the House in 2000 under self-imposed term limits, but was elected to the Senate in 2004.

In the 1993 Virginia elections, both George Allen and attorney general candidate Jim Gilmore won by wide margins, with only the lieutenant gubernatorial candidate, Mike Farris, falling short. Farris faced bitter anti-Christian bigotry from his opponent and other liberal Democrats, and was also the victim of negative comments made by Virginia's senior U.S. senator, Republican John Warner, who refused to endorse him because Farris was too far right—and likely far too religious—for the senator's taste. On election night, George Allen began his acceptance speech by thanking God, and all was well in the Old Dominion.

One day just after Thanksgiving Guy Rodgers summoned me to his office. I thought it might have something to do with my November annual review, which was correct, in part. Guy's words were, "Ralph approved your raise . . . but you're going to have a new boss." After three years as national field director, Guy was leaving the Coalition and starting a political consulting firm.**** I realized that a new era—with new challenges—would soon be dawning on the field division.

A search for a new national field director would begin soon. In the meantime, Steve Jordan and I were responsible for carrying on field operations. Basically, the job was just to keep the lid on everything until a replacement for Guy was found. No heavy lifting would occur in the meantime. Or so I thought.

About two weeks before Christmas, as I was planning to take some vacation, Ralph informed me that Pat wanted to host a formal dinner for Governor-elect Allen on the evening of the Commonwealth Inauguration. "Could you put on an event like that?" Ralph asked me as we discussed Pat's plans.

At first, we were not even sure whom we should invite to the dinner. The governor-elect and attorney general-elect were obvious, of course, as were Allen's Cabinet designees, and our like-minded friends among Virginia's congressional delegation and in the General Assembly. But that left about seventy-five openings in our desired audience of about one hundred. Ralph contacted a couple of Party insiders who supplied the "who's who" list we were looking for, and the invitations hit the mail. The resulting event was good for Pat, good for the governor-elect, and—most of all—good for the Coalition.

---

**** One of Guy's first clients, a board member from a Christian Coalition affiliate in a Southern state, was elected to Congress the very next year.

The dinner would usher in a new year that would, in retrospect, be the "golden era" of Christian Coalition.

6

# The File's for Ollie

NINETEEN NINETY-FOUR WAS *THE* year for Christian Coalition. The country had survived one year of Clinton-Gore and we had seen our budget and membership totals increase dramatically. President Clinton's health care bill was going down to defeat and many of his other liberal social programs were struggling as well. With conservatives poised to make huge gains in the November mid-term congressional elections, we eagerly anticipated the coming of fall, with scores of competitive seats in the House and several in the Senate, with one in particular being in our own back yard. But could we flex our Virginia muscle once again?

The year's first order of business was the Inauguration dinner for Virginia Governor George Allen. Over one hundred people had accepted Pat Robertson's invitation to attend the black-tie affair at Richmond's Valentine Museum, just a stone's throw from the Capitol and Governor's Mansion. Ralph was planning a memorable event at which all the essential GOP officials in the Commonwealth would come to acknowledge the new governor.

Watching the attendees file into the museum was impressive: Conservative icon Oliver North and his wife, Betsy; Attorney General— and future governor—Jim Gilmore; both the current and previous state GOP chairmen; former U.S. Attorney General William Barr; one congressman; and eleven members of the Virginia General Assembly. The governor and his Cabinet only stopped by for a toast before leaving for another event—however, the statement was made.

Ralph always was emphatic that there be no empty seats at our events where a meal was served—and heaven forbid there be any empty tables. This night was no exception. He and I were the only staff at the event, and long after the attendees were in the banquet room, yet while several were up talking but not seated, he instructed me to go around and remove the empty chairs. "Ralph," I protested, "I've just checked the name tag at every empty place. *Each person is here*; they're just not seated yet." They eventually sat down and all was okay; to the last seat, each was filled. A few months earlier, at the 1993 State Legislative Policy and Campaign Institute, Pat was to speak at the concluding dinner and Ralph even wanted me to have an entire table removed from the room upon realizing that the hotel had set ten places that would not be needed. Optics were crucial and he did not want it to seem as if we had "no shows."

Earlier, on Friday afternoon, Ralph and I sat in the hotel discussing the difficulty he had been having in locating a new national field director to replace Guy Rodgers. Then, early Sunday morning, Ralph drove just over an hour north on Interstate 95 to Fredericksburg, Virginia, to speak at a church service at the invitation of local Coalition leaders. I checked out of my room, and before leaving, policed Ralph and Jo Anne's vacated room to be sure he had not forgotten anything in his rush to make the speaking engagement. There, I ran across an opened Federal Express envelope that had been delivered to him at the Marriott. The envelope was empty except for a note from Heidi Scanlon of our Washington, D.C. office. She had written, "Ralph—Here's the info on D. J."

David J. Gribbin IV, a tax analyst with the National Federation of Independent Business and son of Dick Cheney's long-time chief of staff, was soon hired to take over the field organizing and training aspects of Guy's former position. The voter guides were split off into a new "voter education"* division and would be produced by our new director of voter education, Charles H. "Chuck" Cunningham, who had come from the National Rifle Association and, before that, the National Right to Work Committee, and was steadily accumulating the most right-wing résumé in America. He had spoken at our state legislative candidate seminar the previous year.

Chuck was an enigma. On one hand, he was a bearded, gun toting, SUV driving, flannel-shirt-wearing, right-wing activist, whose license plate read, "I AM NRA." But he had a bit of a "green" side, also. He was vocally disapproving of anything he considered extravagant in the Coalition budget, to the point of refraining from using his Coalition-provided cell phone until the lower evening rates were in force. He also hated waste and was the office advocate of recycling. Many times I saw him fish an empty

---

* Ralph felt that "political" would send the wrong signal to outsiders.

soda can out of the garbage receptacle that someone else had thrown away. Basically, Chuck was a Christian version of Andy Sipowicz, a tough yet gentle, no-nonsense guy who did his job and wanted everyone else to do theirs.

Chuck was the first guy anyone would want in his foxhole when under attack. And he could go on the offense as well. He once burst into a Road to Victory planning meeting to inform Ralph of a late-breaking political happening. As Chuck left the room, Ralph remarked with admiration, "That guy's an *assassin*." It happened that a few weeks earlier Ralph had asked Chuck to utilize our nonpartisan voter education practices in a particular primary election in a Southern state. Ralph explained: "The next thing I knew, one of the candidates was calling me, pleading, 'Please make him stop!' Chuck had been doing voter guides, post cards, phone calls, just beating the guy† to a pulp."

Christian Coalition's major legislative focus of 1994 was our opposition to the proposed government takeover of the nation's health care system. In a February 15 news conference at the National Press Club, Ralph Reed promised that Christian Coalition would spend $1.4 million and engage its then one million members and over 850 local chapters to combat the health care plan.[1] While recognizing that health care should be made more available and more affordable for all Americans, we opposed Clinton's plan on the primary basis that it would have placed a government bureaucrat in the middle of the cherished doctor-patient relationship. The Clinton plan would have instituted rationing of health care and government-funded abortion. It would have restricted the consumer's choice of a health care provider and would have cost jobs by placing undue payroll taxes on small business owners. Finally, anyone seeking to go outside the government's prescribed system could have faced Federal prosecution.

We printed 30 million four-color post cards depicting a family visit to the doctor with a caption that read, "Don't Let a Government Bureaucrat in this Picture." Our state directors distributed the cards to their supporters, who signed and mailed them back to their respective congressmen and senators. Our campaign included print and radio ads, direct mail and telephone contacts with our activists, and more post cards sent to voters and to churches for their members to sign and return to

† I.e., his record on the issues.

their own representatives in Congress. Further, each of our state directors identified a "health care coordinator" to head up post card distribution in their respective states.

In the end, the bright prospects for Republican candidates in the upcoming November elections signaled the end of nationalized health care. As summer turned to fall, and with Democrats' chances of victory in November's congressional elections looking slim, so did the fortunes of the Clinton plan.

For the third year in a row, the first Saturday in June found several of our staff at the Virginia Republican Convention. This year's agenda was the U.S. Senate nomination contest between two figures from the Reagan Administration, former National Security Council operative Oliver North and former Reagan budget director Jim Miller. The establishment was firmly behind Miller, with movement activists and leaders behind North. Support among our staff was heavily for North, although, not entirely.

Most notably, the overwhelming majority of our activists were for North. In fact, earlier that year Miller had traveled to Chesapeake to meet with Ralph. He received a warm welcome but left disappointed. Ralph and Pat both strongly supported North for the nomination, but regardless of their personal desires, Ralph was able to tell Miller in all honesty, using our in-house term for the mailing list of donors, "The *file's* for Ollie."[2] And he was correct. Even though the statewide support among our people was not as widespread for North as it had been for lieutenant gubernatorial candidate Mike Farris the year before, most of them were in the North camp. Like the previous two years, of course, our mailings and phone banks to our activists did not show support for one candidate over the other, but simply encouraged our activists to go to Richmond and vote.

Chuck Cunningham ran our state convention delegate recruitment that spring, and his contacts in the pro-family and conservative Republican communities across the Commonwealth were enormous due to his years as a state legislative specialist with the NRA, as well as his life-long political involvement in the state. Thousands of Christian Coalition contacts and other pro-family voters registered as delegates, bringing the total delegate count equal to—if not more than—the previous year's 13,000 when homeschoolers for Mike Farris swarmed the Richmond Coliseum.

Friday evening of convention weekend provided an opportunity for receptions hosted by candidates and activist groups, and this year, Ralph decided that the Coalition would host our own. Chuck, D. J., and I plastered the hotel and adjacent convention hall with handbills that read, "Christian Coalition Reception—Come and Meet Ralph Reed." This was our first indication of the drawing power of Ralph's name. The reception was packed from start to finish. We quickly ran out of food, and hardly another body could have been squeezed into the room, with several spilling out into the hallway.

The excitement was heightened by the fact that almost all the people at the reception were anticipating Oliver North's coronation the next day. Finally, his supporters would get back at the liberals in Washington who had harassed their stalwart for so many years. After what had been done to him and the conservative movement by Democrats in Washington during and after the 1987 Iran-Contra hearings, this was a must-win battle. Establishment Republicans had no right to tell him—or us—that he should not run. It was payback time.

The lion's share of our statewide activists supported North and they were not bashful about it. Later that summer I drove to Manassas, Virginia, to speak at a Leadership School. As soon as I drove into the parking lot of the facility where the event was being held, it seemed that every car proudly sported a North bumper sticker—*North for Senate, Sportsmen for North, Ollie by Golly!*—letting me know right away that I was in North country. I began my speech by joking that at first it seemed that I had arrived at a North rally by mistake.

North's support for the nomination was not unanimous among Coalition members however, with several backing Miller and a small pocket of southwestern Virginia activists threatening to switch from North to Miller if the North campaign served alcohol at its reception the night before the vote. And they succeeded. Ralph coaxed, and possibly even pleaded, but they would not budge, so he gave North's people the news. And North's handlers caved in. I remember visiting the almost empty North reception and picking up one of the many unopened *non-alcoholic* beer bottles on display.‡

Between the nominating convention and Election Day, Senator John Warner struck again, tipping the 1994 Virginia election away from North and the Republican Party. Warner used his statewide popularity,§

‡ I am a non-drinker myself but thought the move by our activists was over the top.

§ Warner, a former Navy secretary who had been elected in 1978 as the husband of Elizabeth Taylor, was a three-term senator, a leading member of the Armed Services Committee and, thankfully, able to keep Virginia's many military bases open and its ship-

along with his endorsement of a feeble candidacy from former attorney general and two-time gubernatorial candidate Marshall Coleman, to take just enough Republican votes away from North and re-elect Robb,¶ just as he had torpedoed Mike Farris's lieutenant gubernatorial candidacy the prior year.

Some conservatives considered supporting North to have been shortsighted, however, feeling that Miller, equally conservative as North, would have provided much less of a target for liberals in November. After winning the nomination, North became the object of Democrat and liberal media fury from Portland, Maine, to Portland, Oregon, and everywhere in between. Possibly more than any U.S. Senate race in history, donors nationwide sent their checks to Virginia, some to help elect North and some to defeat him. Miller would have not faced the media opposition, moderate Republican betrayal, and nationwide vehemence of the Democrats and, therefore, would most likely have beaten Robb handily, who had been plagued by rumors of Clintonesque personal behavior and accounts of a bitter intra-party fight with one of his successors as Virginia governor. Had he won the nomination over North, Jim Miller could have been in the Senate for multiple terms.

As the fall election season approached, national Democrats had decided to brand religious conservatives as "fire-breathing Christian radical(s),"[3] with Christian Coalition and Pat Robertson targeted for much of the criticism. Among other things, conservative candidates were called "card-carrying members of the flat earth society"[4] by Democrat leaders.** In addition, a South Carolina gubernatorial candidate with huge support among Coalition members was castigated by opposing forces in a Republican primary who said that his only qualifications for office were that he handled snakes and spoke fluently in tongues[5]—a blatant slap at Pentecostal and charismatic Christians, the former association being gross hyperbole and the latter mocking a central tenet of their faith.

Democrats, especially at the national level, have exalted far too many leaders who are hostile to Christians. It is little wonder, then, that the type

---

building operations funded.

¶ There actually were four candidates in the race. Former Governor L. Douglas Wilder, a Democrat, ran as an Independent due to a deep feud with Robb, which actually would have assured a victory by North had Warner not persuaded Coleman to run.

** In these examples, respectively, by Rep. Vic Fazio, then chairman of the Democratic Congressional Campaign Committee, and by Democrat consultant Mark Wellman.

of voter who identified with Christian Coalition preferred Republican candidates. Of course, the Democrats tried to play both sides of the fence. They allowed radical liberals to chase conservative voters into the Republican Party during the 1960s, '70s and '80s, and then in the 1990s complained that Christian Coalition was a Republican partisan organization because it sought to mobilize those same voters.

This all just gave us more fodder to use in fund-raising letters and for Ralph to include in speeches. In fact, after the Republican sweep of the 1994 elections, Ralph was able to add a new applause line. He'd wind up by repeating the above examples of anti-Christian bigotry, and then, on behalf of Christian voters, deliver the knock-out punch: "But *we* have different names for our candidates. We call them 'Governor!' 'Senator!' 'Mayor!'" as adoring crowds cheered jubilantly.

It seemed that every year Democrats somewhere attempted to stigmatize Christian candidates because of their faith. And on many occasions they tried to take the focus off of the candidates themselves and, regardless of the state where they were running, onto Pat Robertson. From a Virginia Beach state senate election in 1991, to the Los Angeles mayor's race in 1993, to Senator John McCain in the Republican primaries of 2000, Democrats and moderate Republicans tried again and again to take voters' attention off of their opponents and place it on Pat. And each time, they went down in defeat, hoisted on their own petard. These candidates just did not seem to understand the near impossibility of motivating voters against a person who is not directly involved in the contest. Whenever this happened, after the pro-family candidate had won the election, Pat would flash his inimitable smile and say, "They just can't get it in their heads that I'm not on the ballot."

The approach of an election meant that it was time for voter guide production, and in 1994 our voter guides excelled to a new level. While earlier, we customarily settled for a "no response" in the column of candidates who did not return our issue questionnaire,†† Chuck and his staff pressed forward, researching their issue positions through public statements and voting records, insisting that each candidate was represented on every issue we included. In the end, Christian Coalition printed 33 million voter guides for distribution across the country in 1994.

†† A few northeastern Republicans and most Democrats.

The campaign manager for a third-party candidate for lieutenant governor in Pennsylvania once called me to loudly complain that Christian Coalition was not including his candidate on our voter guide. Because, legally, we had to include only candidates who met objective viability standards, such as polling percentages and money raised, only the two major party candidates were slated for our guides. This campaign threatened to hold a press conference denouncing our "unfair tactics." After attempting to dissuade him, but not succeeding, I passed the call to Chuck, who just hit the speaker button on his phone, heard the threat for himself and simply replied, "Okay," and that was it! Chuck knew full-well that their threat, even if carried out, would have no impact whatsoever. We did, however, understand the reason for their insistence. Appearing on a Christian Coalition voter guide would have given a heightened—although ersatz—legitimacy to their party and to their candidates.

Election Day 1994 was an emotional roller coaster. In the morning and early afternoon we were elated; in the early evening, depressed; and by midnight we were ecstatic. The reason for our euphoria early on was our mistaken belief that Oliver North had won. Out of a desire to know what the results would be long before the polls had closed, we set up what we felt was a sophisticated volunteer exit poll operation around the state. By noon we had received glowing reports of a clear win by North and, as I recall, Ralph called Pat with the good news. We had not counted, however, on the tremendous number of voters who waited until after work to vote and who, when they had voted, reversed our predicted results. North's defeat left most of us with the fallen countenance of a child upon learning that Christmas had been cancelled that year. Needless to say, this episode put an end to volunteer exit polling at Christian Coalition.

Little did we know that within just a couple of hours actual poll results from around the country would be better than we could ever have dreamed. By evening's end, Republicans—the large majority of whom were conservatives—had control of both houses of Congress and two-thirds of the nation's governorships. Liberal governors like Mario Cuomo of New York and Ann Richards of Texas had been sent packing. Pro-family conservatives were elected to the Senate, including John Ashcroft in Missouri, Rod Gramms in Minnesota, and Rick Santorum in Pennsylvania. In Tennessee, surgeon Bill Frist defeated incumbent Jim Sasser, who would have been the likely choice for majority leader had the Democrats retained control of the Senate.‡‡ And even the Democrat Speaker of the House, Tom Foley of Washington, lost not only his position as speaker, but also his seat in Congress, to challenger George Nethercutt. Governors Cuomo and Richards losses were significant in another way. They had given the respective 1984 and 1988 Democratic National Convention keynote speeches and had become national personalities as a result.

The anti-Clinton, anti-Democrat reaction among America's voters had sounded a shot heard round the world. Our post-election telephone surveys§§ showed that the percentage of the electorate made up by religious conservative voters increased from 24 percent in 1992 to 33 percent in 1994.[6] Further, almost half of those religious conservatives who said they had voted for winning candidates had seen a Christian Coalition voter guide before voting.

What had begun with the 1993 GOP victories in the mayoralty elections in New York City and Los Angeles, and picked up steam with Christian bookstore owner Ron Lewis's win in a 1994 special election to fill a vacant U.S. House seat from Kentucky, swept over the land like a tsunami,¶¶ leaving Democrats quaking in their boots and hoping Bill Clinton really meant it when he said, "I feel your pain." And also elected to Congress in that watershed year was a young state representative and former 1988 Robertson campaign volunteer from Puyallup, Washington, Randy Tate, who would later succeed Ralph Reed as executive director of Christian Coalition.

Christian Coalition's experience after the election was the direct opposite of being blamed for Bush's defeat in 1992. The Coalition began being named among the top lobby groups in America; Pat became a welcome face in the leadership offices of Congress; and Ralph began appearing in magazine articles and on television talk shows boasting about the clout of the Coalition. As University of Virginia professor Larry Sabato recalled in an A&E network *Biography* on Pat Robertson: "There's no question that Robertson and the Christian Coalition had a great deal to do with the Republicans taking over the House of Representatives and the United States Senate. The voter guides passed out by the Christian Coalition alone swung many House districts."[7] Years later, according to his own Web

---

‡‡ Frist became majority leader eight years later.

§§ Using professionals at Luntz Research, unlike our volunteer exit poll operation that had gone so far askew.

¶¶ As Ralph often described the election.

site, Ralph Reed called the Republican takeover of Congress in 1994 "the biggest thing I have ever been involved with accomplishing."[8]

As Ralph described to PBS's David Frost, self-identified voters who voted Republican in 1994 comprised a three-legged stool made up of traditional Republicans, disenchanted Perot voters from 1992, and religious conservatives.[9]

Use of the term "religious conservative" was a masterstroke. Rarely did the media adopt our terminology, preferring to brand Christians with negative words like "anti-abortion" rather than our much preferred "pro-life," but primarily due to usage by Christian Coalition "religious conservative" became an accepted way to describe our movement.

The year ended with a senior staff Christmas party at Ralph and Jo Anne Reed's new home in a secluded, wooded neighborhood near the North Carolina border. As the holidays passed, we were filled with anticipation of a new, conservative Congress with Republicans in the majority for the first time in most of our lifetimes. As the calendar turned to 1995, Christian Coalition was poised for an altogether new prominence and a greater degree of influence in American politics.

7

## A Place at the Table

IN 1995, U.S. POLITICS were dominated by newly enthroned Speaker of the House Newt Gingrich and his *Contract with America*. As liberals bemoaned the Republican initiatives—passed with lightening speed—Christian Coalition and its activists worked around the country to put pressure on members of Congress to enact family-friendly legislation. Our phone banks and newly created post card mailings were like not-so-stealth bombers supporting Gingrich's battleships and twenty-one inch guns. And for the first time in its history Christian Coalition was welcome in the majority offices of Congress.

The euphoria among conservatives over the transfer of power from the Democrats to Republicans after more than forty years was almost beyond belief. Other than a brief six-year period when Republicans had taken over the U.S. Senate on Ronald Reagan's long 1980 coattails, liberals had enjoyed a strangle hold on Congress for almost a half-century. During a December, 1994, visit to our Capitol Hill office, Government Affairs Director Marshall Wittmann told me that the excitement among conservatives in Washington regarding Gingrich's ascendancy was not unlike the inauguration of a president.

In mid January, our D.C. office staff arranged for our entire group of state directors and field staff to meet with Gingrich in the Capitol, around which we planned two days of meetings where our state leaders and national staff received updates from Senate and House leaders. Early in the morning, our state directors, a few tag-alongs who had come with them, and about ten staff members squeezed into a conference room in the Speaker's suite in the Capitol.

I stood just a few feet behind Gingrich's right shoulder as he welcomed us and laid out his legislative agenda for our state leadership, and I remember looking curiously at the half-inch-wide border of dark hair above his shirt collar at the end of his otherwise silver mane. As the new House speaker talked about his plans for a Balanced Budget Amendment to the U.S. Constitution, one of our tag-alongs asked a clueless question: "But wouldn't a Balanced Budget Amendment be *unconstitutional*?" As our staff cringed, Gingrich searched for a kind way to say, "That's why they call it an *amendment*."

We were thrilled as the House passed bill after bill during Gingrich's first hundred days. Ralph felt that we needed to put our own mark on the new congressional term and, after many hours of hard work from our D.C. staff, including excellent writing by Policy Analyst Susan Muskett, he unveiled Christian Coalition's *Contract with the American Family* in a flashy Capitol Hill press conference on May 17, flanked by our state directors, along with Gingrich, Senate Minority Whip Trent Lott, soon-to-be 1996 presidential hopeful Senator Phil Gramm of Texas, and a host of other leading House conservatives. A *Washington Post* headline the following day proclaimed, "Gingrich Vows to Pursue Christian Coalition Agenda," and the accompanying article pointed out that after the press conference Ralph had a meeting with Senate Majority Leader Bob Dole, including a photo of Ralph about to walk into Dole's Majority Leader's office in the Capitol.[1]

According to reporters Dan Balz and Ron Brownstein, "[B]ehind [Reed] stood a legion of coalition state directors silently testifying to the organization's grass-roots network . . . Reporters and other guest packed the room like a rush-hour subway, all sweltering under the hot television lights."[2]

Months earlier, we had commissioned a poll called the "Survey on American Values," which showed that church-going Americans listed among their top priorities, not only hot-button issues like abortion, but the same issues most other Americans were concerned about, the two "E's", education and the economy. Therefore Christian Coalition realized that we had to redirect our agenda somewhat. We had always included a breadth of issues on the voter guides, but more discussion was called for.

That summer, Ralph built on the survey and authored a landmark article in the Heritage Foundation's *Policy Review*\* publication, called "A Wider Net."† He wrote:

---

\* Now published by the Hoover Institution at Stanford University.

† Notice the subtle biblical reference in the title.

The most urgent challenge for pro-family conservatives is to develop a broader issues agenda. The pro-family movement has limited its effectiveness by concentrating disproportionately on issues such as abortion and homosexuality. These are vital moral issues, and must remain an important part of the message. To win at the ballot box and in the court of public opinion, however, the pro-family movement must speak to the concerns of average voters in the areas of taxes, crime, government waste, healthcare, and financial security.[3]

Hence the broad agenda in the *Contract with the American Family* when it debuted in 1995. Ralph called the ten planks in our contract "ten suggestions" for Congress to consider after the first hundred days. In his opening remarks, Ralph said:

Today religious conservatives play a vibrant and vital role in our public discourse. We have gained what we have always sought: a place at the table, a sense of legitimacy, and a voice in the conversation we call democracy . . . This agenda is not a Christian agenda, a Republican agenda, or a special interest agenda. It is a pro-family agenda that is embraced by the American people, Republican and Democrat, Christian and Jew, Protestant and Catholic, black and white.[4]

And Ralph was right. Our internal surveys showed that the issues in our *Contract* were supported by more than 60 percent of the American people. These included calls for restrictions on abortion, removal of tax-payer support for obscene art—despite President George H. W. Bush's removal of its president in 1992, the NEA still was alive and well—and what we called the mothers and homemakers I.R.A. Why should women who chose to stay at home not have the same right to save for their golden years as did women who held down jobs outside the house?

As early as August either the U.S. Senate or the House of Representatives had passed four key provisions in our *Contract*: bills restricting pornography, strengthening local control of education, reducing tax-payer funding for the arts, and restrictions on Medicaid-financed abortions. "We never expected to make so much progress so quickly," Ralph said in a media statement, and continued, "We (nonetheless) recognize that the wheels of legislative progress turn slowly. Our grassroots will stay engaged until the final item is passed and signed by this or a future president."[5]

By the spring of 1998, just three years after the *Contract* was introduced, fourteen bills coming under the broad initiatives within our agenda had been passed by Congress and become law. These included: a ban on national testing of school students; a $500 per-child income tax credit; the mothers and homemakers IRA; income tax credits for adoption; adoption and foster care reform; prohibition of Medicaid-funded abortions; a ban on Federal funding of abortion for District of Columbia employees or through Federal employee health benefit plans; a ban on abortion in tax-payer funded military hospitals; a ban on the sale of pornography in military PXs; a ban on Internet pornography; and a bill encouraging restitution for victims of violent crime.[6] While a few of these initiatives later were weakened by further legislation, and one, the Internet pornography ban, was struck down by the U.S. Supreme Court, these were huge successes in such a short period of time and portrayed to a great extent the lobbying potential of Christian Coalition and other pro-family organizations. The *Contract* was so successful that our state affiliates began authoring their own versions targeted at their respective state legislatures.

A publisher offered to turn the *Contract with the American Family* into book form and paid Christian Coalition $50,000 in advance. We had pledged that the proceeds from sales of the book would be given to charity, which led to an appearance by Ralph on *The 700 Club* where he presented a $50,000 check to Pat Robertson to be used for CBN's Operation Blessing International relief ministry.

Not all of our allies in the pro-family movement agreed with the *Contract*, however. After it was released, Judie Brown, president of the American Life League, wrote an article entitled *Rhetoric vs. Reality: The Christian Coalition's Failure*. She was especially displeased with our abortion restrictions, emphasizing that our focus on stopping late-term abortions fell far short of protecting *all* unborn children. Mrs. Brown felt that our proposals invited politicians "to focus on less than one percent of the 1.5 million human beings who are killed by decriminalized abortion."[7] She wrote that a few "cheap and meaningless political victor(ies)" gotten from our *Contract* would inaccurately brand many politicians as "pro-life" when they actually supported most abortions, and that it placed far too little emphasis on stopping other forms of abortions.[8]

Christian Coalition could not have disagreed more. As Ralph told PBS's David Frost later that year, Christian Coalition's goal was to stop all abortion, other than in cases where the mother's life is in danger. But he added that we had to *start* in a place where there was *some* chance of success, rather than going for an "all or nothing" strategy.[9] As Ralph was later quoted in *U.S. News & World Report*, "By failing to achieve the perfect (initially), you have not failed or sinned (ultimately)."[10]

Christian Coalition, therefore, would lobby for restrictions on abortion "as early as we could get the votes,"[11] Ralph told Frost. We wanted to stop as many as possible, as soon as possible. Without enough votes on the Supreme Court to overturn *Roe v. Wade* and with a Human Life Amendment falling far short of the two-thirds vote of Congress necessary for approval, the "all" strategy was out, at least until a pro-life president made several pro-life Supreme Court appointments or until many more pro-life members were elected to Congress. While pro-lifers made up a majority in Congress they still did not possess enough numbers to pass sweeping laws against abortion. Even when Congress did pass a ban on partial-birth abortion it was vetoed by President Clinton; and while the House of Representatives easily voted to overturn the veto, the Senate fell three votes shy, on three separate occasions.[‡]

With pro-life Republicans controlling Congress, the abortion issue was defended by liberals as never before. Finally, conservatives had the key committee chairmanships that would allow our bills to come up for serious debate in Congress, and the pro-abortion movement knew that it was only a matter of time before abortion would be greatly restricted if they did not act quickly to paint the pro-life GOP as extremists in the mind of the people.

Richard John Neuhaus, author of *The Naked Public Square: Religion and Democracy in America*, once wrote in the Catholic journal *First Things* that the abortion debate is "undoubtedly the most fevered question in our public life."[12] The issue divides American citizens unlike any since the War Between the States, often with, as in that war, members of the same family fighting on opposite sides. Otherwise-calm people vehemently disagree on what liberals call "a woman's right to choose" and pro-family activists call "a child's right to life."

As the Coalition's reputation and profile grew, so also did its opposition. In fact, a new organization of liberal ministers, The Interfaith Alliance, partially funded by the Democratic National Committee, was organized in late 1994 just to counter our efforts. Coalition spokesman

‡ The partial-birth abortion ban was passed again in 2003 and was signed into law by President George W. Bush only to be held up by at least three liberal Federal judges.

Mike Russell officially "welcomed" The Interfaith Alliance into American politics: "The organization's sole objective is to attack religious conservative groups, using the thin veil of religion to mask a Democratic controlled, Democratic funded assault on people of faith."[13] For the remainder of the decade, The Interfaith Alliance commented on our every move, calling for America's Christians to flee from our influence. They even had the endorsement of American icon Walter Cronkite, who signed a fund-raising letter in which he vehemently attacked our movement in general and the Coalition in particular, writing that we espoused "a militant ideology—one that encourages deep hostility toward those who disagree with its agenda."[14] Conservative icon William F. Buckley took the most trusted man in America to task in a column entitled "The Cronkite crusade vs. the Christian right," sub-headed "Demonizing Pat Robertson."[15]

Liberal columnists and reporters continued their opposition as well, with headlines such as one in the *(San Antonio) Express-News*, "Christian coalition [sic] subverts democracy."[16] These critics seemed to take a biased view of conservative Christians being taught to exercise their rights as Americans citizens. Evidently, they felt that only liberal Christians or non-Christians had the right to hold office, join political parties, or even vote. Christian Coalition remained undaunted, as Ralph told a Road to Victory audience: "We are Americans too, and we have First Amendment rights, and we're going to exercise them."[17]

The negativity perhaps reached its depth when minister and former Atlanta Mayor Andrew Young told a West Virginia audience, "Unless Jesus was lying, the Christian Coalition is likely to go to hell."[18] Mayor Young's words were particularly alarming, I felt, especially considering that they came from someone professing to be a Christian.

Our Road to Victory conference even was parodied in a 1995 movie, *The American President*, which trumpeted the virtues of all that was liberal in America. The president sat and made catcalls while watching on television his outspoken, and made-to-seem harsh and intolerant Republican opponent speaking to a banquet for the "Conservative Coalition for America." "That's supposed to be us!" I exclaimed when I first saw the film.

Often, Christian Coalition was judged by people who had no idea of our position on an issue. In 1997, I was invited to speak at a local Virginia Beach middle school. A librarian called and asked me to participate as one of two speakers in a forum on the subject of censorship. She told me they already had a representative of the local branch of the National Education Association coming to speak against censorship and wanted me, on behalf of Christian Coalition, to give the *pro*-censorship position. After telling her that Christian Coalition was not a pro-censorship organization, we agreed that I would still speak, where I included an explanation of the reasons parents should be involved in deciding what their children read in school.

Among other things Christian Coalition was called Nazis and likened to Adolph Hitler by enemies and "friends" alike. A *Pueblo (CO) Chieftain* headline screamed "Robertson's rantings [sic] recall words of Third Reich."[19] Even the Reverend Jesse Jackson got into the fray, telling an editorial board at the *Chicago Sun-Times*, "The Christian Coalition was a strong force in Germany ... The Christian Coalition was very much in evidence there."[20] A former member of the *Republican* National Committee referred to the Coalition as "Nazi-like,"[21] and not to be outdone, a former Republican Party local chairman in Virginia called Pat Robertson "the Christian Ayatollah."[22]

Yet *we* were labeled as intolerant, and bigots. As Jewish columnist Don Feder later wrote: "The cover story in the May (2005) issue of *Harper's* magazine screams of 'The Christian Right's War On America.' Try to imagine a reputable publication doing a story about 'The Jews' War On America' or 'The Hispanic War On America.' Again, hatred of Christian conservatives is the last respectable form of bigotry."[23]

Christian Coalition was referred to as "Merchants of Hate,"[24] "Prejudice[d],"[25] "haters of homosexuals,"[26] and "gay bash[ers]."[27] And a flier distributed in Oregon in 1992 threatened violence by portraying the Christian "fish" symbol roasting over an open fire with a caption that read, "You burn us, and we burn you."§ At the time our state affiliate was supporting passage of a ballot initiative to curtail government sanction of special rights for homosexuals.

The harsh feeling about Christian Coalition was in no small part related to our support of legislation like that above, including others in Colorado and Maine. Our position on "gay rights" was one of the most debated, misunderstood, and stereotyped of all our activities; therefore it merits an explanation here.

§ The reader should not conclude that this flier was distributed by homosexuals. It may have been, although, this would not have been the first time far-right wing groups went to great extremes to cause further enmity between Christians and the gay community.

Christian Coalition sought to address the issue only as it related to public policy, neither citing Scripture to make our case nor opposing homosexuals as individuals. But we actively opposed what we felt was a radical agenda based on the premise that a person should merit special protection under the law simply due to the manner in which he or she engaged in sex.

Christian Coalition did not seek to remove the ability of homosexuals to vote, organize, or be active citizens. In fact, we could not have agreed more with their right to be politically active. *Our* activity, of course, placed us at odds with the gay community, as well as with their proponents in the media, the entertainment industry, and the government, a consequence we faced in order to stand in opposition to that agenda, which we believed was as much propaganda as real. There was evidence that on average homosexuals already lived more affluent lives than most other Americans.[28¶]

Nowhere was the debate more highly portrayed at the ballot box than in the 1993 elections for school board in New York City, where 60 percent of pro-family candidates who ran were elected, with the homosexual agenda being the focal point in the campaign. Further, led by grandmother Mary Cummins, pro-family voters called for and received the removal of school superintendent Joseph Fernandez due to pro-homosexual curricula used in the city's public schools, including elementary school textbooks called *Daddy's Roommate* and *Heather Has Two Mommies.*

Sadly, many on both sides of the issue, Christians and homosexuals alike, have demonized the other without even knowing them. And Christians are not without responsibility in this heated debate. It takes a delicate balance to show Christ-like love to a person while, at the same time, disapproving of his or her way of life.

Jesus Christ has often been called a "friend of sinners" but He in no way was a friend of sin, sexual or otherwise. He even died a horrible death in order to pay the price for all sin and to provide reconciliation between God and mankind. Jesus accepted every individual, but they came to Him on His terms or not at all. His parting words to the woman caught in adultery, "I do not condemn you," were followed by, "Go and sin no more."**

¶ A 1991 *Wall Street Journal* article made the point that homosexuals ranked near the top of the scale of demographic groups in many socio-economic factors, including income, education, travel frequency, and housing value.

** See John's gospel, Chapter 8.

One Christian leader who walked the balance quite well was the late John Cardinal O'Connor of the Catholic Archdiocese in New York City. While fighting the city over encroaching gay rights ordinances and sternly warning from the pulpit against the dangers of homosexual behavior, he nonetheless opened an AIDS ward in a Catholic hospital and even went himself to minister to AIDS patients, often washing their hair and emptying their bedpans.[29]

# 8

# The Right Hand of God

A s Christian Coalition's public profile rose so did Ralph Reed's at an equal, if not greater, trajectory. His first book, *Politically Incorrect*, had been done by a Christian publishing house in 1994, but he became an attractive prospect for secular shops by 1995, with his sequel, *Active Faith*, hitting bookstore shelves in 1996. In late 1994 Ralph was offered his own monthly television program, *Christian Coalition Live*,* on the new National Empowerment Television network,† and *Time* magazine featured him on its May, 1995, cover under the somewhat pejorative headline "Right Hand of God,"[1] having already named him in a December, 1994, cover story, along with others including Microsoft founder Bill Gates and television mogul Oprah Winfrey, as one of America's fifty most promising leaders under age forty.[2] *Newsweek* featured Ralph, along with television commentator and former Dan Quayle chief of staff Bill Kristol, and Republican pollster Frank Luntz, in an article, "The GOP's Three Amigos," subtitled, "Idea Men: They have PhDs, Newt's gratitude—and a big stake in the party's future."[3]

Ralph was featured in Christian and secular magazines alike, including pop culture publications such as *People* and *Vogue*. And in what was perhaps the most public acknowledgement of his new fame and notoriety, in the Jodie Foster movie *Contact*, Ralph was portrayed by actor Rob Lowe. On a subsequent episode of *The Tonight Show*, Lowe said that since he first had become aware of Ralph he had wanted to play him in a part.[4] Lowe's "Ralph" was quite lacking, however, including an exaggerated attempt at a Southern accent, which Ralph did not even have. The producers

* Beamed over Ku-band satellite to our local chapters, which national reimbursed the $100 cost of the small dishes.

† Founded by Paul Weyrich. NET eventually changed its name to America's Voice. I believe it no longer exists.

should have hired Michael J. Fox instead.‡ Also, that year, Ralph's stature nationally was recognized at home as he was elevated to the Coalition's board of directors.

Ralph's abilities before a television camera were sharp arrows in Christian Coalition's quiver and were displayed perhaps at their finest when he was interviewed in the Founders Inn's Presidential Suite for the Public Broadcasting System's *Talking with David Frost*, which aired on May 19, 1995. Frost's political reputation had been established in 1977 when he secured a series of frank and revealing interviews with disgraced former President Richard M. Nixon. Several of Ralph's answers to Frost's questions are referenced throughout this book because his responses were a virtual tutorial on how to handle an interview, and a masterful showcase of Ralph's talents.

Frost asked Ralph who was the boss at the Coalition, he or Pat Robertson. Ralph answered by comparing their relationship to that of a senior partner with a junior partner in a law firm. Each trusts and respects the intelligence and abilities of the other, recognizing that the firm benefits greatly by the talents of each.[5] Frost followed Ralph's explanation with his original question as to who was in charge. "He is,"[6] Ralph responded.

Ralph and Pat contrasted each other quite well. Both were dedicated to advancing a pro-family, conservative political agenda. They differed, however, in that although the son of a U.S. senator, Pat became re-involved in politics after almost thirty years as a Christian minister, whereas Ralph was a veteran political operative *before* accepting Christ.[§] This difference in experiences gave each a slightly different outlook, along with a perspective not totally enjoyed by the other, and created a symbiotic relationship that furthered the fortunes of Christian Coalition.

Destiny seemed to have waited at their respective doors many years earlier. Ralph was born (prematurely) in Portsmouth, Virginia, in June, 1961. And while his military doctor father was eventually transferred, Ralph was just over three months old when CBN had its initial broadcast on October 1, just across town in a run-down studio on Spratley Street.

‡ See Chapter 2.

§ As (future Pulitzer Prize nominee journalist and Regent University graduate) Mark O'Keefe wrote in *Charisma* magazine's October, 1993, issue: "Reed says God still wanted him to play political hardball—but he was not allowed to hit below the belt anymore." The mixed sports metaphor notwithstanding.

Ralph was sure that the Coalition always looked out for Pat's interests. For instance, the day after each election found the staff at headquarters coordinating a mailing to each pro-family candidate who had been on the ballot, either in a Federal election or for a Virginia post, offering either Pat's congratulations or his condolences.

Sometimes, however, we just looked out for Pat. Each election day either a staff member or a representative of our local chapter stood outside Pat's polling place, Brandon Middle School, passing out Christian Coalition voter guides. The person was instructed to remain there until Pat had voted, and then he or she was free to leave, knowing the boss had seen his troops at work. Pat must have been pleased to see the Coalition volunteers each year.

Unless Pat happened to be around, Ralph was always at the center of whatever situation presented itself, and due to his consuming personality, others often blended into the woodwork. We staff members were amused when we got copies of *Time* with Ralph on the cover, and an inside photo of Ralph and spokesman Mike Russell walking down the halls of the New Hampshire State Capitol along with Governor Steve Merrill, as Ralph was about to address the New Hampshire Senate. Ralph was in the middle, leaning over, talking with Mike, as the governor walked along, effectually by himself.[7] When Pat was present, however, everyone else was a staffer, including Ralph.

Ralph never eclipsed Pat in terms of media attention, but he garnered his own share with certainty. While NBC's Tim Russert introduced him as "Ralph Reed of Pat Robertson's Christian Coalition"[8] during a 1992 broadcast of *Meet the Press*, and a 1993 CBS exposé on the Coalition by Connie Chung did not even mention Ralph's name, his public profile had grown so by 1995, that reporters began referring to the organization routinely as "Ralph Reed's Christian Coalition."

By the September, 1995, Road to Victory conference, Ralph even had his own protesters, as homosexual rights activists marching outside the Washington Hilton carried signs with his picture (not Pat's) adjacent to that of House Speaker Newt Gingrich. Ralph wanted one as a souvenir, so I asked one of the hotel's managers to commandeer one of the signs as she observed the protesters. We had it framed for display back at headquarters, however, it never was hung due to concerns over the impression it might give visitors.

David Frost also brought up the subject of critics who said the Coalition claimed to speak for all Christians. Ralph debunked that one by stressing that, to the contrary, we neither claimed nor aspired to speak for all Christians; but, nonetheless, we *were* Christians and would continue to say so. Ralph paraphrased Dr. Martin Luther King's motto, it's not only what you stand for but how you advance it,[9] in explaining a major reason that faith is important in the public debate. And Ralph even gave credit to Christians of the liberal persuasion for leading the way in this country in support of child labor laws, for abolition, and against segregation, while their conservative counterparts sat idly by.[10]

Ending their session together, Frost teased that the interview needed to be hurried along due to the fact that the potential GOP candidates for president were waiting outside to talk with Ralph. His joke was not totally inaccurate, as we will see later.

On Sunday, May 21, Ralph appeared on NBC's *Meet the Press* versus his virtual opposite in everything but age, George Stephanopoulos. Our staff had long anticipated a match-up between the two on television. The face-off on Tim Russert's program was akin to a debate between two candidates for the same office. The topic was our recently announced *Contract with the American Family* and Ralph did a brilliant job, countering the Clinton aide at every turn, even using Clinton's own words in our favor when discussing the blessings of voluntary prayer at public school functions.

Another famous Democrat nearly his age with whom Ralph brushed shoulders was the late John F. Kennedy, Jr. On a late spring day in 1997—after Ralph had announced his resignation from the Coalition but before he actually left—I received a call from a jubilant Camille Mitzner of our Washington office. She and the rest of the women in that office were as thrilled as schoolgirls, awaiting a visit by JFK, Jr., to interview Ralph for *George* magazine's July, 1997, edition. The article included a bit of banter between the two, plus Ralph's recently announced plan to start a consulting firm⁵, and ended with each man raising the possibility of a future run for office by the other. Kennedy concluded by saying, "Who knows, maybe I'll have a (political) conversion, and when I do I'll give you a call." Ralph responded, "Listen, if you ever decide to switch to our side, you *should* give me a call."[11]

---

⁵ See Chapter 10.

I saw Ralph Reed flustered on television only once. It happened during an interview alongside the Reverend Jesse Jackson. Ralph had gotten the best of Jackson for the entire show and at the end was explaining how the media and the Democrats in government had a double standard regarding Christian involvement in politics. While Christian Coalition was lambasted for reaching Christian voters through churches, Jackson often campaigned in churches, even taking up offerings for his presidential campaign. Ralph described the generic white buckets in which money was collected as "chicken buckets."

Jackson saw an opportunity to cry racism and leaped on Ralph for using what he felt was a stereotype. How did Ralph know they were *chicken* buckets? Jackson asked. Ralph, not accustomed to being accused of racism, was stymied. His only reply was that he was sorry if he had offended Jackson, who countered that it was Ralph's comment, rather than his own offense, that was at issue. He repeated his call for an explanation from Ralph, who could only repeat the earlier defense.

I remembered seeing news footage of Jackson passing the white buckets down the aisles of a church during his 1988 campaign. Ralph was correct in his identification of the double standard. Had Pat Robertson attempted to raise money in churches when he ran for president, his campaign and the churches involved would have figuratively been buried under IRS headquarters in Washington, D.C. Ralph certainly had not intended to exhibit racism, but merely fell victim to his own use of an unfortunate term. "If only he had said *popcorn* buckets," I thought.[12]

From 1994–1996 the staff at headquarters and in the Capitol Hill office functioned like a well-oiled machine, with a common purpose and camaraderie unmatched in American politics. In a strategically organized effort each person on our staff did his or her job with the assurance that they had played a distinct part in the whole. Of course, the spiritual element of our organization added a bond that other political groups did not have.

Because of the Coalition's prominence and the fact that the next presidential election cycle was gearing up, the interest and organization at the grassroots was at an all-time high and headquarters felt the years 1995 and 1996 might be Christian Coalition's last big window of opportunity to train large numbers of activists. Therefore, Training Coordinator Steve Jordan scheduled as many Training Seminars (our new name for the Leadership Schools) as he could get the state affiliates to sponsor.

By year's end we had trained almost 15,000 activists in seminars held around the country, plus those who came to the Road to Victory conference.

The other chief field division goal of 1995 was to reach a total of 2,000 local chapters. We fell about twenty short but crossed the threshold in 1996.

Our prime training opportunity was the annual Road to Victory conference, with its breakout training sessions.** Friday, September 8, was opening day for Road to Victory '95 in Washington, D.C. Each year had presented a new boost for the conference, whether it was having the president (Bush) in 1992, or moving the event to the nation's capital in 1993, or our fifth anniversary gala in 1994.

This was the year for a dramatic increase in attendance. (We had started with approximately 800 people in 1991, with about 1,500 coming the next year. The first year in Washington, 1993, saw a significant increase, bringing out 2,200 attendees, with the total growing to over 3,000 activists from across the nation in 1994.)

This first year of Newt Gingrich as House speaker brought an explosive increase in attendance, with approximately 4,000 people registering for the event, and numbers swelling to 5,000 people in the ballroom Friday morning as Gingrich spoke to our conferees, Hill staffers, and Beltway insiders who had come just for his appearance. The setting was as inspiring as anything I could have imagined. As I walked through the ballroom while Gingrich was speaking, people were seated on stairways and in the aisles, with standing-room-only crowds packed on the terrace surrounding the sunken conference floor. It brought tears to the eyes of more than one staffer who had worked so hard to see such a marvelous happening. However, that very Road to Victory may well have been the apex of the lifespan of the Christian Coalition.

A summer senior staff retreat at the historic Williamsburg Inn, just on the outskirts of Colonial Williamsburg, provided a memory that seemed trivial at the time, although was not so insignificant a few months later. Ralph had invited the Coalition's outside fund-raiser, Ben Hart, to join us, and one afternoon, Ben and I were walking to our cars before a round of golf when I asked how much mail his company, Hart Conover, actually produced. As I recall, he said that they had done something akin to 30

** Afternoon sessions where attendees "broke-out" of the large general session into smaller groups to attend specialized training on issues.

million pieces of mail in a recent twelve-month period and added that over 20 million of those had been on behalf of the Coalition, which told me that we were responsible for most of his revenue. I knew that Ralph and Ben were friends and, while I suspected no inappropriate dealings between the two, I could not help thinking, "This might not look good to anyone looking to find trouble." And regrettably, I was right.

Soon, others became suspicious of the Coalition's relationship with Ben Hart, and their actions proved devastating to the organization. A few months after the staff retreat, Don Black, then marketing manager for our *Christian American* magazine, in a move totally independent and unknowing of my discussion with Ben, raised the question of impropriety when he learned that two other companies involved in the Coalition's direct mail program, Federal Printing and Mailing, and Universal Lists, appeared to be shadow companies, and were owned by Hart.[13] This sparked a scenario that resulted in the Coalition's only brush with scandal during the Reed era, as well as the loss of Hart as a consultant, the departure of two Coalition employees, and possibly one of Hart Conover's, who mysteriously†† left that company around the same time.[14]

The controversy decimated our fund-raising program and was critical in the Coalition's ultimate downfall.‡‡ Unfortunately, personalities and ambitions got in the way, which greatly exacerbated the situation; therefore, the fallout was much worse than whatever was thought by Don Black to have been done wrong in the first place. Feelings were hurt, which led to mistakes in the way people reacted and to how they handled information in their possession.

As was reported in an article entitled "HART Ache"[15] in *Mother Jones* magazine, Black raised the issue with our director of finance, Judy Liebert, who took the information to Ralph. Ralph said he would handle it, but Judy either was not convinced or not satisfied, and took the matter to Federal authorities,§§ as well as to the Christian Coalition board of

††  This scenario was not widely known at the Coalition at the time. Most only knew that it seemed as if one day she worked for Hart and the next she did not.

‡‡  I report the narrative of this story from memory; and the quotes and facts as cited in the notes.

§§  Judy's actions in disclosing internal documents to Federal authorities may have resulted from her fear of being implicated, as the organization's director of finance and its corporate secretary, in any official governmental investigation that might have arisen out of Black's findings had he himself chosen to expose them.

directors in a hastily convened meeting in early 1996, after which she was placed on indefinite leave and later fired by the board for the breach of corporate confidentiality. Don Black later resigned.[16]

Soon, there was a Grand Jury investigation, as well as an outside audit of the Christian Coalition-Ben Hart relationship. The audit resulted in a payment by Hart Conover to the Coalition⁵⁵ for irregularities in billing. Hart Conover was also required to submit competitive bids on future Coalition projects, breaking the virtual monopoly it had enjoyed. Whether because their price was too high or due simply to a lack of interest on their part, Hart Conover subsequently handled few, if any, direct mail projects for Christian Coalition.

Ralph and Christian Coalition were cleared of any impropriety, and in her book, *Gang of Five*, Nina Easton even noted Judy Liebert herself as telling the Coalition's board that she had no knowledge of any improprieties by Ralph in the matter.[17] Further, Coalition lawyer Dave Ventker told *The Virginian-Pilot* that the audit confirmed that "no [C]oalition employee or officer personally benefited from the organization's relationship with any outside vendor,"[18] and that Judy's attorney admitted that Judy "had absolutely no evidence or knowledge of criminal activity on the part of anyone at the [C]oalition."[19] Ralph's mistakes in the matter appeared to have been allowing Ben to work without a firm contract— which would have placed strict controls on how much he could charge for his services—and failing to assure Judy that her concerns were receiving his full, and sincere, attention.

Judy evidently saw herself as a woman scorned, and later gave negative newspaper and television interviews, and even became a hostile witness in the Federal Election Commission's 1996–1999 lawsuit against the Coalition, during which she disclosed confidential operational and financial documents that she had been retaining over the years.[20] Many of the documents held illusions of smoking guns, which Judy (or someone advising her) hoped would damage our case.[21] She even hired as her lawyer Moody Stallings,[22] the Democrat former state senator from Virginia Beach, who, according to *The Virginian-Pilot*, "blame[d] his [1991 re-election] loss in large part on Pat Robertson."[23] Stallings had publicly acknowledged his contempt for Christian Coalition and helped organize a demonstration outside our Road to Victory conference in 1992.[24]

⁵⁵ I withhold the amount out of respect for a confidential agreement between Christian Coalition and Hart Conover.

As for our employees, some defended Judy—even in the media[25]—believing her to be the victim in the matter, but most disapproved of the way she handled the information in her possession. Later, after Judy's account appeared in the local newspaper and on ABC's *Nightline* sympathy for her around the office waned dramatically. Few knew of Don Black's involvement, although as the scenario was being played out Judy and her husband were observed having lunch with him at the local Lone Star steak house.[26]

According to *The Virginian-Pilot*, Judy testified to the FEC that she had become afraid of (unnamed) officials with the Coalition.[27] However, it was Ralph who was believed to be in need of protection, and an armed guard appeared outside his office door the same afternoon that Judy made her accusations to the board of directors. I was aware that the board meeting was in progress at the Founders Inn, just a few miles away from our headquarters, and then saw the guard later that evening. In fact, I remember hearing later that someone had been sitting in a car outside Ralph's office window at night, watching him work. The Reeds, as Easton learned from Jo Anne, even began to practice escape drills at their home,*** making it like a game so as not to startle the children.[28]

Until the Hart incident, Judy appeared to adore her business relationship with Ralph, later telling Easton she considered him brilliant and loved him like a member of her family.[29] In an odd coincidence, some twenty years earlier Judy had worked as a young secretary in the office of local philanthropist Fred Beasley, who was an early benefactor to both Pat Robertson and to CBN. She once told me of how she remembered Pat coming to the office to meet with Mr. Beasley.

The entire Hart-Liebert scenario dealt a tremendous blow to our direct mail program. Ben was a brilliant writer who, while evidently profiting handsomely from our very aggressive direct mail fund-raising efforts, was quite adept at appealing to conservative Christians to support our cause. His letters were hard hitting on liberals and, along with an enclosed copy of our *Congressional Scorecard*, proved to be the most successful direct mail campaigns in Christian Coalition history—and possibly of any political fund-raising tool during the decade of the 1990s. The loss of his capabilities was significant and proved to be the first crack in the dam that held back Christian Coalition's financial problems that were to come.

*** I am not relating the escape drills to the Judy Liebert scenario, although they are juxtaposed here as they were by Easton in her book (386–88).

93

Had the Coalition's income not been so closely tied to direct mail, we would have weathered the storm much better. There really is no viable alternative for such organizations than direct mail,[†††] however, which is a two-edged sword, and can become its own worst enemy. Success necessitates the continual acquisition of new donors as well as the solicitation of the core supporters with incessant mail requests, which also cost the organization a high percentage of the income to pay for the postage and production. Donors often tire of repetitive mailings, leaving them weary in receipt of future letters.

The series of events reared its head again in 1997 when Christians across America (many of whom were our supporters) began receiving fund-raising letters that looked quite similar to Christian Coalition letters, but were from a new organization called the Christian Defense Fund, a group that most likely existed only on paper. Ben Hart, who had left (or was soon to leave) his company, Hart Conover, had signed the letters as president of the organization. The letters looked and read strikingly similar to those he had written for the Coalition over the years. Earlier, Judy Liebert (and her loyalists) publicly alleged that Ralph had tried to supply Ben with the Coalition's mailing list at no cost,[30] which was an odd accusation, considering that as our direct mail vendor Ben naturally would have had access to the list.

Christian Coalition filed another law suit, which was ultimately settled out of court with the details undisclosed.[31] There was forgiveness, however, between Christian Coalition and Ben Hart; and as an indication of our desperate need for cash in 1997, he was again retained to write fund-raising letters for the Coalition. His former company, Hart-Conover, protested, however, and we stopped using his services.

One humorous incident—unrelated to the above—involved Ben Hart. Our membership services department once received a copy of one of our direct mail letters that had been returned by its intended recipient. Circled amidst the text was a typographical error that Ben and his proofreaders had overlooked, and that had been mailed to millions of people

---

[†††] Large six and seven figure gifts from major donors are the primary alternative, but those go mostly to 501(c)(3) tax-deductible organizations. Christian Coalition could have started a sister (c)(3) to receive those gifts—and pay for non-lobbying activities—but it did not. Further, due to the lobbying nature of 501(c)(4) organizations, affiliated (c)(3)s may not legally transfer money to them. All (c)(4) lobbying activity and (c)(3) education activities would have had to have been separated between the two sister groups. Nonetheless, it was not an option the Coalition chose.

over the past few months. What they had failed to see was the embarrassing assertion that Christian Coalition felt it necessary to reform America's
"pubic" schools. When Ben learned of the mistake, probably after receiving a call from Ralph, he assembled his staff, gave each one a copy of the
letter and told them to "find the typo." After ten minutes the staff still had
not located the missing "L."

At the national and state level, there were no major elections to be
conducted in 1995 for the first time in the Coalition's existence.‡‡‡ As au-
tumn drifted into winter the Coalition was poised for what would prove
to be its number one year of activity, both financially and politically.

‡‡‡ In the midst of a national and state Republican juggernaut, the Virginian General
Assembly election did not need our attention as it had in 1991.

9

## For Such a Time as This

THE DAWNING OF 1996 brought significant promise for Christian Coalition. The next presidential election was just around the corner and America would hopefully be rid of the Clinton-Gore Administration. Finally, I could remove the red bumper sticker I had affixed to my office door just after the 1992 election that read: "Is it 96 yet?"

Clinton was still on the retreat from the 1994 mid-term congressional elections and was faced with the possibility of losing additional seats in Congress in 1996. He had no serious prospects of defeat himself, however, having spent the last year catering to the voters by adopting popular programs from the Republican agenda. This had been the brainchild of strategist Dick Morris, who, according to George Stephanopoulos's book, advised Clinton to "steal the popular-sounding parts of the Republican platform, sign them into law, and you'll win."[1] When I read that, it reminded me vividly of how we often had criticized Clinton for doing that very thing.

By spring, the Republican presidential primary season was in full gear with eventual nominee Bob Dole fighting off challenges from publisher Steve Forbes, commentator Pat Buchanan, Senator Phil Gramm, and former UN Ambassador Alan Keyes. Several of our state affiliates had planned candidate rallies, hoping to capitalize on the opportunity to make a good deal of money to further their activities in conjunction with appearances by the candidates.

I handled the advance work at one of these events, which was held in Detroit on March 16. National headquarters was directly concerned because Ralph would be speaking. I arrived in Detroit on the day prior to the event and met with our local directors, as well as with Secret Service agents who were there to protect Pat Buchanan, the only candidate who had accepted our invitation. The rally was to be held in a large suburban church.

That evening, I drove to the Detroit airport to pick up Ralph and National Field Director D. J. Gribbin who were flying in from a donor reception in Minneapolis sponsored by the Minnesota Christian Coalition. When we arrived at our hotel we saw the large tour bus of the Buchanan campaign parked in the hotel lot. After chatting for a few minutes with *Human Events'* Terry Jefferies, who was working on Buchanan's staff at the time, we went to Ralph's room to plan the next morning's order of events.

The rally went very well with both Ralph and Buchanan making rousing speeches to a large crowd. That was the rally, itself, however; events earlier in the day were more complicated. Upon arrival at the church, Ralph retired to a private office to work on his remarks. D. J. and I were just outside the door when Buchanan's Secret Service detail arrived, with the candidate waiting outside in his bus.

"I need that room for my protectee," said the agent in charge. D. J. explained that Ralph was just working on his speech and, since he spoke before Buchanan, he would be out of the room in plenty of time for Buchanan to use it. The agent protested, insisting that he must have access to the office *immediately*. D. J. countered again. After all, it was *our* event. They could wait. Or so we thought.

"I need him out of that room *now*," said the agent, "and if *you* don't get him out, *I* will," implying that Ralph would most likely prefer to leave of his own power rather than be ejected by the United States Secret Service. So, upon learning of the situation, Ralph left the room and went back stage in search of continued privacy, only to be accosted by yet another Secret Service agent. "I'm paying for this event!" Ralph demanded, perhaps purposely paraphrasing one of Ronald Reagan's most famous quotes, but there was no arguing with the Secret Service.

The San Diego Republican National Convention in August was an all-hands-on-deck operation. Approximately thirty headquarters staff members, along with two interns, traveled to the west coast, either as delegates or alternates for the convention, or to work on behalf of Christian Coalition's efforts there, which included a huge, outdoor rally, a daily newsletter, a major donor luncheon, and, most importantly, a "war room" to support an organized and sophisticated floor whip operation.*

The rally, called the Faith and Freedom Celebration, was held at San Diego's Balboa Park. Over 3,000 attendees, including pro-family local activists, and delegates and alternates to the convention, came on a very hot afternoon to hear speakers that included Pat Robertson and Ralph, along with former Vice President Dan Quayle, House Speaker Newt Gingrich, Oklahoma Congressman J. C. Watts, Bosnian war hero Scott O'Grady, the Reverend Daniel De León, host of CBN's Spanish *El Club 700*, and surprise guest Joanne Kemp, wife of recently announced vice presidential candidate, Jack Kemp, who contrary to predictions after the 1992 GOP convention had decided to forego his own candidacy for the top office.

We had been working all year to instruct our state and local leaders on the intricacies of running for delegate and alternate to the convention either at the Congressional District level or on a statewide, at-large level. And they went out and got themselves elected from coast to coast! When combined with other pro-family delegates not associated with Christian Coalition, we had a clear majority. Our pre-convention phone surveys of the delegates showed that 1,087 of the 1,990 total delegates supported a Constitutional amendment protecting unborn life and opposed efforts to change the strong pro-life plank that long had been in the Party's platform.

The whip operation was brilliantly managed and engineered by Chuck Cunningham and D. J. Gribbin, both of whom, along with Ralph, went out to San Diego a week early for the all-important platform hearings. By week's end, they had so convinced the Dole campaign of our strength to control the convention floor that, by the time the rest of us arrived, the job was done. Dole had no choice but to select a pro-life vice presidential candidate; although his selection of Jack Kemp was quite a surprise to Coalition leadership.

*Newsweek* ran a story about Dole's choice of Kemp as his vice presidential nominee. Their sources confirmed the long-rumored dissention between Pat Robertson and Kemp,† to the tune that the Dole campaign was allegedly forced to get Pat's approval beforehand for the choice of Kemp.[2] Actually, both Bob and Elizabeth Dole had checked with Pat for

---

* The term used for people stationed throughout an audience for the purpose of disseminating information or "whipping" up support for a vote or demonstration.

† See Chapter 5.

his suggestions of a running mate in weeks leading up to the convention but they did *not* get his sign-off on Kemp, whose choice came as quite a surprise, therefore.

Kemp provided some degree of balance to the Dole-led GOP ticket. He was known as a staunch conservative, and was a decade younger, along with the image of being a former NFL quarterback who still kept a football close at photo ops.

At a Sunday afternoon rally for "our" delegates, Ralph and Pat sat on the dais, along with Eagle Forum founder Phyllis Schlafly and Gary Bauer, head of Family Research Council. Ralph needed to show Pat that the pro-family delegates strongly supported Dole's choice of Kemp and, as he kicked off the rally, began drumming up an ovation for the ticket. When he asked the overflow crowd's opinion of Kemp for vice president, they cheered wildly. Standing in the back of the room, I easily perceived Ralph's motive and looked instantly to Pat's face. He nodded decidedly toward the delegates, as if to say, "Ok, I get it."

The convention itself was far different from the previous two GOP national conventions.‡ For starters, the week's activities were orchestrated to correspond with east coast prime-time television coverage, which meant that all festivities were completed by eight o'clock on the west coast. That left plenty of time for dinners and receptions each night, and for our graphics and writing staff, more work. For each of the four nights of the convention, Mike Ebert and his *Christian American* staff produced a newsletter and took it to Kinko's for copying. The copies were fanned out among approximately thirty-five hotels (where the delegates and alternates were staying) by local activists provided by Sara Hardman, our state chairman in California, as well as by volunteers from among our delegates who attended the convention.

By the first night of the actual proceedings at the San Diego Convention Center, a smaller than usual venue for such an event, our delegates and whips were in place with pagers on their belts and in their purses, capable of receiving instant messages from the war room. Specially selected whip leaders supervised approximately twenty whips each, while carrying state-of-the-art Motorola mini-computers, about one-third the size of today's laptops, although, much larger than the BlackBerrys that keep thumbs buzzing all over Washington, D.C. today. This was all made

‡ I attended 1988's convention as a Robertson campaign staffer, and 1992 and 1996 as an alternate delegate from Virginia.

necessary by the fact that party leaders had—in what seems unrealistic today—banned cell phones from the convention floor. But our pagers proved to be much more effective, and provided more media interest, than cell phones would ever have. Streams of network camera crews revolved in and out of the war room during the convention, broadcasting reports of our technology, along with shots of our smiling—and exhausted—tech wizard, David Ballard, around the globe.

One evening after the convention had adjourned, as I walked the short distance from the convention hall to the Marriott where our operation was based, I heard someone call my name as I passed a sleek, dark Cadillac with opaque, dark-tinted windows. "Hey Joel," the voice quietly called from a partially opened rear driver's-side window. I stopped, as the window powered the rest of the way down, to see the familiar face of none other than Ralph Reed. "How's it goin'?" he asked, as I stopped briefly to chat. Ralph and Jo Anne were waiting with their driver for the traffic to thin before returning to their hotel.

Ralph was a celebrity among celebrities in San Diego that week. Reporters and pundits alike knew that Christian Coalition wielded considerable power among the delegates and were lined up to interview Ralph. In a setting where even unrecognizable governors of small states walked about with body guards, Ralph and Pat were in far greater media demand than chief executives of many states, commanding hoards of reporters and taking back seats only to the highest echelon of Republican leadership.

This reminds me of something that happened a few months later at the January, 1997, winter meeting of the Republican National Committee, where Christian Coalition hoped to weigh in on the committee's choice of a new national chairman. Ralph, Chuck Cunningham, and I traveled to Washington, where Ralph worked behind the scenes, Chuck maintained a presence on the meeting floor, and I served as a liaison between the two.

Many prominent Republicans had come to the RNC meeting, including then House Speaker Newt Gingrich, outgoing RNC chairman Haley Barbour of Mississippi, and a host of congressional leaders. Also present was Arkansas Governor Mike Huckabee, a great friend of Christian Coalition. Elected as lieutenant governor, he had succeeded to the governorship when Jim Guy Tucker resigned after his conviction in the Clinton-Whitewater investigation.

On Friday evening, after the voting was over and Colorado national committeeman Jim Nicholson had been elected as the new RNC chairman, Ralph and I were talking on the phone when I mentioned that Huckabee had just walked past me in the hotel lobby. Ralph said he wanted to talk with him, so I had to set up the meeting.

I approached the Arkansas special agent in charge of the governor's security detail and suggested that "Ralph Reed" would like to meet with the governor. The agent did not seem familiar with the name and told me they had to hurry to the airport to fly back to Little Rock, to which I added, "The governor will *want* to meet with him," which I am sure was not the first time he had heard that one.

Bodyguards for public figures are quite set on keeping to their schedule. Therefore, he was not about to wait, which meant we had to move quickly. I called Ralph back and explained the situation, telling him that Huckabee would be leaving any minute. He had to get down there fast. In a few minutes, Ralph walked off the elevator and up to Huckabee, who, as I had predicted, was delighted to see him.

As the two men stood and talked, a crowd of ten or twelve onlookers quickly huddled around to enjoy the moment. Ralph recognized someone in the group and also began chatting with that person, and as a metaphor for the tremendous profile Ralph carried at the time, the rest of the crowd began to shift their attention to Ralph's tangential conversation, leaving the governor of the home state of the President of the United States standing aside.

One last story about Ralph's presence at the 1996 GOP convention occurred during platform week, when a group of reporters were interviewing Phyllis Schlafly and Gary Bauer. Whether Ralph was a late arrival, a party crasher, or an accidental tourist, I am not sure, but as the story goes, he walked in a door on the other side of the room, prompting the throng of reporters to leave the two stunned leaders and swoop over to Ralph like a flock of birds on a fresh piece of bread.[3]

Such was the political and media power of Ralph Reed in San Diego that summer. Not only had Christian Coalition arrived, Ralph was driving the bus. Of course, Pat Robertson still owned the bus and we had practically enough delegate strength at that convention to have made a serious run at nominating Pat for vice president, had Dole chosen a pro-abortion running mate.

Road to Victory preparations were already well underway even before we left for San Diego. The most memorable occurrence of the conference that year was related to the September 14 appearance of the Republican presidential nominee, Senator Bob Dole, who had resigned from the Senate during the campaign as a sign that he was 100 percent focused on the presidency. The Dole campaign had not accepted our invitation to speak that year but he dropped by "unexpectedly" during our Saturday morning session. I am sure they had planned the appearance all along but had kept it a secret so as to heighten the excitement of the crowd.

Vice presidential nominee Jack Kemp had already spoken to our group that morning when we learned that Senator Dole was about to arrive. Pat Robertson was located, and quickly came to our speaker holding room before going on stage to do the formal introduction of Dole. With the polls all but guaranteeing President Bill Clinton's re-election victory, Pat evidently felt our audience needed special motivation to pray for the hapless Dole campaign, and he, therefore began his introduction by saying that only by a miracle from God could Dole win the election.

Such terminology was not out of the norm for a man who hosted a daily religious television program and hoped to inspire his followers to pray and work extra hard over the next few weeks. But to the former senator, who was desperately trying to win what would be his last campaign for the presidency, at a time when his campaign hoped to get some enthusiasm going, it probably sounded like a pronouncement of certain doom.

Dole was so surprised by Pat's words that he would hardly go out on stage to speak, and did so only with the encouragement of his staff and, I assumed, Ralph Reed. As he began his speech Dole pointed out that his name was not on the official conference agenda: "I was just driving by and saw all the cars," he said, which brought laughter from the audience. They gave him a rousing reception and his appearance was a huge hit.

With the arrival of fall, most thoughts turn to the World Series and football, most except for politicians, that is, due to the fall campaign season. Roberta Combs, chairman of the South Carolina state affiliate, called Ralph, saying that she and Pat had been talking and, with the campaign in full swing, Pat wanted to get out in the grassroots himself and had asked her to work with our office to put on a few events for him.§ Three Christian

§ Whenever someone told you "Pat wants" something, you never really knew whether the idea originated with Pat or if that person planted the idea, only to have Pat agree that it was a good thing to do.

Coalition rallies soon were planned for Houston, Montgomery, and Orlando, with Pat as featured speaker and the respective Texas, Alabama, and Florida state affiliates having opportunities to use the events as fund-raisers. I did the advance work for Pat in Houston and Montgomery, each a rousing event. Houston was somewhat complicated, however.

I arrived on Friday, October 11, via U.S. Air[5] and went to the Sheraton Astrodome Hotel, the same hotel we had used for the God and Country Rally in 1992. Roberta's daughter, Michele, an event planner, was already there working on the program, and press spokesman Mike Russell would arrive with Pat the following day on Pat's Learjet. Before coming to Houston, Pat spoke at three Columbus Day events in other parts of the state, which were targeted for Hispanic audiences. When they arrived at the Sheraton, all was ready as I escorted Pat and security aide John Rea to their rooms so they could freshen up and get a little rest before the rally, while Mike went to check on the press arrangements.

A hearty crowd of about 500 people was expected at the rally, which was wonderful, except for the fact that the room was big enough for a thousand. I had the hotel staff close an air wall (separating the two ball-rooms we had reserved), which made the room appear to be packed for Pat's speech.

Earlier in the week, I had asked Pat's administrative assistant of about thirty years, Barbara Johnson, if it would be okay for me to ride back from Houston on the jet with Pat. That would get me back home in Norfolk almost twenty-four hours earlier than the U.S. Air return ticket I was holding. Barbara said that as far as she could tell, there would be room on the plane, which was good for me.

Of course, I still had to approach Pat about my joining him on the flight, but I procrastinated. Actually, my luggage already was loaded on the plane when Pat and I crossed paths in the terminal and he asked, "Joel, are you going back with us?"

"If there's room, I'd like to," I answered, knowing that would leave him the option of saying it would be too crowded if he really preferred that I not tag along. But Pat encouraged me to join them for the flight back.

A local chapter chairman had volunteered to chauffeur Pat while he was in Houston, and as he drove us in his van back to the airport after

___

[5] Later renamed U.S. Airways.

the rally, he was obviously pleased to be able to spend time with Pat, and went into great detail telling Pat about his chapter's success with precinct organization. He had done a superb job and was delighted to be able to share his chapter's success with the Coalition's founder.

By then it was about ten o'clock back home in Virginia and the lateness of the hour, coupled with my concern as a staffer for Pat's certain fatigue after a long day, did not leave much room for me to appreciate the conversation. "Pat sure is listening politely through all this," I thought, assuming he had feelings similar to mine. I was delighted at the chapter's success, but after a long day and a tense event, I had had enough politics.

Mike and I sat in back seats of the plane, with Pat just ahead, while bodyguard Rea, a former Navy SEAL, sat near the door, at the ready should anything go wrong. Just before takeoff, Pat unexpectedly turned around in his seat and looked me square in the eye. "That guy's story of his precinct activity really got me excited," he said, much to my surprise. He continued, saying that organizing precincts was one of the primary reasons he had founded Christian Coalition, but that it had not been done. We had held events, won electoral battles, and garnered much media attention, but had never located those ten activists per precinct. I later learned that both Ralph and D. J. soon received the same exhortation from Pat.

Unbeknownst to Pat, the field division had pretty much given up recruiting precinct coordinators** by that time, choosing instead to identify volunteer liaisons in as many churches as possible. The political parties already had their own precinct captains, and most that we could have recruited would have been Republicans, so the result seemed duplicative and, D. J. felt, virtually impossible. Therefore, finding liaisons to distribute our voter guides in their churches seemed to serve a similar purpose.

"Pat won't like that if he finds out," I thought, even though I understood the reason for the decision. Considering that our constituency spent at least one hour in church every week, that seemed to be the best place to reach them. "The advantage we have is that liberals and feminists don't generally go to church. They don't gather in one place [two] days before the election," Ralph once told reporters Dan Balz and Ron Brownstein.[4] Of course, the church liaisons had to do their work in a nonpartisan manner in order to protect the church's tax status.

---

** The essential link in finding the ten activists per precinct.

After the plane had taken off, we began eating boxed meals of chicken strips and fruit, which the pilots had secured while waiting during the event. Also, each meal contained a slice of pecan pie. After eating his piece of pie, Mike accepted Pat's offer of his, which gave Pat material for a funny one-liner later on. Somewhere along the way the pilot asked Pat if we wanted to stop to refuel. Before he could answer, Mike, who was in a hurry to get home, said, "No," which prompted Pat to show a bit of restraint. "Wait," he said, "We don't want the headline in *The Virginian-Pilot* to say, 'Robertson's plane runs out of gas and crashes a hundred yards short of the runway, with a sugar-crazed [press] guy in the back seat,'" as we all laughed. The pilot assured us that we had enough fuel and we made it safely home. When we landed in Norfolk, at approximately two o'clock in the morning, Pat was careful to check to be sure Mike and I had our cars, offering to give us rides if we did not.

As Election Day approached, prospects for a Dole victory were no better than they had been at Road to Victory. Therefore, the mood around the office in anticipation of four more years of the Clinton Administration was quite disheartening. Clinton's re-election was all but assured, although with Republicans firmly in control of Congress and no national elections the next year, the Coalition did not expect the tremendous growth it had experienced after Clinton's first election. Our donations would likely lag in 1997, as they had the first year after the Republican takeover.

As Christmas bells rang, little did I know that my most vivid memories of Christian Coalition were yet to come—as well as my most difficult.

## 10

# Transition

AFTER ALMOST SIX YEARS in the field division, in late January, 1997, I was assigned to the executive office to assume the newly created position of special assistant to the chief operating officer. COO Ken Hill had approached me a few weeks earlier to see whether I was interested in working with him. He certainly had no idea that, for me, his offer was an answer to prayer. In the latter part of 1996 I had become very dissatisfied in the field division and realized the need for a change. By Christmas I almost had given up and was considering leaving the Coalition. Therefore, I was delighted and relieved when Ken told me of his idea. Steve Jordan replaced me as deputy field director, while at the time neither of us had any idea that a much more significant staff change was just around the corner for the Coalition.

Ken was a much-needed addition to the Coalition, starting work in August, 1996, while most of us were at the Republican National Convention in San Diego. Until Ken arrived Ralph had been spread far too thin for much too long and needed someone to help with day-to-day operations at headquarters. He traveled most every week, which left no one in charge to make decisions that were not appropriately made by one of the division directors. In announcing Ken's hiring, Ralph said, "With Ken on board, we have another senior manager who can make the trains run on time so that I have more time to focus on strategy and large issues vital to the organization."[1]

For the staff it was a blessing, too. Shortly after Ken's arrival, Mike Ebert, editor of our *Christian American* magazine, remarked to me in a light-hearted way, "It's kind of nice to have a grown-up around," commenting on the fact that Ralph and our division directors were in their thirties, while Ken was just shy of fifty, with the quintessential sign of maturity, gray hair. Also, Ken had seen action at the highest levels of government, having been deputy chief of staff for the National Security Council.

My association with Ken started with a bang, so to speak. One Monday morning, a message from the weekend on our main number voice mail was in a man's voice: "Wednesday, seven a.m., you will be bombed." This was not our first bomb threat, with at least two others preceding it. After consulting with Ken, I called the city police, who referred me to the fire inspector's office, which I thought was an odd referral but soon learned was standard operating procedure for bomb threats. Soon, two plainclothesmen and one uniformed agent appeared at our office.* Since our mail was delivered at seven o'clock each weekday morning, it appeared that a mail bomb might be in Wednesday's delivery. We had only two days to prepare.

An attempt to trace the phone number came up empty, so the agents canvassed our complex, looking for places where a bomb could be hidden, and also devised a plan to monitor our mail delivery on that particular Wednesday. They informed me that they would be present outside our building well before seven that morning, in order to see if anyone approached our front, back, or side doors to place a bomb. In the end, there was no bomb, in the mail, in the building, or otherwise. Thankfully, it had been a prank.

Security became tighter after that experience, although it had been increasing for the last several years, including the already mentioned escort for our bank deposit run. And in mid-1996 we began retaining guards to patrol our offices during business hours. These men became like Coalition family, making coffee, opening doors for employees and even delivering messages throughout the building. One, a former plumber, even fixed our toilets when needed.

While praying one evening in early 1997, I felt impressed to get my Bible and read a passage in the Apostle Paul's first letter to the church at Thessalonica: "And we urge you, brethren, to recognize those who labor among you, and are over you in the Lord and admonish you, and to esteem them very highly in love for their work's sake."† As I read those words I felt God was speaking to me specifically about Ralph, although I had no idea why. Soon, it made perfect sense.

---

* A subsequent bomb threat brought a visit from the FBI as well.

† (vv. 12–13).

There had been earlier discussions among the staff that Ralph might leave the Coalition, going back to the GOP convention in San Diego the previous summer. He just seemed "different," more relaxed. Even state directors noticed the change when they were around him at Road to Victory in 1996. But when 1997 came and Ralph was still around, our concerns were allayed.

My antennas went back up one night in March when, as I worked late, Ralph telephoned and asked me to drop by his house with a folder containing some "highly confidential" documents he had left in his office. The first thing I saw upon arriving at his home in Chesapeake's Timberwood subdivision was a For Sale sign. I mentioned the sign as I was leaving, after a visit that lasted about an hour and included conversation with Ralph and Jo Anne as we watched the Academy Awards. They seemed somewhat uneasy when I commented on the sign, and asked me to not tell anyone about their house being for sale. I dutifully complied, and was not too skeptical as I knew that Ralph had wanted to live closer to a golf course for quite some time.

All remained quiet for the next month or so, until one Tuesday in late April when Ken Hill instructed me to set up a conference call for Ralph to speak with our state directors the following morning, April 23. I had not been assigned a field-related task since leaving that division and wondered why he had delegated it to me. The call was to be at nine o'clock in the morning, which was especially early for our state leaders in Alaska and Hawaii. Ralph was to be in Washington during the call. "Why did it have to be so early?" I wondered. I soon learned that Ken knew something that day that no one else knew, although having only a day or so notice, himself.

On the afternoon prior to the conference call, Ralph, who had been in another Southern state, interrupted a flight to Washington with a stopover in Norfolk, where he drove the ten or so miles to our office, meeting Jo Anne there. The senior staff was asked to report to the conference room, where Ralph informed us that the next day he would announce his resignation as Christian Coalition executive director, effective September 1. His plans were to start a political consulting firm. Jo had tears in her eyes during the brief meeting, as we all searched for the appropriate expression, knowing one thing for certain: for better or for worse, Christian Coalition would not be the same without its young leader.

Early the next morning, Ralph met first with the staff of our Capitol Hill office, and then held the conference call with the states before facing the media. Our entire staff gathered in the conference room to listen in on Ralph's call with the states. What was for us a very solemn occasion seemed bittersweet for Ralph. He was leaving the organization he had started from birth, and driven to great national prominence and success, but was also going on to a new venture, itself ripe with the seeds of personal and political fruition.

The staff had mixed reactions to Ralph's leaving. Most understood his desire to become more directly involved in campaign politics, but more than a few felt he was making a mistake. What about holding the team together until the 2000 presidential elections? How could he leave now? What about the mission? I shared in those sentiments but remembered the preview that I was now certain God had given me from I Thessalonians.

Ralph certainly had his personal reasons for leaving Christian Coalition, while others speculated. Skeptics believed that he saw the writing on the wall, and knew that the organization was headed for serious financial and legal problems. One unnamed (yet bitter) Coalition staffer told Nina Easton for her book, *Gang of Five*, that he "bought low and was selling high" that he knew the Coalition was "crumbling from within" and wanted to leave while he could.[2] They said he was getting out while the getting was good.

Even Jo Anne realized that others might attribute negative motives to Ralph, telling Easton, "I didn't want him to leave at that time. I didn't want people to think he was leaving under a cloud with the Judy Liebert thing or that he was being forced out because of it. He wasn't."[3]

Most likely Ralph simply needed a new challenge, having become complacent. We had been unable to tip the scales regarding the election of a president in two successive elections, a win in either of which might have led to a presidential appointment for Ralph or a heavy role in policy selection for the Coalition. With Dole's loss in 1996, Ralph may have just felt there was nothing left to do.

Or, he may have wanted to broaden his image for future political purposes. Easton told a political blog that in an interview with her Ralph once expressed mixed emotions about being known as a leader of religious conservatives:

Ralph Reed is deeply ambitions, and always was so. There was a time when he . . . in one of my interviews, said he pondered running the Ross Perot campaign,[‡] and he wasn't sure he wanted to do the Christian Right thing, he was worried that it boxed him into a corner. And he took the Christian Coalition as far mainstream as he could, and then he got out. I really think in that case it was about Ralph, and his vision for being a mover and a shaker in the Party.[4]

I later learned that Pat's reaction upon learning that Ralph was resigning was one of defiance. "Ralph, you can't leave," he probably said. Then, upon seeing Ralph's resolve, he reportedly contacted other pro-family leaders, encouraging them to try and convince Ralph to stay, before finally accepting his protégé's decision.[5]

From the outset, newspaper headlines and press releases from our critics sounded Ralph's announcement. "The Religious Right loses its most skilled tactician," wrote *The Virginian-Pilot*.[6] "Is there life after Reed for Christian Coalition?" asked *The Washington Times*.[7] And Coalition nemesis People for the American Way boasted, "Reed Returns to Political Roots—Pat Robertson Loses Talented Front Man."[8]

Immediately speculation began in the office and in the press about possible replacements. An April 26 front page piece in *The Virginian-Pilot* offered the following "want ad":

> WANTED: Committed, pro-life, pro-family evangelical Christian, with ability to play hardball politics. Passionate about conservative causes like school prayer and banning abortion, but pragmatic about political agenda. Able to rub shoulders with the suits on Capitol Hill, without losing touch with the little guy at the grassroots. Must be independent-minded, but not too independent. Articulate, but not too smooth. Previous national exposure a plus. Salary: About $192,000. To apply: Send résumé to Pat Robertson, president, Christian Coalition.[9]

The names of Regent University Dean Kay Coles James and former U.S. Senator William Armstrong of Colorado were mentioned in early press stories, as were the names of our own Chuck Cunningham and Brian Lopina, director of our Capitol Hill office, neither of whom wanted the job. In addition, several lesser-known individuals surfaced from time to time, and others, both inside the Coalition and outside, promoted

‡ Obviously Perot's 1996 rather than 1992 campaign.

themselves for the job. Our staff began to pray that God would lead Pat Robertson in this all-important choice of a new leader for the Coalition.

Another name came to my attention that spring, for different reasons, but it soon proved to be very significant to the entire country. A few weeks after announcing his departure, Ralph was invited to address a college class via videoconference. My task was to find a site in our area with the technology to facilitate and I located the local PBS affiliate, WHRO, in Norfolk. There, Ralph could link up with the class, which was being held in Texas.

In early May, I accompanied Ralph to the studio. As we drove from Chesapeake to Norfolk via Interstate 464 and through the winding streets of downtown Norfolk, we discussed his decision to leave the Coalition, which was poignant considering that I was one of the very first people he met upon moving to Virginia almost eight years earlier. This was the first time I had been alone with him since the announcement.

He told me that in teaching this class he was helping out a friend, Karl Rove, a name I was unfamiliar with at the time but, along with millions of other Americans, would come to know quite well a couple of years later as President George W. Bush's closest advisor. Ralph lectured the class and took questions, after which we drove back to the office to complete an otherwise uneventful day, but one on which I often reflected in the early days of the Bush Administration.

In 2002, *The New York Times* alleged that at the same time that spring Rove had secured a job for Ralph's consulting firm with the scandal-ridden Enron as an indirect retainer for his clandestine services in the upcoming Bush presidential campaign.[10] The reports concluded that due to Ralph's high profile as a leader of religious conservatives, having him as an official advisor might backfire.

Upon hearing the news I thought back to the day five years earlier when Ralph and I had gone to WHRO. Also, I knew the accusation of George W. Bush wanting to keep Ralph at a distance was not true. Ralph was far from a "clandestine" advisor to Bush. In 1999 and 2000 he often appeared on television news programs on behalf of Bush's campaign. I remembered it was common knowledge around our office in 1997 that Ralph supported Bush, and many expected him to work for the Texas governor in some fashion.

As Ralph told CNN's *Inside Politics* when the stir arose:

[O]ur firm was paid both by the Bush campaign and the Republican National Committee (to do voter contact—telemarketing, direct mail) . . . I met with George W. Bush in April of 1997 before obviously he had made any kind of decision. And I said, "Look, I don't know that you're going to decide, but I want you to know that I'm excited about you, and if you run, I want to be on your team, and I want to help you in whatever capacity I can."[11]

In the *Times* piece Karl Rove's memory was uncertain, saying, "I think I talked to someone (at Enron) before Ralph got hired," but that it "may have [been] afterward."[12] And he explained his admiration of Ralph: "I'm a big fan of Ralph's, so I'm constantly saying positive things."[13] According to the Associated Press, the White House soon confirmed that Rove spoke to Enron about Ralph's company, Century Strategies[14] but it was nothing illegal. The Federal Election Commission eventually investigated the Reed-Rove-Enron connection, but found nothing of an inappropriate nature, as stated in a February, 2003, ruling.

On Mothers Day weekend, 1997, Christian Coalition sponsored an event highlighting a new initiative. Over the prior year or so, we had raised and distributed over $750,000 through a charity we founded, Save the Churches, to help rebuild African American churches that had been destroyed in a string of arson attacks.[§] Ralph decided to use that momentum to form a new, inner-city outreach called The Samaritan Project, which he had announced three months earlier in a January press conference in Washington, D.C.

The idea was on the cutting-edge, considering it came from a group with close, although informal, ties to the Republican Party, and would provide an answer in the future when Christian Coalition was included among liberals' false accusations of conservatives as not caring about the poor. Among its eight-point plan The Samaritan Project promised "a bold and compassionate agenda designed to combat poverty and restore hope."[15] As Ralph said at the January news conference:

Now that we have ended the welfare system as we know it, it is incumbent upon us as people of faith to provide a positive alternative to the welfare state. We believe that the welfare programs of the past should be judged not by the height of their aspirations, lofty though they may have been, but by the depth of their failure and the magnitude of their human casualties . . . The crisis of the soul

§ Not all were African American churches but the large majority were.

presents us with what Martin Luther King, Jr., called "life's most persistent and urgent question: what are you doing for others?"[16]

Ralph often exhibited a strong consideration for race relations, as Nina Easton quoted him in *Gang of Five*: "It is a painful truth that the white evangelical church was not only on the sidelines, but on the wrong side, of the most central struggle for social justice in this county."[17] And a 1999 article in the *Atlanta Jewish Times* focused on Ralph's multicultural outlook:

> Reed inaugurated two sort-of initiatives which reflect an awareness of the problems of evangelical Christians in politics in American history. One was (the) outreach to Roman Catholics. The other reflects Southern evangelical issues. (Christian Coalition) raised a bunch of money for rebuilding the black churches that burned down. So he was determined to, at least, make it clear that the Coalition was not going to be narrowly sectarian and possess any of these sort of unattractive racist or religious dimensions of some previous manifestations of Southern evangelical politicking.[18]

The article quoted Ralph himself on his feelings about discourse between Christians and Jews:

> I tried to spend as much time as I could building mutual respect and trust, so when those flash points came along that provided an opportunity for division between Christians and Jews, you could pick up the phone and get through it based on your trust and friendship . . . There were times when some in the Jewish community said things that were hurtful to Christians, and times when some in the Christian community said things that were hurtful to Jews.[19]

The Samaritan Project's founding event was held at a waterfront hotel in downtown Baltimore, just a stone's throw from the new Camden Yards baseball stadium. Several churches we had helped financially through Save the Churches brought busses full of people to the event from places as far away as Milwaukee (Wisconsin) and Charlotte (North Carolina). In addition, a cadre of Baltimore pastors served as hosts for the event, which culminated in a Baltimore inner-city church on Saturday evening.

Ralph would speak in a morning session at the hotel and Pat would close the event with a message that evening at the church, which would be followed by a dinner for all participants. The Reverend Earl Jackson, Sr., an African American pastor from Boston and a Harvard-educated lawyer, who once hosted a conservative radio program and was already on staff as Christian Coalition's liaison to African Americans, was chosen as national director of the Samaritan Project.

Things went fairly well at the conference until Saturday afternoon when the North Carolina pastor decided to leave early with her busses— and people—rather than attend the church event that night. This meant that our evening crowd would be missing well over one hundred people, which would not be acceptable. The last thing we needed was a lackluster event, especially considering that Pat was the speaker. To make matters worse, the driver of another bus got lost en route from the hotel to the church, causing much consternation before he finally arrived in the knick of time.

Hours before the evening event was to begin, another staffer and I canvassed the neighborhood in our business suits, white shirts, and ties in hopes of finding people to fill the empty pews at that night's event. Amazingly, I was carrying $3,000 in cash inside the breast pocket of my suit. The money was to pay for the Milwaukee busses before they returned home. When we arrived at the church I temporarily hid the money inside a desk drawer in the church office.

One of the pastors of the church offered to drive me in his car, and would stop at street corners while I went door to door asking people if they would like to "come to a free dinner and listen to a message by Pat Robertson, host of *The 700 Club*." The pastor kindly pastor knocked on a few doors as well.

On one corner, however, the pastor stood by the car as I began walking down the street, after which I learned that this was not exactly the safest neighborhood in Baltimore. And as we drove past a particular alley I noticed several people lined up, which the pastor identified as a drug buy about to go down, but for me it was just another new experience in service of the Coalition. Finally, we were back at the church, praying that the lost bus would arrive in time and the sanctuary would be filled for Pat's message.

In such church settings with a very famous speaker, he or she often slips off the podium early, during the closing prayer, in order to avoid the crowd that would surely gather otherwise. Trained counselors come to the front of the sanctuary so that people needing personal ministry have someone to talk with. Far more people can be helped than if only the one minister had remained, in which instance all the people would want to be prayed for or counseled by him personally.

It was a very long service, and after Pat spoke, he began shaking hands with several area pastors who were standing in a semi-circle on the platform, while Reverend Jackson made closing comments. As Pat reached the last pastor between himself and the hallway leading to his exit out the church's back door where his car and driver were waiting, he was about to step quietly off the platform and turn the corner. Suddenly, however, Reverend Jackson innocently, but boldly, with microphone in hand, pointed toward him and asked, "Are you leaving?"

"No!" a startled Pat responded. And he was correct! He was definitely *not* leaving at that point, having to walk back to the pulpit as if that had been his intent all along, where the other pastors gathered around him for a final prayer. All in all, his exit was delayed by about fifteen additional minutes. Reverend Jackson's question and Pat's aborted exit caused me to smile wryly where I sat in the back of the church. "Now, *that* was funny!" I thought.

Unfortunately, the event in Baltimore proved to be the high point for The Samaritan Project. Contributions were far less than the money we had raised to rebuild churches the previous year.⸭ The organization struggled along for the next few months before becoming a casualty of the Coalition's overall financial problems, as did another off-shoot of the Coalition, the Catholic Alliance.

⸭ Almost nothing in comparison.

## 11

# Welcome to Arkansas

RALPH REED'S LAST MAJOR legislation-related project as executive director was a series of press conferences highlighting the need for a Religious Freedom Amendment to the United States Constitution. Due in part to the efforts of Christian Coalition, such an amendment received a majority of votes in the U.S. House of Representatives approximately one year later, but fell short of the necessary two-thirds vote in both houses of Congress, before being passed to the states where it would have required ratification by three-fourths of the fifty state legislatures.

We planned three press events for a warm, sunny day in mid-May, 1997, which were to be held in three cities: Washington, D.C., Cincinnati, and Nashville. Washington was chosen as the site for the first event of the day for obvious reasons; Cincinnati was second, because we wanted to highlight a group of nearby Kentucky school bus drivers who had faced job discrimination for dressing as Santa Claus during the Christmas season; and Nashville, because it was near the home of Brittney Settle Gossett, a young woman who, as a teenage school girl, had been the victim of religious bigotry, receiving an "F" on a term paper because she chose Jesus Christ as her subject.

Cincinnati was my event. The evening before, I sat cross-legged on my airport-hotel-room bed with my ever-present copy of the Coalition's state directors list, a legal pad, and a telephone, desperately trying to locate one of the bus drivers to appear with Ralph the next day. Our projects often included last-minute activities of one sort or another, desperate and otherwise. I called one of our former state chairmen in Kentucky, and was referred to the head of another pro-family statewide group that had taken a role in defending the drivers. He gave me the number of an activist who would probably know one or more of the men.

Finally, I reached one of them. I explained that we were there to speak out in their defense and invited him to come to Cincinnati the next day, an invitation that he politely but definitely declined. "That stuff is all over" he said, "and I don't want to bring it up again. Everything's okay now." We proceeded with our plan, but none of the bus drivers were present.

The next morning, I rose early and after breakfast went to supervise the set-up of the hotel room where the press conference would be held. We had chosen a hotel on the grounds of the Cincinnati metro airport* in order to enable Ralph to land, hold the press conference, and take off again in quick fashion.† What followed was one of the best events I had personally been connected with. Ralph arrived in the van of Phil Burress, one of the top pro-family activists in the area, to see the microwave trucks of two local television stations, along with a camera from a third, and other media representatives, including radio and newspaper. I knew this event was going to be a home run. It would provide lots of local coverage of our message. And about fifty of our local Cincinnati activists had come to show their support for Ralph, lending a homey flair to the press conference.

I had flown to Cincinnati via US Air and had a return ticket that would have gotten me back home in Norfolk in time for dinner, but I had the option of joining Ralph on the charter flight to Nashville for the day's third event. The day was so well that it made perfect sense to go on with Ralph—or so I thought. The remainder of the day did not go quite as smoothly, although it provided me with one of the most vividly memorable afternoons of my entire Christian Coalition experience, as well as a story to tell over and over again.

Upon arrival at the Nashville airport, our pilot taxied up to the wrong FBO.‡ Coalition staff member Sharon Helton, a native Tennessean, had to commandeer an airport van to drive across the tarmac and pick us up. Little did we know that this was just a sample of what was yet to come.

As soon as we parked at the correct FBO, Ralph went into a meeting with some local executives from nearby Thomas Nelson Publishers who were awaiting our arrival. This gave me time to check the setting for the press conference.

* Actually located in northern Kentucky.
† For this reason, many political events are held at airports.
‡ Fixed Based Operator, i.e., private terminal.

We had requested an airplane hangar in which to hold the event. But much to my alarm, we were given a hangar that looked large enough to hold a Goodyear blimp, rather than the small private-plane-type hangar we had expected. Our local leaders had brought about the same number of supporters as in Cincinnati, but in such a large hangar, they were hardly enough to make an impression, spread throughout hangar in several small groups. I had to try and do something about the crowd. The television cameras would have portrayed the event as having only a sparse turnout, which would have looked terrible, notwithstanding the fact that news conferences normally don't have audiences. I was also concerned about Ralph walking around the corner, through the huge, sliding doors normally used to close the hangar, but which on this day were open, and seeing the virtually empty hangar. That would surely dampen his enthusiasm and, possibly, hinder his performance.

First, I went to the microphone and announced for the crowd to gather right in front of the lectern, as we were about to begin. This would concentrate their numbers and provide the allure of mass. Second, I noticed a normal-size door behind and to my left. We could bring Ralph in that way and due to the (new) density of the rearranged audience he would not notice the emptiness of the rest of the hangar.

And it worked. When Ralph walked in to open the press conference, he was followed by Brittany Settle Gossett and Dr. Richard Land, president of the Nashville-based Christian Life Commission of the Southern Baptist Convention, both speaking in addition to Ralph, and from floor level, the crowd looked acceptable.

There was a new problem, however. Since the very large sliding doors at the back were open, each time someone started the engine of one of the privately owned planes sitting nearby,[§] the noise would interfere with the audience's ability to hear the speaker. I spent my time near those doors asking pilots to wait until our event was complete before starting their engines.

That afternoon, however, *private* planes were the least of our noise problems. The hangar sat adjacent to a seldom-used runway, which, for reasons unknown, was being utilized that afternoon. I remember watching a large Boeing 727 taxi up, waiting for the signal from the control tower to take off. The pilot set the huge engines to full power just about

§ One was piloted by country singer Roy Clark.

the time Dr. Land was leading up to an applause line carefully placed in his speech. A Baptist preacher, Land's cadence ranked with the best of them. But to his dismay, just as he uttered the line, a burst of engine noise encompassed the hangar, swallowing his words as they left his mouth. Somewhat amused by the situation, I looked at Ralph who, with a big smile on his face, was clapping vigorously in a much-exaggerated fashion as if he were oblivious to the roar of the plane and had understood every word.

After the press conference, several of our local supporters present wanted to capitalize on the opportunity to meet Ralph. One such woman had ridden the bus to the airport, but had to walk two miles from the bus stop down the secluded road that led to the FBO to attend the event. She was thrilled to meet Ralph, the popular movement leader she had seen so often on television. Such was the affection that Coalition supporters had for Ralph.

Finally, we were ready to head back to Virginia, or so we thought. We were supposed to fly to the town of Hot Springs, in the mountains of extreme western Virginia, where we would drop off Ralph to have dinner with Pat at his home near the famous Homestead resort. As we boarded the plane and waited for clearance from the tower, Ralph lamented that the dismal Nashville press conference "would be [his] last event as executive director of Christian Coalition."

As the small plane took off for Virginia, I sat to Ralph's left, with part-time press secretary Larry Cirignano and newly-hired communications director Arne Owens facing us. Larry was across from Ralph, and Arne and I, both over six feet tall, sat with our knees almost bumping in the tight space. Few words were spoken on the flight. Everyone was tired and talking would have reminded us of the less than desirable event we had just completed. Personally, I regretted my decision to accompany Ralph to Nashville, rather than using my airline ticket from Cincinnati back to Norfolk.

About an hour into the flight I looked out the window and could see that we were approaching a fairly large city below. It had to be Charleston, West Virginia, I surmised. Soon, however, I noticed a lake, which did not fit with the familiar Appalachian Mountain scenery I had expected.

"Ralph, I didn't know there was a lake up here," I said. "Yeah," Ralph answered a bit absently, as he looked out the window on the plane's starboard side. But as the plane began descending, he became more aware.

"Hey," he exclaimed, "We're supposed to be landing on a mountain! There's no mountain here!" Then he sprang from his seat and bounded to the cockpit, opening the doors that separated the pilots from the passenger cabin. All that I saw next was akin to a baseball pitcher's view of the umpire's rear end as he bends over to sweep the dirt off of home plate. Ralph was leaning into the cockpit, his head gyrating, obviously talking furiously.

Then, he turned and started back to his seat. "We're in Hot Springs, *Arkansas!*" he cried, with almost palpable desperation.

Without a doubt, Arne, Larry, and I all immediately were consumed by the same emotion, and it was not frustration, but hilarity. "Don't laugh," I silently told myself, hoping they would maintain their composure as well.

As the plane taxied up to the Hot Springs FBO, Ralph already was on his cell phone to headquarters to find out what had gone wrong. As it turned out, the account representative of our Norfolk-based charter company was new to the area and had no knowledge that a town called Hot Springs, Virginia, existed. So, when she was told to route the pilots from Nashville to Hot Springs . . . well, you can fill in the rest. While Ralph was on the phone, the three of us found a convenient place to release our pent-up laughter.

The delay meant that Ralph was going to be very late for his dinner meeting with Pat, so he called the number to Pat's house and explained our plight to the caretaker. We refueled and took off again, this time, flying *back over* Nashville and on to Hot Springs, *Virginia*, where we left Ralph before continuing to Norfolk. During the flight Arne and I resisted the temptation to make eye contact, the briefest instance of which caused each to sputter and look out the window while fighting back laughter. Of course, we then convulsed in laughter once Ralph deplaned and was safely out of earshot.

Just prior to the 1992 presidential elections, the late Ron Brown, then chairman of the Democratic National Committee and Bill Clinton's campaign chairman, filed a complaint against Christian Coalition with the Federal Election Commission,⁵ an agency made up of presidential-

---

⁵ In an October 21, 1992, DNC news release announcing his complaint, Brown alleged that Christian Coalition had "infiltrated all levels of the Republican Party" as well as "the American political system." He further accused us of having a "hidden influence" and "deceiving the American public with hidden political agendas and activities." Amazingly

appointed commissioners, including an equal number of Democrats and Republicans. The complaint asserted that Christian Coalition had violated Federal laws in regard to the 1992 elections and requested that the FEC investigate the Coalition. As irony would have it, a Democrat U.S. senator from Georgia, Wyche Fowler, who had gone down to defeat in 1992, had been given a job as U.S. Senate liaison to the FEC. The fact that Christian Coalition had distributed tens of thousands of voter guides in his defeat may not have helped our status with the commission.**

We already had an ongoing investigation by the Internal Revenue Service. It seemed that even with the White House in Republican hands, our conservative organization had not been immune from being targeted by Federal agencies. We had wondered how much worse our fortunes would be under a Democrat president—and we soon found out. The FEC investigation went on for over three years under what was called the Matter Under Review (M.U.R.) stage before they officially filed a civil lawsuit against Christian Coalition in July, 1996. With unlimited taxpayer dollars at their disposal, this was destined to be a long, drawn-out and expensive process.

Lawsuits like these begin with what is called the "discovery period" when each side requests information from the other. Between the IRS and FEC investigations, and later the FEC lawsuit, Christian Coalition received numerous "Requests for Discovery," which consisted of several pages of detailed questions relating to every conceivable aspect of our activities. No one who has been spared this process can imagine the difficulty and expense of complying with such requests. Looking back, it might have been easier had they just said, "Send us a copy of everything."

One effect of the searches was that they caused us to spend countless man-hours sorting through files and copying documents. Each piece of paper had to be copied three times—one for the FEC, one for our attorneys and one for the Coalition's internal files relating to the lawsuit, before the original document was re-filed where it had been found—in addition to a similar procedure for copying audio and video tapes. Controller Jeanne DelliCarpini had the responsibility for supervising the document

the letterhead on which his words appeared bore the words "Democratic News" while his text complained that we were participating in the democratic system.

** In 1999 the Coalition filed its own FEC complaint against the Democratic National Committee, asking the commission to investigate then Vice President Al Gore's fundraising activities at a Buddhist Temple in Los Angeles.

searches early in the process. She passed out copies of the document requests to staff members who she thought might know where to find the papers but, as I recall, gave only the questions which she thought applied to a given individual.

Even though several boxes of photocopies, and audio and video tapes were provided to the FEC, they complained that we had not supplied enough documents and requested the judge to allow them to furnish us with another Request for Discovery shortly thereafter. It arrived in June, 1997. In the meantime, Jeanne had left the Coalition and it fell to me, as special assistant to the COO, to handle the new search. Because of my position at Christian Coalition during the years with which the case dealt, I possessed knowledge that Jeanne, an accountant who had joined the Coalition only in 1995, did not.

Basically, the FEC's case, which after four years had grown far beyond the DNC's original complaint, dealt with five specific campaigns: Jesse Helms's 1990 U.S. Senate race; the 1992 Bush-Quayle campaign; a 1992 House race in South Carolina where Republican challenger Bob Inglis defeated an incumbent Democrat congresswoman; Oliver North's 1994 Virginia U.S. Senate race; and Arizona Congressman J. D. Hayworth's House race that same year. All in all, there were thirty-nine categories of document requests directly or indirectly relating to these five campaigns. Before discovery was over, we had given the FEC over 100,000 pieces of paper, in addition to scores of audio and video tapes. I eventually took over a small conference room in which to house the documents as I searched through them.

In addition to document requests, the discovery period included depositions of staff members, where FEC attorneys had the opportunity to question witnesses under oath. During the M.U.R. stage and lawsuit process, around twenty Coalition staff and board members were deposed, as well as several of our state directors. In addition, the FEC took depositions from several representatives from the political campaigns and committees listed above. All total, eighty-one testimonies were extracted by the Federal government, and paid for by its tax payers, before the case was decided.

I began the document search by listing the areas of activity covered by the request and making note of which file cabinets might contain relevant information. For instance, documents relating to the 1990 Jesse Helms U.S. Senate race could be found in one of four locations: the Helms file, the North Carolina file, the National Republican Senatorial Committee file, or the 1990 elections file. Ralph had begun Christian Coalition with one set of files and as new divisions were created—field, communications, voter education, etc.—each started its own filing system. To make matters worse, Ralph had several secretaries between 1989 and 1997. Beginning with his wife, Jo Anne and former Robertson campaign staffer Karen Pierce, a succession of women had worked for Ralph in that capacity, each evidently having her own filing system.

For example, the FEC was particularly interested in reviewing Ralph's desk calendars, which I located in a cabinet outside Ralph's office. Some earlier ones were missing, but I later accidentally found them while looking for something else, filed in a different cabinet under the letter "B" where one of his assistants had filed them. Why "B"? The way she had labeled the file provided the clue. You see, not only were they desk calendars, they were "back-dated" desk calendars. An exasperated Ralph once lamented after being informed by a secretary that a document he needed could not be located, "I wonder why we even bother to file anything."[1]

The FEC case reached a media high in mid-1997 when the Republican National Committee turned over documents from the 1992 Bush campaign archives that detailed meetings that senior campaign staff had with Ralph Reed and Pat Robertson. At about the same time period, a Federal judge ordered CBN to release internal documents supposedly showing details relating to Coalition activities. This put our legal struggle on television news for the first time, with dubious looking documents being highlighted for all America to see.

What the media did *not* report was that each account was composed more of press hype than actual substance, and both the RNC and CBN documents proved to be innocuous. Nevertheless, proceedings in the case escalated, with the judge granting the FEC permission to depose additional persons, as well as to re-depose others, due to the release of so many new documents, primarily those from our own files.

A surprising, yet welcomed, event occurred during the final months of the case, when our local critic, *The Virginian-Pilot*, published a lead editorial in our defense. Entitled "Let them speak," it included an endorsement of our voter guides: "The guides do not urge voters to vote for or to defeat specific candidates . . . socially conservative voters who generally receive the guides at their churches will select the candidate whose views most closely mirror their own—almost invariably a Republican. We have a word for that: democracy."[2]

The *Pilot* went even further, encouraging our critics to come to our aid:

> Critics of the Christian Coalition are rejoicing over the suit, but they would be wise to remember that the next ox gored could be theirs. If the FEC prevails, what's next? Labor unions—which spend millions of dollars of dues money (not PAC money) on "issue advocacy" and outright endorsements—ought to be watching this case closely. They would be wise to file friend-of-the-court briefs on behalf of the [C]oalition.[3]

And file they did. Both the AFL-CIO and the American Civil Liberties Union wrote amicus briefs in support of our position. Each group was an avowed enemy of Christian Coalition and we were quite surprised by the move, which, I assume, was masterfully coordinated by lawyer Jim Bopp. While leaders of the groups may not have gotten their motivation from *The Virginian-Pilot*, certainly each had their own interests at heart. The AFL-CIO, America's largest labor union, had planned to spend over $30 million in grassroots electoral activities in the upcoming 1998 elections in order to defeat incumbent Republicans.[4] Second, the ACLU supported our activities on grounds of free speech, which was an interruption of their normal practice of defending flag burning and government funding of anti-Christian "art." As they say, politics makes strange bedfellows.

While we eventually won the case, its long, drawn-out nature, the expensive attorneys fees, and the intense press scrutiny it caused the organization to undergo all played heavily in the Coalition's continuing financial woes: mounting debt, coupled with a shrinking income due to Ralph's absence. Hopefully, his replacement would be able to turn the situation around . . . quickly.

# 12

## Washington Comes to Chesapeake

LATE ONE AFTERNOON IN early June, 1997, just over a month after Ralph's announcement, and with no real evidence of who might replace him, Chuck Cunningham and I were in his office discussing the possibilities, when Ken Hill joined us. "Might be a former Cabinet secretary," he said, almost in passing.

Immediately I thought, "Don Hodel," who had been both Secretary of Energy and of the Interior under President Ronald Reagan. I remembered hearing that name several times during Pat's campaign and, other than the very slight possibility that it could be former education secretary William Bennett, I knew he had to be referring to Hodel. Chuck agreed. Ken was just guessing, as Pat and Ralph had kept the selection process to themselves, but something evidently had occurred that put the idea in his mind.

I later learned that Ralph's reason for meeting Pat in Hot Springs a few weeks earlier had been that Secretary Hodel had flown in from political retirement in Colorado's ski country, at Pat's request, to discuss the possibility of assuming leadership of Christian Coalition. Of course with Ralph's late arrival, Pat and Hodel dined without him.[1]

Pat took the lead at a June 11 Washington, D.C. news conference announcing the selection of Hodel as president, and former U.S. Representative Randy Tate of Washington as executive director.* Showing that he, not Ralph, was in charge that day, Pat stepped in front of Ralph toward the microphone to make the announcement.[2] "Don Hodel brings the stature due a man who led two [C]abinet agencies in the Reagan Administration; a strong family man and a man of faith that America can look up to as a true role model. Randy Tate is one of the brightest and

---

* Tate's name had leaked the day before.

most talented political leaders in the nation,"[3] Pat concluded of the two men he had hired.[†]

The appointments of a Cabinet officer and a congressman were very prestigious and signaled bright things in store for the Coalition. As Americans for Tax Reform President Grover Norquist told *The Washington Post*, "What you've got is Reagan and Gingrich. Hodel is a Reagan Republican and Tate is a Gingrich Republican."[4] And the reporter also quoted Gingrich himself, saying that it was "like a baseball team that just lost Cal Ripken announcing that it picked up Ken Griffey, Jr., and Barry Bonds to take his place."[5]

I quickly began researching my new bosses in order to learn as much about them as possible. Tate was young and energetic, two qualities that had aided in Ralph's success. Hodel, as already mentioned, had done two tours of duty as a Cabinet secretary in the Reagan Administration. I was delighted at the opportunity to work for men of their background.

Don Hodel was experienced in building coalitions among pro-family leaders and organizations, partly due to his long-time friendships with leaders like Phyllis Schlafly of Eagle Forum, Charles Colson of Prison Fellowship, and Dr. James Dobson of Focus on the Family. His best relationship was with Dobson, having served on the board of Focus on the Family for several years, and volunteering for seven months as a Focus's executive vice president in 1996.

The two men first met when Hodel was Secretary of the Interior. Upon learning that Dr. Dobson enjoyed basketball, Hodel invited him to play in the department's gymnasium and a close friendship developed in the ensuing years. In fact Dobson agreed to be the keynote speaker at Road to Victory '98 before having to withdraw after suffering a stroke earlier in the year.[‡]

On June 13, I drove to Norfolk International Airport to pick up Randy Tate, who was making his first trip to Chesapeake. He told me it actually was his *second* flight to Norfolk International Airport, as a few weeks earlier he had flown in, unbeknownst to any of the Coalition staff, to be interviewed by Pat for the job.

---

[†] This was hardly Pat's main activity of the day. After the news conference he was sequestered in a conference room at the Coalition's D.C. office to hammer out the final agreement to sell The Family Channel to the Fox network for $1.9 billion.

[‡] From which he experienced a miraculous recovery.

As Tate walked off the plane I greeted him with the familiar one-word title, "Congressman," and escorted him to my car en route to the Founders Inn where he would spend the next few nights. I later learned that the first time he and Don Hodel had met was at the Denver airport only a couple of weeks earlier, Tate having flown in from Seattle.

First, however, Tate wanted to go by Coalition headquarters. We toured the building and, afterwards, dined at a nearby restaurant, and began getting acquainted. He told me that his parents were long-time viewers of *The 700 Club* and that Pat's campaign for president had been his first political experience. He had been a delegate to the 1988 Republican National Convention before running and winning an election for the Washington state legislature while still in college.

Two evenings later, I repeated the same procedure, including a midnight visit to headquarters, with Don Hodel. At first, I was less at ease with Secretary Hodel, who was a generation older than Tate and me, had served at a higher level than anyone I had ever worked for, and seemed quite more official than Randy.

Ever a conservative, Hodel was concerned about using donor money for his comfort and asked why we had purchased a first-class ticket for him, rather than coach. And he soon moved out of the Founders Inn to the less expensive Wellesley Inn, located next to our office. Randy moved also, of course.

In addition to frugality, another quality the staff noticed early on in Don Hodel was punctuality. If a meeting was scheduled to begin at ten o'clock, anyone arriving two minutes after ten would find himself or herself entering in the middle of a conversation. He moved through an agenda with rapidity, although he was always willing to discuss any matter an employee felt was pertinent. I respectfully called him "Mr. Hodel" for the first day or so, but soon I heard, "Call me 'Don,'" as I left his office one day.

Each time I walked into "Don's" office it was like stepping back in time to the 1980s when Reagan was president and most all seemed right with America. Pictures of him with Reagan graced almost every wall. I especially remember a large bowl, decorated with gold and blue presidential insignias. "This guy is a heavy hitter," I thought.

Soon, it seemed as if I had known Hodel for years. He was quite Reaganesque, always affable and solicitous to the staff, and quite easy to get to know, portraying that same avuncular disposition as the Gipper.

As long as he was in charge at the Coalition, we knew that things would be okay. The money may have been tight and the media on the attack, but there was a sense of peace and expectancy.

Not long after arriving, Hodel decided to decline his Coalition salary, in favor of contributing his services to the organization on a volunteer basis due to a vow he had made to the Lord several years earlier. He even paid his own travel expenses, which included an average of one flight each week for him and his wife, Barbara, who worked as his unpaid personal assistant.

In addition to their volunteering in the office, the Hodels made a practice of hosting small groups of staff for lunch or dinner several times each month. These outings sometimes occurred at the best restaurants in the area, but they were just as comfortable at Nathan's Deli or the Old Country Buffet around the corner. And one of their favorite spots was Pungo Pizza and Ice Cream, tucked away in a secluded part of Virginia Beach, a restaurant that could be described as rustic at best. Rarely have I met a political figure as equally at home with strip mall buffets as with filet mignon.

It was an average afternoon at Christian Coalition, except that Ralph was there, yet no longer in charge, Don Hodel having begun his presidency. Ralph was spending his last few days at headquarters, his attention already in Atlanta with his new consulting company, Century Strategies. But there was one last speech to give to a local audience, the Virginia Beach Jaycees.

"Joel, could you go with Ralph tonight to handle any press that might be there?" asked Ken Hill. "Arne (Owens, the communications director) has family responsibilities and can't go." I did not know, however, that there was a particular reason Ralph could not go alone that evening. A producer from *20/20*, ABC's news-magazine show, had been calling earlier in the day in an attempt to set up an interview with Ralph. The show had recently conducted an interview with hostile former employee Judy Liebert and wanted Ralph's response to her allegations.[§] As with most such television programs, Ralph was sure to be placed in a "Have you stopped beating your wife?" situation and had no obligation to comply.

I arrived at the Virginia Beach Museum of Fine Arts approximately half an hour before the event was to start. That would be plenty of time to

§ See Chapter 8.

see the room and perform routine advance work before Ralph arrived. A couple of camera crews already were there. I explained to them that Ralph would not be doing any interviews that evening but that they could cover his speech.

People were slow in arriving and I already could tell this was going to be a very small crowd. I called Ralph on the cell phone to let him know that the crowd was trickling in. That would allow him to arrive late, taking advantage of the tardiness of the attendees. He already was on his way, however, and said he would be there in about ten minutes. Then he asked what I thought to be an odd question: "Is Brian Ross there?"

Brian Ross was the "attack journalism" reporter for ABC. I well remembered his jump-in-your-face attack on Pat (and Dede) Robertson and Ralph a few years earlier at our Road to Victory conference in Washington. Only the close proximity to the elevator and the strong presence of CBN security kept the Robertsons and Ralph from a very unwelcome, impromptu interview with the ABC reporter.

I had not seen Ross there that evening in Virginia Beach, but quickly surveyed the parking lot to see if he was anywhere around. "No," I said. "What about Rhonda Schwartz?" Ralph continued. I had never heard that name and had no way of knowing that the petit dark-haired woman standing by the door to the museum was Ross's producer for his exposé reports.

Shortly, Ralph's sleek, white Acura wheeled into the parking lot and he quickly got out. Suddenly, at the opposite side of the parking lot I saw out of the corner of my eye a tall, skinny man emerge from a car that had been inconspicuously parked among others. It was Brian Ross. Ralph and I already had hung up our cell phones and before I could warn him, he was walking toward me—and Ross. I couldn't shout to him, so I began walking ever so briskly in his direction trying to head him off. "Ralph, go back," I *wanted* to yell. By then it was too late, however, as Ross and his crew were heading toward the point where the entrance walk to the museum met the sidewalk.

There was nothing Ralph and I could do but walk up to them, acting as if we expected their presence. Ross began shouting rapid-fire questions at Ralph without even giving him a chance to answer, as the cameraman held the lens about two feet from Ralph's face. "I'll talk to you live," Ralph said, "but I won't give you anything on tape." Ralph was all too familiar with television journalism and its carefully spliced-together footage.

"What about the accusations against you," Ross continued to shout, as Ralph and I calmly approached the door. "I'll only talk to you live," Ralph repeated.

As we reached the door the cameraman stopped with his back to the door, thus blocking the entrance. I'm sure they thought they had Ralph trapped at that point. But I opened the door with my left hand, sweeping the cameraman out of the way in the process. Ralph walked through in front of me and I stepped between him and the ABC crew, taking hold of each side of the doorway, thinking I would hold them off until Ralph could get inside and out of their reach. Then, however, I heard a voice that sounded to me like Ross exclaim, "Get the [expletive] out of my way," as someone kneed me from behind and shoved me through the door, only to have Ross then accuse *me* of shoving *him*. "Is this your henchman, Reed? Is this guy with you?" he asked, obviously hoping to give Ralph the impression that it was I who had gotten rough.

Once inside, Ralph had been stopped in his tracks by the event host, who was very startled by the commotion and did not know what to do. So, by the time I came stumbling through the door with Ross hot on my heels, Ralph still was standing there and had to endure more questions from Ross. After the struggle, I remember walking past a young, new reporter for the Norfolk ABC affiliate. She seemed shocked at what had occurred, and actually apologized for the actions of her "associate" from the network's national bureau.

After one more encounter in the lobby, Ralph finally made his way to the stage, only to have Ross and his crew set up their cameras in the back of the auditorium, awaiting his exit. I had to act, and act quickly. Another confrontation could not happen!

First, I called Ken Hill on his cell phone and filled him in on the situation. Ken had done security and advance work for both the Reagan and Bush Administrations. If I had not come up with a solution by the time he arrived, he would surely have one. As Ken got in his car and began the twenty-minute drive to the location, we kept the phone line open so I could keep him briefed on any further events.

As Ralph began his speech, I went backstage, searching for another door leading outside. If there were one, we could take Ralph out that way, keeping him away from the grasp of the reporter. I peered through a break in the backstage curtains and noticed two double doors just to the right of the stage. They were fire exits. "This might be the solution to *this* hot situation," I thought. After being assured and reassured again by the center's director that these doors would open if the panic bar handle were engaged, I knew we had our solution. The key would be to park a car close to that door and have a driver waiting so we could pull away as soon as Ralph was in the car.

About that time Ken arrived and entered the museum. I filled him in on the scenario and we agreed that I should wait in the driver's seat of his car with the motor running, as he escorted Ralph out. The advantage to this plan was that Ross would not know who Ken was and, therefore, would not be suspicious about seeing him walk through the auditorium.

So I left and Ken went inside so that Ralph would see him and realize the situation was under control. Ralph, who had been speaking for far longer than planned, later told us that he had decided just to keep talking until he saw a signal that it was time to escape. Ken's presence in the room told Ralph that the time had come to make his exit.

As Ralph concluded his speech, Ken walked toward him and, as Ralph came off the stage, quickly ushered him to the fire exit and they walked to the car. They could not run, of course, which would have made it seem as if Ralph had something to hide. We drove onto the Interstate and took the next exit, leaving Ralph at a Wendy's restaurant while Ken and I returned for Ralph's car. Ken then took the precaution of driving Ralph's car one additional exit before doubling back, just in case he was being followed. After Ralph was peacefully on his way home, Ken and I went back to the museum to my waiting car, where we learned from museum staff that our exit was so clean that Ross had no idea that we had even left.

The next morning when I arrived at the office, the same ABC camera crew had their tripod set up in a grassy area adjacent to our parking lot. I entered the building and learned that Ken had gotten there early, saw the cameras, and called Ralph on his cell phone to alert him. So Ralph parked on the other side of the complex and walked through the back door by the loading dock. Don Hodel also had to enter through the back entrance in order to avoid the camera crew, who soon folded up their tripod and left. I then drove the fifteen miles or so to Ralph's house to be sure they were not there hassling Jo Anne and the children.

The story ran approximately three months later⁵ but on a different ABC news program, *Nightline*, as part of a segment featuring their earlier

⁵ One month prior to the 1997 Virginia election for governor, along with New Jersey, the only major elections occurring that year. One might wonder why ABC held the piece

interview with Judy Liebert, bringing up old accusations of impropriety in our activities, which she alleged were related to the FEC lawsuit.
Fortunately, ABC allowed our attorney, Jim Bopp, to appear, and he came
off as much more credible than Judy. As Ken Hill once said, "All they do is
make allegations about Ralph, while Jim argues the law."**

Bopp, who has likely done as much in the courtroom to protect
both political free speech and unborn life as any living American, even
received one fan letter, which was mailed to our office a few days after the
interview. Just for fun, I faxed it to his office in Terre Haute, Indiana, along
with a note congratulating him for his new celebrity status.

The remainder of the summer saw Don Hodel and Randy Tate
settling into their new roles, as Ken Hill kept the lid on the Coalition's
continued legal problems and conducted searches for new senior staff
members to replace several who left soon after Ralph.

First to leave was *Christian American* editor Mike Ebert, who had an
offer with the prestigious Southern Baptist Convention. Chief Capitol Hill
lobbyist Brian Lopina accepted a position with a Washington, D.C. law
firm, and Director of Administration Tom McDonald went to work for
a local Jewish organization. Finally, Field Director D. J. Gribbin resigned
just after Road to Victory in September to take a corporate post. With
press spokesman Mike Russell already having left in December, 1996, and
Finance Director Liebert having been fired earlier that year, only Voter
Education Director Chuck Cunningham and two other division directors
remained from the Reed-era group of the Coalition's division heads.

---

for three months unless they hoped it would reflect negatively on Republican candidates
that fall.

** Conversation with Ken Hill, ca. 1999.

# 13

## Farewell

ROAD TO VICTORY '96 had been such a huge success that we knew topping it in 1997, a year with no national elections, would be next to impossible. So a decision was made by the board of directors to instead hold three *regional* Road to Victory conferences in 1997, one in Atlanta, one in St. Louis, and one in Los Angeles, each spaced about a month apart. This would alleviate the need to exceed 1996 in terms of attendance in Washington, D.C., but at the same time it would permit us to pass the previous year in terms of perception, by having three events, rather than just one.

The idea sounded good only at headquarters, however. The grassroots activists across the country enjoyed the annual trip to the nation's capital and were not excited about replacing it with a journey to another destination. A large number of our activists, as well as four of our best state affiliates—Texas, South Carolina, Florida, and Alabama—were located in the South guaranteeing that the Atlanta event would be somewhat successful, so that one seemed less volatile. Nevertheless, by mid-summer it was apparent that registrations were lagging even there.

We were faced, therefore, with the possibility of one lackluster event in Atlanta and two disasters in the other cities, which was far from acceptable. With Ralph Reed's resignation and the premature media obituaries on the Coalition that followed, Road to Victory(s) '97 had to be hugely— and visibly—successful. Recognizing that one RTV would be hard enough and that three would be essentially impossible to pull off, the decision was made to cancel Los Angeles and St. Louis, focusing all our attention on Atlanta. Since Georgia was Ralph's home state and Atlanta was his new hometown, this was a perfect fit. We would hold a farewell dinner in his honor, which would justify the condensing of the three events into one.

The result of canning the other two events was a successful conference in Atlanta. There were fewer attendees than we had been accustomed to in Washington, but, nonetheless, it was a full ballroom in a major hotel with all the headline speakers we could have hoped for.

Ralph was there, too, of course, and the Brian Ross-20/20 problem still was lurking; therefore, Ken and I were busy securing Ralph's entrances and exits at the downtown Marriott Marquis hotel where the event was held. Fortunately, there were no mishaps, which allowed me to focus most of my attention on Pat Robertson.

First was the arrival at the Atlanta airport. We had arranged for a local limousine company to pick up and deliver our speakers from and to the Atlanta airport. And we decided to use the same service for Pat and Dede when they arrived on Friday afternoon in time for the evening banquet saluting Ralph.

The limo was supposed to pick me up at the hotel so that I could ride to the airport to greet the Robertsons. But when I walked outside the hotel, the tasteful—and most importantly—*inconspicuous* black or navy Lincoln Town Car we had ordered was nowhere in sight. There was this eye-sore, a white "stretch" version, which I learned, much to my chagrin upon talking with the driver, was the car that had been sent for Pat and Dede. This would not do. I could not put Pat and Dede into a limo that would have looked more appropriate transporting a rock star or an NBA player. They had to bring a different car. So I instructed the driver to take me to the airport in that car and to radio his office to send the appropriate car to meet us there.

And they got it half right. They sent a black Town Car but it was another stretch version. This was little better than before; and Pat's plane would be landing soon. There was no time to order another car, so I just had to wait and tough it out.

As Pat's Learjet touched down, I made my way out on the tarmac and the limo driver made the mistake of following me as I walked toward the plane. Pat was less than thrilled to see such an ostentatious car rolling toward him. But upon hearing my explanation that we would be entering the hotel via an underground parking garage, out of sight of onlookers and television cameras, Pat got inside the car, along with Dede and body-guard John Rea.

As we approached the Marriott, however, it turned out that my consternation had only begun. The stretch-limo's chassis was so long and the slope of the underground garage entrance so steep, that when the driver turned the wheels into the hotel's driveway to start down, the car bottomed-out against the pavement. As my life began whizzing before my eyes, the driver was able to generate enough power from the rear wheels to push us over the high spot in the pavement and soon we were safely underground.

At the time, I would not have cared whether the driver scraped the entire underside off the car or if he ever was able to get the limo out of that garage again. We were there and that's all that mattered. As I showed the Robertsons to their suite, forty-five floors above, and turned to leave, Pat said, "Joel, you did good," which was music to my ears considering the limo debacle, making me smile as I entered the elevator and descended to the hotel lobby.

Ralph's farewell dinner later that evening was quite entertaining with warm tributes to Ralph offered by former Virginia Cabinet secretary and Regent University Dean Kay James, Congressman John Kasich, and former vice presidential candidate Jack Kemp, among others, along with a video tribute to Ralph featuring congressional leaders such as Senate Majority Leader Trent Lott and House Majority Leader Dick Armey. Don Hodel emceed the event, and pointed out that, as irony would have it, less than a decade earlier Ralph had worked as a waiter in that very hotel.

Jack Kemp's appearance was quite memorable to me. I met him at the hotel entrance, escorting him downstairs and through the long hallways of the hotel's kitchen to the curtain in back of the dais. Don Hodel joined us at the bottom of the escalator in order to greet Kemp and walked with us along the way. Being a former Cabinet secretary, Don had many good relationships with national leaders (on both sides of the aisle), and I remember meeting none except that they paused to tell me of their respect for him.

As we walked, Kemp ran over his planned comments about Ralph and mentioned that Ralph had supported his 1988 presidential candidacy. He stopped himself, saying he would not mention that fact during his remarks and wanted to be sure Don did the same when he introduced him. Kemp felt that would be in bad taste because Pat, also a candidate in 1988, was sitting at the same head table and Ralph had gone on to work for him. Of course, I'm sure Pat already knew that Ralph had been a Kemp supporter, but nonetheless, most of the crowd did not and this was a genuine gesture from Kemp.

During Kemp's remarks he told a story of legendary Brooklyn Dodgers baseball players Jackie Robinson and Pee Wee Reese. When Robinson courageously broke baseball's color barrier in 1947 he received a very negative response from racially prejudiced fans. On one occasion, when the fans and even the opposing manager were pelting Robinson with insults, Reese, shortstop to Robinson as second baseman, walked past second base and put his arm on Robinson's shoulder in a show of support. Kemp concluded that Reese stood by his teammate in part due to being a Christian. It was a very touching story. Later, however, as I accompanied him back through the long kitchen hallway to return him to his waiting car, Kemp leaned over to me and said in an uncertain tone, "I *think* Pee Wee Reese was a Christian." Either he was just kidding me or he had gotten carried away in telling the story.

At six o'clock the next morning, Ken Hill and I both were up and out of our rooms early to see Ralph off, as he left the hotel, and the Coalition. He remained on the organization's board of directors until 1998. But with the Coalition's problems with the IRS and the FEC escalating, the board felt the partisan nature of his political consulting business might bring us even more scrutiny, and asked him to resign. Don Hodel flew from Norfolk to Atlanta at his own expense to deliver the request.

My next duty that day in Atlanta was to go to Pat and Dede's suite and escort them to a breakfast of about 250 Christian Coalition state and county leaders from around the nation, a breakfast that had been scheduled purposely so that our top activists attending Road to Victory could hear directly, and confidentially, from Pat. As we descended in the elevator, I explained the makeup of the audience and told him he could share "from his heart"—which he did.

Tragically, however, and totally unbeknownst to me, a significant security breach occurred that morning, and our plan to verify each attendee at the door by nametags to a pre-printed list of invitees was not enacted. The doors were left wide open and *no one* was screened before entering the room.

By the time Pat, Dede, and I arrived, someone had slipped in with a hidden cassette recorder, a fact we did not learn of until a week or so later when our nemesis, the liberal Reverend Barry Lynn of Americans for Separation of Church and State, went public with the tape. His face was well-known to all of our employees so there is no way he was in the breakfast that morning, but one of his associates evidently slipped in.

At the time we felt that Lynn hated Christian Coalition, which was paradoxical considering that we were his reason for being, his best opportunity to garner press attention, and his meal ticket.

When Reverend Lynn later released the tape of Pat's comments, it caused quite a stir. In his speech Pat made it clear that if our supporters came out in such large numbers that they dominated whatever local or state Republican Party meetings they attended, the result would be a powerful national political machine reminiscent of other legendary political machines, including New York's Tammany Hall.[1] No election laws would be in jeopardy of being transgressed; it would be strictly a matter of numbers and strategy.

If not couched in colorful metaphors Pat's point would have provided no ammunition for Lynn to use against us. Finally, Pat mentioned that when he offered Don Hodel the Coalition presidency, he included that Don's acceptance might result in the two together selecting the next President of the United States.[2] That comment gave the news media the opportunity to squawk for months.

Back home, the November Virginia elections brought a Republican sweep of the three statewide offices, which became the top political story of the nation. On election night, Pat, Randy Tate, and I traveled to Richmond to attend the GOP's victory celebration at the Party's customary hotel of choice, the downtown Marriott. I arrived early to meet Pat's security staff, while Randy flew up with Pat. This was going to be a great night and I was delighted to be there.

As hundreds of excited Republicans eagerly awaited the arrival in the ballroom by Governor-elect Jim Gilmore, Lieutenant Governor-elect John Hager, and Attorney General-elect Mark Earley, Pat came in and was immediately surrounded by a throng of reporters. For almost an hour he walked from camera crew to camera crew, doing interviews about the results, flanked by three security men and press handler Gene Kapp.

*The Virginian-Pilot* later reported that Pat had swept into the ballroom as if he himself had been elected governor.[3] That was okay. Pat deserved to bask in the victory. He had been made an issue in the election by the Democrats, who inserted him into their television and print advertisements. Their plan was to paint Gilmore as a pawn of Pat Robertson and religious conservative values. True, Pat personally had given $50,000 to Gilmore's campaign, as he had when Gilmore ran for attorney general in 1993, but the comparison was unfair. Like any other private citizen,

Pat had every right to support the candidates of his choice with his time, talents and finances.

Christian Coalition had mailed post cards to over 60,000 voters around the state in opposition to what we felt were bigoted characterizations of religious conservative values by the Democrats. As described in an earlier chapter, Democrats in Virginia had used similar tactics against Pat in 1993 and before that in 1991. In 1997, as usual, their bigotry backfired. Our tracking polls showed that in 1997 Gilmore actually hit an upswing just as the Democrats began their attack against Pat.

The final month of 1997 saw Christian Coalition reach both highs and lows. First, the good news: the December 8 issue of *FORTUNE* magazine featured *Washington's Power 25*, a rating of the twenty-five most influential organizations in politics. An accompanying article by reporter Jeffrey Birnbaum began: "Which pressure groups are best at manipulating the laws we live by? A ground-breaking *FORTUNE* survey reveals who belongs to lobbying's elite and why they wield so much clout."[4] We were elated when Christian Coalition was chosen as number seven on the list, right behind the powerful National Rifle Association, which had a annual budget multiple times larger than ours.

On the "power" list, Christian Coalition was ranked ahead of such groups as the American Medical Association and the U.S. Chamber of Commerce. Further, we were seen as more influential than an arch-enemy, the ninth ranked National Education Association. Only one other pro-family group, the National Right to Life Committee, made the list, at number ten. We also were voted the Republicans' fourth-most-loved group and the Democrats' twelfth-most-hated organization.[5] "Only twelfth?" we lamented.

Even though the poll had begun before Ralph Reed resigned, this was a huge indicator that the Coalition's standing was still strong in the eyes of those surveyed by *FORTUNE* and that we were still considered a major player in Washington. It refuted the opinions of many newspapers and political magazines, which had begun writing the Coalition's obituary when Ralph announced that he was stepping down. And as a tribute to Randy Tate's and Don Hodel's leadership, one year later, Christian Coalition retained its seventh-place finish in the 1998 *FORTUNE* poll.

The news in late 1997 was not all good, however. A significant drop in income occurred just after the 1996 elections, when the Republican Party retained control of both houses of Congress, even despite the

626628228865828

re-election of Bill Clinton. This helped lead to a serious amount of debt that began accumulating on the Coalition's books in the early months of 1997, which became quite unmanageable shortly after Ralph Reed announced his imminent departure, as income fell even sharper. This involved several components.

First, we faced an immediate and significant loss in direct mail income. As an example of the tremendous personal appeal Ralph had with our membership, Pat Robertson's name had been replaced by Ralph's on the fund-raising letters a couple of years earlier. But with no immediate replacement announced at Ralph's resignation, donors seemed to be holding their money, waiting to see who Ralph's successor would be. Pat later told *The New York Times Magazine*, "The direct mail wasn't good . . . and Ralph was in transition and not focusing."[6]

The Coalition's cash flow was already so bad by May, 1997, that Ken Hill sent an e-mail to the senior staff placing a halt on all spending in order to get things back under control, division by division. Ken's succinct memo included the words, "As of today, you no longer have a budget."[7]

And when Hodel and Tate began to get our direct mail program geared-up again, results were far less than we had hoped. The money simply was not flowing in as well as in the past. Basically, the direct mail program in 1997 barely paid for itself.

Don later told me that when he took over the helm in mid-June, 1997, and learned of the Coalition's debt, he should have gotten a tighter grip on the situation and should have been more pro-active to cut spending. At the time, however, our direct mail consultants were insisting that revenues would increase dramatically by fall. What they did not take into account was the lack of a national election cycle, which had been the reason for the tremendous upswing in our revenues the previous fall, in addition to donor confusion over the Christian Defense Fund's apparent cloning of our mailings.*

From the expenditures side of the ledger, debt began to increase with a steep trajectory due to a backlog of invoices for goods and services from earlier in the year. And they just kept coming. The result of all the above factors was that the Coalition's total accounts payable skyrocketed by about $1 million during the first two months of the Hodel-Tate era.

* See Chapter 8.

Making matters much worse, overall spending was at an all-time high. Coming off the record fund-raising year of 1996, spending at the Coalition had ballooned. We were supporting two additional organizations, the Catholic Alliance and The Samaritan Project, in addition to paying for the *Christian American*, which had grown from a tabloid newspaper to a glossy magazine. Staff size was also high, with a total of about 120 employees between the national headquarters and the Capitol Hill office. In February, 1997, we had increased our headquarters office space by 5,000 square feet, mostly to provide more space—including a "war room"—for the field operation.

In 1996, the Coalition even considered purchasing an airplane, a small Learjet, which would have allowed Ralph to maximize his time much better, cutting hours and delays out of most trips. This is not as unusual as it might sound, as many well-known religious figures ignore the extravagant impression and travel in airplanes owned by their ministries. Doing so might be considered to be a flagrant use of donated funds but is not illegal as long as ministry monies do not pay for personal trips made by ministry employees.

The tremendous cash flow the Coalition had been blessed with over the past three years had allowed the organization to relax spending controls.[†] The momentum was too great, however, and the bills, coupled with payroll, outpaced cash receipts. The result was that by the fall of 1997 the debt had reached almost $3 million. Pat Robertson later said that he did not know the extent of the financial problems Don and Randy would inherit.[8] Communications Director Arne Owens told *The New York Times Magazine*, "Don and Randy took over and that's what they were greeted with."[9]

The Coalition also lacked a senior financial analyst at the time. Finance Director Judy Liebert had been dismissed in 1996 for divulging confidential information, a successor had not been located, and her backup, our controller, was released less than a year later for embezzlement—actually, on the same day Ralph's leaving became public. "I was in a meeting with the D.C. office staff while Ralph was telling them he was leaving and my cell phone rang," Ken later told me. It was a member of the

---

† One senior staff member told me with delightful amazement, ca. 1995, that he'd never worked anywhere where money was so abundant and that budgets were of so little concern. That may have been only *his* impression, however.

accounting staff informing him they had run across serious irregularities in the books, which meant that the controller had to go.

In October, Ken located and hired a new director of finance, Steve Wolkomir, whose background was as an auditor. Steve's initial survey of our books showed that we were in a financially desperate state and he immediately began instituting corrective measures, chief among them being a tight hold on our purchasing habits, insisting that goods and services be encumbered as they were ordered, giving him forewarning that the invoice would be arriving, which for the most part was new to the Coalition. Of course, it was not noticeable when income was bountiful.

Upon seeing Steve's initial audit of the books, Don called an emergency board meeting in order to inform them of the financial situation. Even though Don had been interceding with the Coalition's creditors for several weeks, he was concerned that the patience of several was wearing quite thin. Lawsuits could be imminent. The board had to be made aware.

When Don told me he was calling the board together, I warned that the result would be board-mandated layoffs—a fact he reminded me of afterward. And at a December 16 meeting, the board of directors, which consisted of Pat Robertson, Billy McCormack, Dick Weinhold, and—at the time—Ralph Reed, mandated a dramatic slashing of the budget, including the loss of four entire divisions of the organization,‡ which were not directly related to our core mission of organizing precincts and distributing voter education material, as well as the termination of various consulting contracts. In addition, the field budget was reduced by a sizeable amount. The changes brought a total staff loss of twenty-seven, reducing our total work force by 20 percent. While a pre-Christmas layoff seemed harsh—and it was—worse still would have been losing their jobs after the holidays, after having spent much more money on Christmas gifts and other festivities than they otherwise did.

Other remedies considered in addition to cutbacks in spending were bank loans and loans from major donors, a method that had provided start-up funds for the initial kick-off event for the Robertson presidential campaign in 1986,[10] as well as the rental or sale of the Coalition's mailing list.

‡ The development division, the *Christian American* magazine, the Catholic Alliance, and the Samaritan Project. I later learned that during the meeting Ralph lobbied to save the Samaritan Project, which stood out, considering that when he launched the initiative the previous January his plans to resign in April had already likely been made.

Christian Coalition had always refused to allow other organizations to use its mailing list.§ But eventually, the lapsed donor portion of the mailing list was put on the market for rental. The Coalition also received loans both from Pat Robertson and Don Hodel, each of whom later forgave the amount. Don made two personal contributions of $100,000 each, while Pat put in $500,000 in late 1997, along with another half-million in 1998. Together, they kept the Coalition afloat during those months.

Just a few days after the board meeting, Barbara Hodel asked me to come to Don's office where I learned that my next task was to investigate and make a list of those among our departing employees who were in the most serious financial need. After checking with our human resources manager, Connie Melton, and asking a few confidential questions, I was able to present Don and Barbara with a list of names the next afternoon. In a couple of hours, Barbara returned from the bank with an envelope containing thousands of dollars in cash, which I was to distribute to the names on my list. This was followed a few days later with another envelope and instructions to keep my eyes open for future needs. Randy Tate also made a gift to at least one of the employees.

Seeing the looks on the faces and the tears of joy in the eyes of the parting employees was a highlight of my Christmas that year, and I later told Don and Barbara what a blessing it had been to assist with their benevolence. Don responded in his inimitable humor. "Joel," he said, "that just shows that you would make a good congressman—because you enjoy giving away *other people's* money." The Hodels insisted that their generosity be anonymous, so that is how I left it—until now.

We at Christian Coalition ended 1997 with a significant amount of trepidation, but at the same time, with a positive expectation of what the New Year held in store. Little did we know that we were about to be labeled as a key component of a "vast, right-wing conspiracy" attempting to bring down President Bill Clinton.

---

§ Although we did rent the list to a few candidates over the years, notably the Georgia portion to George H. W. Bush in 1992 and the Virginia portion to Oliver North in 1994. These rentals were totally within the law.

# 14

# Holding It All Together

THE ONLY COMPLETE YEAR of the Hodel-Tate era was a wonderful time to be working at Christian Coalition. Soon after Don and Randy came to town I began to handle projects for them, including briefing them on matters related to the local Hampton Roads area, as well as details about CBN and Pat Robertson. Because of my years of service to Pat and the Coalition, I was a repository of historical and organizational facts that provided them with a quick reference point. I immensely enjoyed working alongside Don, Randy, and Ken Hill, and during the year was promoted to the position of assistant to the president, a title familiar to Don from his time in the Reagan Administration.

In January, 1998, Don and Randy began co-hosting their own weekly television program on the National Empowerment Television cable network. Don asked me to be executive producer for the show, which consisted of lining up guests and choosing topics for each Monday's weekly edition. The new show, *Christian Coalition Weekly*, was similar to, although less scripted than, Ralph's monthly program on the same network had been.* Each week, Don and Randy would ad-lib back and forth about current events and issues before the Congress, as well as interview a guest. This was going to be a great year working alongside our two new leaders. The year, politically and otherwise, however, was dominated by a young, former White House intern and her affection for a man in power who had a weakness that has plagued leaders for centuries.

On January 19, we all watched the news coverage on CNN about the latest scandal that had attached itself to President Bill Clinton, an alleged affair with a White House intern. He, only two days earlier, had testified in

---

* Although, by the time, NET was carried on some cable systems and on the Dish Network, alleviating the need for the Ku-band downlink to our local chapters.

THE RISE AND FALL OF THE CHRISTIAN COALITION

the Paula Jones lawsuit, where he finally admitted to having an affair with Gennifer Flowers. Little did we know then that the Monica Lewinsky soap opera would lead to the initial tug on the thread that would ultimately cause Christian Coalition to unravel.

As more and more details surfaced in the Lewinsky scandal, pro-family organizations around the country called for Clinton's resignation. By the time of Road to Victory '98 in September, almost every speaker worked a Lewinsky related anti-Clinton punch line into his or her speech.[†] The best came from House Majority Leader Dick Armey of Texas, who commented on how his wife would respond if he committed similar actions: "You'll wake up in a pool of blood, with me standing over you saying, 'How do I reload this thing?'" Armey's line was picked up by CNN and run almost every half hour throughout the weekend on CNN's *Headline News*.

Throughout the summer and into fall we had been collecting signatures on petitions calling for the president's resignation or impeachment. Such a disgrace to the Oval Office and to the executive branch of government could not go unchallenged. The White House and the presidency had to be cleansed. Petitions poured in by the thousands, filling boxes in our mailroom that were labeled with the names of members of Congress awaiting shipment to Capitol Hill.

Shortly after taking over the helm of the Coalition, Don Hodel came to the conclusion that he should not be the organization's chief spokesman, since he planned to stay only about three years, just through the 2000 elections. Therefore, when he left, the Coalition should not have to undergo another transition in its public persona. In addition, he felt that he was of the wrong generation to "replace" Ralph Reed in representing the Coalition on television. So, he insisted that Randy Tate be the organization's only "front man."

While the executive directorship of Christian Coalition transferred from Ralph Reed to Randy Tate, much to our dismay the mantle of primary spokesman for religious conservatives did not automatically go with it. Randy certainly had his share of television and print media in the early days, but leaders of other conservative groups suddenly realized Ralph's absence on the scene might open up airtime for them.

---

[†] The anti-Clinton lines were always there. Only the Lewinsky angle had to be added.

And then there was Gary Bauer, then head of the Family Research Council. For years he had been second to Ralph Reed as a leader of the pro-family political movement in the eyes of the media and among pro-family activists. Ralph was younger and, many felt, came across better on television. He garnered most of the network television interviews whenever they wanted a representative from the religious conservative movement. Bauer, on the other hand, had been active for a decade, having served in the Reagan Administration. But Ralph came out of nowhere, with the benefit of Pat Robertson's already established grassroots infrastructure from his presidential campaign, and surpassed Bauer in terms of perceived effectiveness and media exposure.

When Ralph stepped down from the Coalition, it left a temporary void in terms of publicity for our movement that Gary Bauer quickly filled by scooping up press opportunities that would have otherwise gone to Ralph, and by working very diligently to capture as much attention as he could. As they say, the early bird gets the worm. Bauer's publicity reached a peak in a December, 1997, cover story in *The Weekly Standard* entitled "Bauer Power," which featured a caricature of Bauer in a *Superman* suit on the cover, and in which writer Fred Barnes laid out his claim for Bauer as the leader of the post-Reed Christian Right.[1]

In the Chapter 1, I alluded to a sibling-type rivalry between Ralph Reed and Gary Bauer, who once said that Ralph was on precarious ground in trying to mainstream the Coalition. "Ralph is going to have to be really careful to not end up a leader without a following,"[2] Bauer said. But Gary was quite complimentary of Don and Randy, as well as conciliatory toward the Coalition, in a February, 1998, "Washington Update" daily fax to his grassroots leaders: "The Christian Coalition, under my friends Don Hodel and Randy Tate, is going to emerge stronger than ever . . . We are committed to not allowing the press to divide us nor [sic] to distract us from the pro-family / pro-life agenda."[3]

Considering that in 1998 Christian Coalition had to step out of Ralph Reed's shadow and Randy had to chart his own course for the Coalition, Bauer's rise in popularity did not help, especially in terms of television coverage. But we pressed on, realizing that media attention was more earned than given, and that as soon as Christian Coalition began affecting legislation in ways other organizations, including Gary's, could not, i.e., through those activists Randy described in every Congressional District in America, media exposure would follow. Randy built a solid television image, so much so that he was still seen as a leading candidate to comment on Christian Coalition even after leaving the group in mid-1999.

Christian Coalition released a new set of legislative proposals in 1998 to follow up on our hugely successful 1995 *Contract with the American Family*. Called *New Freedom for America's Families: A Blueprint for the 21st Century*, our 1998 legislative agenda relied on six key building blocks: ensuring education and economic opportunity; reforming Social Security and health care; strengthening national security; preserving the sanctity of life; respecting religious freedom; and demanding tax fairness.[4] Due to the dismal showing of conservatives at the ballot box in November, and to the internal troubles of Christian Coalition, however, the *Blueprint* brought less-than-desired success. There were at least three bright spots, however.

Randy put his experience as a congressman into play, along with the relationships he built while in Washington, to gear up our lobbying activities on three major legislative initiatives, one being spearheaded by Don Hodel and another by Pat Robertson, with the third being Randy's own project. I remember sessions in his office when we pored over target lists showing which congressmen and senators supported our position on whatever issue was at hand, as Randy decided how best to lobby those who were undecided, encouraging them to vote for our position. Most often, this would include three means: postcards mailed to our members in their districts, phone banks to those same members, and encouraging our local leadership to schedule visits with their congressman and senators back in the home districts.

Post cards were written by our Capitol Hill staff, and then designed by graphic artists at headquarters. They were then printed on neon-colored paper and mailed to our supporters in respective Congressional Districts.

Phone banks to those same supporters were conducted by internal phone callers, sometimes with as many as thirty temporary workers making calls, as well as via computerized calls where supporters received a prerecorded message from Randy, Pat, or even a member of Congress, educating them on an issue and asking them to phone their congressman or senators. I once answered one of the calls at my home and the first thing I heard was, "Hello, this is Newt Gingrich."[‡]

---

‡ Recent technological advances far exceed anything available in the 1990s, including automatic phone calls that are able to ask a series of questions, formerly done only by a live caller.

Randy took the lead on one major Christian Coalition legislative interest of 1998, the abolishment of the marriage tax penalty, an arcane income tax law that actually penalized married couples in America, who, when filing jointly, received a lower deduction amount than did their unmarried and cohabiting counterparts, who filed separately.

In 1998, Randy felt the marriage penalty should be included in the *Blueprint* and supported with an extensive grassroots campaign. He brought up the issue in most every interview during his tenure with the Coalition and worked to eradicate the unfair tax burden on married couples in America. "Christian Coalition urge[s] Congress to act now and to end the unfair tax penalty on married couples and demonstrate that our government, through the tax code, values and strengthens families,"[5] Randy said in a 1999 news release, still hammering away one year after the *Blueprint* was released. The marriage penalty was eventually eliminated in 2003, long after Christian Coalition had faded from the scene.

Don Hodel, concurrently, became involved in support of an initiative billed as the Freedom from Religious Persecution Act, which was sponsored in the House by Congressman Frank Wolf of Virginia and, in a bizarre turn, in the Senate by a major Coalition foe, moderate Senator Arlen Specter of Pennsylvania. The act mandated the establishment of an official Federal office to monitor religious persecution in other countries, and instituted restrictions on trade and other private sector business relations between American businesses and those countries.

In late 1997, Don testified in hearings conducted by the House International Relations Committee, where he called for swift passage of the act. "It is time for the Congress, the Administration, churches, and corporate leaders to take this issue seriously and place the full focus of public opinion behind a coordinated effort to end this horrendous abuse of very basic human rights,"[6] he said. Earlier that morning, he met with House Speaker Newt Gingrich and Senate Majority Leader Trent Lott to express his support for the initiative, which was passed by both houses of Congress and signed into law by President Clinton.

In 1998, Christian Coalition attacked religious persecution at home, as well. Since its inception the Coalition had focused on religious bigotry in the United States. This year, we encouraged passage of the Religious Freedom Amendment to the United States Constitution. In fact, Pat Robertson said that support for the amendment would be our major priority for 1998.

As we expected, news of our support brought liberal politicians and leaders of anti-Christian activism groups out of their all-knowing huddles, eager to assert that we *already* had an amendment guaranteeing religious freedom, the First Amendment. We agreed, but unfortunately, while trumpeting the first clause of that amendment, "Congress shall make no law respecting an establishment of religion," government officials ranging from local school principals to Federal judges had ignored the second, "or prohibiting the free exercise thereof," which led to gross infringements on the freedom to practice religion by school teachers with Bibles on their desks, pastors offering baccalaureate prayers, and government employees wearing crosses or Stars of David around their necks.

Pat's dedication to the protection of religious freedom proved to be a boon for the fortunes of the Coalition. We received greater press coverage during the congressional discussion of the Religious Freedom Amendment than we had received in several months, culminating when the House of Representatives passed the measure by a majority. Unfortunately, it fell short of the two-thirds majority required by the Constitution for an amendment to pass. Nonetheless, this was the first time such an amendment had received a majority in the House and only the second time it had come up for a vote in almost thirty years.

On occasion, groups in the pro-family movement joined their ranks in support of important issues. In 1998 the Coalition allowed its name to be included among those of several others on a series of advertisements called the *Truth in Love Campaign*, an outreach to homosexuals sponsored primarily by Dr. D. James Kennedy's Center for Reclaiming America. In the ads, one of which featured football star Reggie White, homosexuals were encouraged to seek Jesus Christ as the pathway away from the lifestyle. The ads referenced a ministry called Exodus International.

As was the case more often than not, whenever Christian Coalition's name appeared on an initiative, the Coalition received the credit. Even though we had put no money and no time into the development of the ads, we received the lion's share of the attention from the media, as well as the scorn from opposition groups who incessantly called our toll-free phone line for weeks after.

Likewise, Christian Coalition often shared in the blame for things actually done by other groups with which we had no contact at all. This occurred particularly when we were lumped in unfairly by the media with other pro-life groups,[§] accusing us, among other things, of approving the shooting of abortion doctors, which we abhorred. Two wrongs do not make a right, and murder was wrong, whether done *to* an abortionist or *by* one.

Christian Coalition wanted no connection with violence, as Randy Tate stated in 1998 when an abortion clinic in Birmingham, Alabama, was bombed, severely injuring a clinic worker. "The bombing of an abortion clinic . . . is a shameful and cowardly act. It is the antithesis of our efforts on behalf of unborn human life,"[7] he said. "We will continue to speak out on behalf of the unborn, but we will do so with the godly weapons of love and mercy, and not with the hellish weapons of violence and terror,"[8] he concluded.

Road to Victory '98 was by most accounts our best ever. After the somewhat less-than-stellar showing in Atlanta the previous year, we were eager to get back to our familiar location at the Washington Hilton. Over 4,000 activists from around the country came to the conference, as well as virtually every speaker we had invited. It seemed that the entire pro-family community was glad our event was back in its familiar setting.

Charles Colson made his second appearance at our annual event, and during his speech he decried religious persecution oversees. Dr. Bill Bright, founder of Campus Crusade for Christ, made his second visit as well. Other speakers included a first-timer, motivational speaker Zig Ziglar, and the usual leaders from Congress: Speaker Newt Gingrich, Senate Majority Leader Trent Lott, House Majority Leader Dick Armey, and House Majority Whip Tom DeLay.

Also present were prospective presidential candidates for 2000, including former Vice President Dan Quayle, Senator John Ashcroft, publisher Steve Forbes, Congressman John Kasich, Gary Bauer, and former ambassador Alan Keyes. And of course, crowd favorite Oliver North was there for the seventh year in a row, along with other perennial favorites Kay James, Rabbi Daniel Lapin, Phyllis Schlafly, and Bill Bennett. And Ralph Reed came back, as well, his first time speaking to our activists in his post Christian Coalition status.

Without a doubt, however, the most notable speaker was actor Charlton Heston, who gave the keynote address at Saturday's banquet. It was quite a coup to host America's most famous living conservative, next to Ronald Reagan, and the closest reminder, in stature and in philosophy,

§ In this case those misguided groups that advocated violence.

of our beloved President Reagan, who was suffering with Alzheimer's at the time, a disease that would claim Heston, as well.

The November election results brought Randy the uncomfortable job of critiquing his Republican former associates in Congress. In spite of backing President Clinton in the impeachment proceedings over his affair with Monica Lewinsky, Democrats held their own on Election Day. Whereas Republicans campaigned only against the president, the Democrats actually laid out an agenda and pulled off virtual magic at the ballot box. "Some agenda beats no agenda every time," Randy often remarked to the press over the next few days in discussing the election results.

As we prepared for the holidays, the House of Representatives had just completed the second-ever vote to impeach a President of the United States. The trial in the Senate would begin in January, 1999. What would be regretful days for the country would also bring on the worst days of the Christian Coalition.

15

## Say It Ain't So

O N WEDNESDAY, JANUARY 20, 1999, Pat Robertson's commentary on
*The 700 Club* focused on President Bill Clinton's State of the Union
speech the night before. In describing the president's speech, Pat told his
*700 Club* audience that Clinton had hit a home run and had put a huge
obstacle on the track in front of the impeachment train being conducted
by Republicans in Congress. "Clinton's won! They might as well dismiss
this impeachment hearing and get on with something else, because it's
over as far as I'm concerned,"[1] Pat said.

Pat was upset that the Republican-controlled Congress had given
the president such a forum in the midst of the impeachment process.
Considering Clinton's theatric skills, his abilities before a television camera, and his knack of spinning a negative story, to say nothing of the soft
treatment he received from the press, Pat felt that the GOP leadership
had blown it by inviting him to address the Congress, and the country.
Pat said the Constitution mandates only that a State of the Union speech
be *delivered* to Congress, not that it be delivered orally, in person, and
especially not live on national television.[2]

Former Clinton aide George Stephanopoulos later wrote in his book:
"The speech was sure to be a winner; it always was ... [Clinton] shot them
a competitor's glare—a look that said, 'You guys can pound me all you
want. Tonight you're mine.' I had to laugh, delighting in the sheer political
virtuosity of Clinton's performance ..."[3]

Although he never practiced law, Pat held a juris doctorate from Yale,
and in an exhibit of his knowledge of arcane elements of the Constitution,
Pat explained that the leaders in Congress instead could have directed the
president to deliver his report in writing, thus removing the public forum,
and the opportunity for him to trump them in the eyes of the press and in

the minds of senators who were undecided as to how to vote during the ongoing impeachment trial.

Article II, Section 3 reads only that the president "shall from time to time give to the Congress Information of the State of the union, and recommend to their Consideration such Measures as he shall judge necessary and expedient," not that his information and recommendations must be given in person, and not in the form of a speech.

In fact, fifty-one weeks later, a January, 2000, episode of NBC's drama *The West Wing* included a similar scenario where White House staffers fretted because, only three days prior to the date of the State of the Union, the Republican Speaker of the House had yet to officially invite their president to come to Capitol Hill to deliver the address. Might *West Wing* creator Aaron Sorkin have gotten that idea from Pat?

Pat considered himself simply a news analyst commenting on a political happening, but many of our grassroots supporters believed it to be a betrayal of their efforts over the past few months. They had written letters to Congress, made phone calls, and collected thousands of signatures on petitions urging the president's removal from office, and were still doing so at the time of the State of the Union. Further, they were not ready to give up. If anything, Clinton's speech, which was little more than pandering for public support, had added fuel to their fire.

We immediately began receiving calls of complaint from state directors, from chapter chairmen, and from donors who threatened to never give money again. CBN received similar calls from their supporters as well, including many who had just made pledges during a *700 Club* telethon going on at the time. I even received a long-distance call from a friend and fellow Regent University graduate who formerly had expressed little interest in politics. "What is Pat doing?" he asked. The next day it became a huge national story when *The New York Times* chose to put Pat's comments on the front page under a headline that read, "Robertson, Praising Speech, Suggests G.O.P. Halt Trial."[4]

Pat was proven correct in his assessment of Clinton's performance and the effect it would have on the Senate and the impeachment process. In hindsight, from a political standpoint, it *was* over. Even though chances of Clinton's losing the Senate Impeachment trial had always been slim, his speech and the play it received made it virtually impossible for House Judiciary Committee Chairman Henry Hyde and the rest of the House managers* to convince enough senators to vote to remove the president from office.

But by declaring defeat, many of our supporters felt Pat had pulled the rug out from under them. They did not know the meaning of the words "give up" and were not about to retreat just because of one speech from Bill Clinton.

Pat previously had made ad-lib comments on his live daily program that caused alarm from the press but this was the first time Pat's words had run afoul of our supporters to such an extent. Enough calls and faxes came that first day to let Don Hodel know we had a major problem.† With depleted numbers of donors and activists, the Coalition's future would be in serious jeopardy. Don attempted on more than one occasion to get Pat to correct the situation, at first calling Pat to let him know what was happening and encouraging him to go on *The 700 Club* the next day to correct his statement. "You don't call the team off the field before the game is over!"⁵ Don stressed.

But Pat just could not get over his disgust with the Republicans in Congress. On *The 700 Club* in following days, he acknowledged the firestorm his comments had ignited, but also repeated his earlier sentiments. Similar results happened the following weekend on ABC's *This Week* Sunday program. "[Your supporters] are madder than hornets," a smiling co-host Sam Donaldson taunted Pat. And Pat agreed: "To say the least, Sam. That's probably the reason I'm here, to clarify . . ."⁶ Pat's clarification was that he had meant only that Republican leaders in Congress had given a huge public relations victory to Clinton, which would make it impossible to convict him. "All I did was state the obvious,"⁷ he said, adding that he had not meant to suggest that the impeachment proceedings should not be carried through to conclusion.

Pat appeared on *This Week* over the strong objections of both Don Hodel and Randy Tate, who were concerned that it would only worsen the situation with our supporters. Pat's opinion was that he had been a television commentator for almost forty years—as he told co-hosts Donaldson and Cokie Roberts—and was capable of handling the situation himself. Don and Randy, however, had received many calls from outraged people—

---

* House committee members acting as prosecutors in the trial.

† The ensuing days (and weeks) brought dismal results in our fund-raising mail, with letters being torn up and returned, while others were faxed with handwritten notes of protest to Pat on them.

and not just from activists. Many of the Coalition's high-dollar donors were miffed, as were leaders in the conservative community.

Don spent the Friday and Saturday between Pat's Wednesday *700 Club* comments and his Sunday appearance on *This Week* in Florida, attending a national meeting of the Council for National Policy (CNP), a group made up of influential conservative leaders, and contributors to conservative causes and candidates. Evidently, the sentiment for Pat's "Clinton's won!" statement was no better among that group than it had been with Christian Coalition activists. The same weekend, Randy Tate was attending the winter meeting of the Republican National Committee, which guaranteed that he received similar negative reactions as Don had at CNP. On *This Week,* Cokie Roberts noted that GOP leaders were upset with Pat, since he—and Christian Coalition—had sounded a strong voice in favor of impeachment early on. Therefore, they had a "You got us into this" attitude.[8]

Don had heard stories of chapter leaders resigning over the national headquarters' implication by association in Pat's endorsement of the socially moderate Bob Dole for president in 1996. He began his tenure at the Coalition in June, 1997, by driving cross-country from Colorado to Virginia with his wife, Barbara, in their white Jeep Cherokee. During the trip, they stopped along the way to meet with state directors and groups of activists, where they learned of their disappointments with headquarters. These people, while not speaking for the majority of our activists, were not exactly few in numbers either. They were quick to express dissatisfaction with headquarters over the Dole endorsement in 1996 and let Don know in no uncertain terms. They wanted to be sure that he, as Christian Coalition's new leader, would not let anything like that happen again. As one state director told *The Washington Times,* "If there is another fiasco like Dole, I would not be surprised if a lot of the leadership left."[9][‡]

Don had a sincere fondness for the grassroots volunteers and, again, was a volunteer himself, having not only given up his Coalition salary but was even paying his own travel expenses. He began his political journey as a precinct captain in Oregon, setting up card tables in his living room with maps of the precinct, and eventually was elected Republican Party state chairman, accepting each post only "because no one else would."[10] His feelings for the activists were made evident at Road to Victory '97

‡ Paul Volle of Maine.

in his first major speech to our supporters, where he made a strong and touching appeal to them:

> It is only by God's grace that we are going to be able to do the task that lies before us ... Where is it written that we are only to attempt to do the doable? We're called to be faithful to God's call. That's why you're here ... That is one of the reasons *I* am here. Not only that I felt God's call on me but that I knew of God's call on *you*. And in that cause we are united strongly to do what is right—because we believe it is right ...[11]

Pat had sought Don's services for over a decade. He had planned to name him as White House chief of staff had he been elected president in 1988,[12] and in 1990 he had sounded Don out regarding the presidency of Regent University.[13] Don obviously assumed that since Pat had asked him to run the Coalition, he would be willing to consider his advice and, therefore, clear up any unintentional impressions that his words about Clinton had given the supporters.

Pat was likely surprised at being questioned so directly by a colleague and probably did not expect the strong resistance from Don. In most cases, whenever any political or religious leader has a disagreement with someone working for him, the leader wins. But with Don's background in the Reagan Cabinet (and Randy's as a former congressman), there was a level of governmental status unlike any Pat was accustomed to in an "employee."[§]

When a former Cabinet secretary says there is a problem, there likely *is* a problem. The donors and activists were very upset at what they perceived from Pat as a call for retreat, and their concerns needed to be addressed. Pat just did not understand why the supporters were so displeased, which explains his manner the next few times he went on television to "clear it up."

In responding to one particular letter of criticism, Pat had a tone of astonishment. "Why does the statement of an obvious fact bring forth such incredible furor?" He wrote that by inviting Clinton to deliver the State of the Union, the "leadership of the House of Representatives totally undercut the position of the Judicial Committee members ... The framers of the Constitution put a high-bar to impeachment. Without bipartisan

§ Pat had at least two former generals who had worked for him. Yet of the four leaders in Coalition history to that point—Robertson, Reed, Hodel, and Tate—only Tate had been elected to public office—repeatedly—and ultimately to Congress.

consent, impeachment will not [succeed]." He concluded by expressing his amazement over the fact that his "unprepared, ad-lib remarks," which had been "somewhat truncated in the press reports and, consequently . . . misunderstood" had caused such a stir.[14]

Pat's initial comments would have had less impact on our grassroots activists and supporters had he amended them more strongly, adding that not only should the trial be carried through to completion, but the senators' constituents should keep sounding the alarm loud and clear, and holding their feet to the fire, fighting for principle. Things would have fared better if headquarters had not been seen as giving up, as long as the grassroots had not done so.

Christian Coalition, coming out of the Robertson campaign for president, had molded the religious conservative political movement of the late twentieth century more so than any other organization. However, when you are responsible *for* a movement, you also are responsible *to* that movement. Of course, the toothpaste was out of the tube, so to speak, so Pat would have had to rectify his comments more emphatically than just once on *The 700 Club* and on other news outlets. It would have required direct communications to our supporters.

On Monday, January 25, six days after the State of the Union, I went for lunch with Randy Tate and Ken Hill to our usual Monday venue, Don Pablo's Mexican Kitchen, just a few blocks down Greenbrier Parkway from the office. As we munched on tortilla chips and salsa, and talked about sports, much was about to transpire back at the office.

After several unfruitful attempts to get Pat to try and correct the impeachment problem Don felt that he was at a point of no return. Due to the serious financial strain the organization was under, fund-raising had consumed the majority of Don's time and energy since he arrived in 1997, which was a tremendous weight on his shoulders and surely caused a great deal of fatigue.

Don later recalled that during the weekend he spent at CNP in Florida he realized that he no longer felt comfortable asking prospective donors to contribute to the Coalition due to his "inability to defend or explain statements and activities [by Pat] that were beyond his control."[15] He had left private life to come to Christian Coalition out of response to an inner call to serve our nationwide grassroots movement. When headquarters became at odds with the movement, he felt the overall situation was beyond repair. He asked for a meeting with Pat for the next day, at which he planned to resign as president of the Coalition.

Having worked for Pat for over a decade, his words were not surprising to me. He often spoke frankly with little worry about political fallout. Ralph Reed had been no less challenged to compensate for such statements and situations, as well as other aspects of Pat's celebrity profile: internal lawsuits at Regent University, a multi-level marketing business that suffered more than one public disagreement, and much-reported gold and diamond mine ventures in Africa, for instance.[§] Ralph had a significant capacity for forbearance, perhaps due to his being so much younger than Pat and owing his political station in life to him, always telling the staff that we had to just "let Pat be Pat."

But Don Hodel had endured accusations and media attacks against the Reagan Administration for eight years, including many biased mischaracterizations of his own Department of Interior—one of the most targeted agencies by the Left due to its relation to natural resources—all having more severity than the issue over Clinton's impeachment. So when this flare-up arose he felt there were better things for him to do with his time than to continually have to put out fires with the media, the grassroots activists, and the supporters. Tuesday afternoon, after talking with the rest of his Coalition inner circle, Don got in his car and drove to CBN for his meeting with Pat.

A few days earlier Don and Randy had discussed—and Don had run past me—that it would be good if there were a way for Pat to speak more freely on television, as well as take personal positions on candidates and political issues, without his words being inextricably linked to the Coalition.[**] Possibly a less visible role in the organization would provide that leeway.

On the surface, it sounded like an interesting idea. If only there could have been a way for Pat to express his personal comments on political and other matters, or endorse a candidate or issue—his support of the North

§ I understood the business related blow-ups above, realizing they were Pat's well-intentioned prospects for future funding for CBN after he passed from the scene, due to his concerns over how revenues dipped when he left to run for president in 1987–1988. I never doubted his sincerity or integrity in these ventures.

** For example, Pat's 1998 sympathetic statements that Texas-murder-turned-Christian Karla Faye Tucker should be spared the death penalty were at stark odds with the Texas Christian Coalition and then Texas Governor George W. Bush.

American Free Trade Agreement had also run afoul of many of our supporters a few years earlier—without those comments reflecting so heavily on Christian Coalition and its activists. This would protect the organization, not only from a backlash in the media and among the supporters, but also from further harassment by the IRS and the FEC. Further, it would provide a buffer from Pat's role as host of a daily live television program where he commented on news as it happened.

Nonetheless, it was an idea that I was certain would not fly—with Pat, or with the other members of the board. They would never want to see Pat's role diminish, in part due to their personal association with him. I prepared Don to expect a negative reaction; and as he drove over to meet with Pat, those of us who knew what was about to transpire left the office with butterflies in our stomachs.

On Wednesday morning I arrived early at the office, eager to learn the results of the meeting between Don and Pat. A group assembled in Don's office, sitting in wing-backed chairs and a sofa around a Queen Anne coffee table,[††] all of us on the edge of our seats. As Don began talking he looked directly at me, probably because he knew that I, most of all, would be surprised that during their meeting Pat *himself* had brought up the possibility of stepping back a bit. My jaw must have dropped as I listened to him relate Pat's words. However, the two men had ended their meeting without reaching any conclusions.

Later that morning, Don wrote a letter to Pat following up on their meeting, in which he referred to the idea as Pat's becoming "chairman emeritus." The letter was faxed (or read by one of his CBN assistants) to Pat, who had flown to Florida on business. In the end, however, Pat was persuaded that he should continue in his role of active chairman. In their Tuesday afternoon meeting, Pat may have been just "thinking out loud," perhaps wondering if his willingness to step back might induce Don to withdraw his resignation; or, since Don had shared the idea with the board members before going to meet Pat, one or more had called Pat to tip him off.

Thursday saw the two men *exchange* letters. After further discussions with three members of the Coalition's board, who by that time were circling their wagons around Pat, Don wrote Pat for the purpose of restating his resignation, which would be effective the next day. Pat—still

---

†† All except the sofa were leftover from the 1988 Robertson campaign.

in Florida—wrote Don a letter at the same time, thanking him for his service and accepting the resignation Don had tendered orally two days earlier. Pat included in the letter that he had come to the realization that if he withdrew from the scene, the Coalition would likely not be able to sustain itself.

Thursday also brought the arrival of new board member Roberta Combs from her home in South Carolina. Roberta was chairman of the South Carolina state affiliate of the Coalition and had been added to the national board of directors by Pat a few months earlier. She had chaired his campaign committee in South Carolina for the concluding weeks before the 1988 primary, and had put on several very good events where he spoke on behalf of the South Carolina Christian Coalition. In addition, she had successfully gotten pro-family activists into leadership roles throughout the Republican Party in her state.

Pat evidently believed that Roberta's expertise would help on the national level as well. A friend of Pat's since the 1988 campaign, and an acquaintance of Don's for about the same amount of time),‡‡ Roberta had come—at least ostensibly—to personally deliver Pat's letter to Don, lending a hand in an awkward situation.

The parting between Pat Robertson and Don Hodel was not so much one of a personal nature but one of principle, as to the direction of Christian Coalition and how it should be run. They both were great men, of similar age, committed Christians, and both successful in business and in politics. I imagine that Don believed Pat should have been more open to his and Randy's advice regarding clearing up the statement on impeachment, while Pat probably felt that his longevity as a Christian leader and television personality should allow him to speak freely without being questioned.

The Hodel-Robertson split was extremely difficult for me personally. While most in Don Hodel's inner circle had been with the Coalition for only a few years, I had been there from the inception, having worked for Pat's presidential campaign beforehand. Pat had been my employer for a decade; and through his auspices he not only augmented my education, both biblically and politically, but also provided the laboratory in which I put knowledge into practice. Yet, at the same time, I had a deep personal

---

‡‡ Due to their meeting when Don, as Secretary of the Interior, spoke at a Republican Party event in South Carolina.

loyalty to Don, with whom I had worked far more closely than I ever had with Pat. I could not imagine the Coalition without either man.

The Coalition's inner conflict around the Impeachment proceedings actually was a by-product of a larger issue, not between Robertson and Hodel necessarily, but involving the entire grassroots organization that made up the Coalition. Christian Coalition's meteoric rise, coupled with the voters' vehement disgust with the first years of the Clinton Administration, had produced great success in only a few years. This success reached its pinnacle with the 1994 congressional elections, and resulted in the passage of many pieces of pro-family legislation, including several items in the *Contract with America* and our *Contract with the American Family*. Pat's descriptions of a government firmly in the hands of pro-family conservatives had excited both activists and donors over the last decade, resulting in the recruitment of hundreds of thousands of activists, as well as multiple millions of dollars in our coffers.

The Coalition's stature, combined with Ralph Reed's celebrity and Pat Robertson's even larger prominence, had made it necessary that we keep "winning" in order to refrain from apparent loss or lack of effectiveness. The liberal media was vicious, blaming the Christian Right, with Christian Coalition as its premier organization, for George H. W. Bush's re-election defeat in 1992 and we did not want to go through that again. So, the "win" concept began to take over, which required *legislative* wins, *large-event* wins, *media* wins, and *electoral* wins.

The Coalition was somewhat of a victim of its own success. It all had begun to unravel beginning with the 1996 elections and into early 1997, as Ralph prepared to depart and a shrinking income no longer could sustain our huge staff and appetite for activity. If we had stayed with the early under-the-radar grassroots strategy, the Coalition might have maintained a much stronger presence over the long-term, although with a much lower profile and more moderate budget.

Christian Coalition's original stated objective was to change America by identifying, training, energizing, and mobilizing our constituency so that they represented a large voting block in support of the candidates and issues of their choice. Eventually, *they* would win the elections, for *their* candidates. As Ralph Reed told David Frost in 1995, the goal was to create a supply of voters that would influence the issue positions of candidates, rather than answer a demand for votes from candidates.[16]

As alluded to earlier, problems resulted when Pat, Ralph or one of our state directors chose to personally support candidates whom many of the grassroots did not. After the disastrous defeat of the Dole-Kemp ticket, Pat himself agreed that the activists had been correct, promising during a summer 1999 appearance on *Larry King Live* to keep his powder dry and not endorse a candidate too early during the 2000 primaries due to the backlash he received from activists in 1996.[17]

Most of our activists actually supported Bob Dole in the Republican primaries in 1996, believing he had the best opportunity to defeat Bill Clinton; but more than enough supported Buchanan, and to a lesser extent, Alan Keyes, to cause a ruckus within our ranks. These were some of our most passionate and active supporters. They tended to support the most hard-line candidates. However, even if Buchanan had been more viable than Dole, it would have found resistance in Chesapeake. As one unnamed Coalition insider told Nina Easton in *Gang of Five*: "We didn't build up this movement so that Pat Buchanan could come along and hijack it."[18]

Larry King asked a question that got to the crux of Pat's philosophy for the Coalition, when he inquired as to whether Gary Bauer portrayed a more ideal presidential candidate in Pat's eyes than did front-runner George W. Bush. As Pat answered, stopping short of endorsing Bush,[19] I was amused. "Larry just doesn't understand Pat," I thought, confident that Pat would choose George W. Bush over Bauer, et al, in 2000. In his own candidacy in 1988, Pat was running for president *to win*, not just to advance a set of ideals.

Friday, January 29, three days after the meeting between Don Hodel and Pat Robertson, and ten days after the State of the Union, I stood in the jam-packed conference room at Christian Coalition national headquarters and looked into the tear-filled eyes of two of my female co-workers. The reason was that Don, tactfully, was announcing his resignation to the staff.

I knew that day that Christian Coalition would never be the same. For the past year and a half we had struggled to overcome the departure of Ralph Reed; and were succeeding, mostly due to Don's enormous clout in the conservative Christian community and Randy Tate's connections inside Congress, not to mention, of course, the approximately $1.5 million given or loaned to the organization cumulatively by Pat and Don, as well as hundreds of thousands more that Don personally raised. Without

Don, however, it looked like it might be only a matter of time before we all would be looking for jobs. A significant amount of debt, plus the ever-present FEC lawsuit, along with continued scrutiny from the IRS presented a one-two-three punch that, while not insurmountable, was formidable to say the least. Finally, Randy might not want to stay either.

Amazingly, the story of Don's departure stayed out of the press for the first few days. When the reports began, however, they lasted for several weeks, each predicting the imminent demise of Christian Coalition. Even the talk of Pat becoming chairman emeritus found its way into press accounts, stated either by someone grossly uninformed or who hoped to belittle Hodel, making it seem as if he had gone to Pat Robertson with an "it's you or me" ultimatum, which was untrue.[20]

Alarming headlines signaled the beginning of the end. A report by political commentator Stuart Rothenberg in *Roll Call*, the leading newspaper dealing with day-to-day congressional activities, led with a headline asking, "Has the Christian Coalition Lost Its Political Muscle?"[21] Veteran reporter Ralph Hallow of *The Washington Times* wrote an in-depth story about Don's departure, which included a strong defense of him by conservative luminary Phyllis Schlafly. "Hodel resigned?" she asked. "He was the best thing that ever happened to [the Coalition]. Hodel had a lot of stature and principled dedication and political smarts . . . He had stature and the ability to work with a lot of people. I'm sorry he's gone."[22]

Randy Tate made similar comments to Hallow: "The thing that has marked Don Hodel's career is integrity across the board. I considered it a privilege to work with him ever single day. He is a selfless individual."[23]

Don, himself, refrained from talking to the media except for one brief interview with the Associated Press, which ran in his hometown paper, *The Oregonian*, where he confined his comments primarily to, "It was time to move on,"[24] and quietly returned to private life.

On the Monday morning following Don and Barbara's last day, Randy called an all-staff meeting and soon the conference room was filled with the same people who had gathered there just three days before—only without Don and Barbara, of course. In their place were Pat Robertson and Roberta Combs. Randy introduced Pat, who began sharing a message of encouragement. He would reassume the title of Coalition president and would be taking a more direct role in the organization's day-to-day activities. He acknowledged an understandable sense of apprehension among the staff and began encouraging us that everything would be okay.

Pat then told a story that that I had heard a few times before, and which I had always referred to affectionately as "the library story." It referenced a situation at CBN in the early 1980s when the burgeoning CBN University had become strangled by growth and there was simply not enough room to house the university's classrooms, offices, and library. The board of trustees voted to break ground on construction of an expensive new library building.[§§]

In order to quell discontent among CBN employees—the university was owned by CBN at the time—who may have felt the money could be used for other purposes, Pat exhorted all with words similar to those he shared with the Coalition staff on this day: "You may not agree with what I'm doing, but please don't complain."

The completion of the CBN University library was a watershed in the history of the university. For certain, Pat and the board had been correct that its building was essential not only to the school's success but to its very existence. And personally, it was in that very library building that I attended every class, and completed every exam and research paper that comprised my master's degree in biblical studies.

One could not argue with Pat's feelings about complaining. The Bible is clear that such attitudes displease the Lord when allowed to run rampant among His people. Murmuring among the Israelites had been a major hindrance to Moses during the march from Egypt to the Promised Land. What should have been about an eleven-days journey[¶¶] took approximately forty years due to their complaining and unbelief. But what changes was Pat planning to make at Christian Coalition? Were his words simply relating to the fact that he knew Don had been highly popular with the staff and he realized a good deal of unrest might lay within us? Or were additional changes planned?

I listened to Pat and purposed to stay the course. I had no idea, however, how quickly my resolve would be stressed in this instance, and must admit that I violated my commitment not to complain far too often. As Pat drove away from the office that day in his shiny, black Corvette, any comfort that his visit had brought left with him.

---

§§  As I remember at a cost of $13 million in 1984 dollars.

¶¶  See Deuteronomy 1:2, a verse Pat has called the saddest in the Bible.

## 16

## *Designing Women* Meets *The West Wing*

R OBERTA COMBS REMAINED IN Virginia "to see us through the transition."[1] Day by day, however, her authority grew—first to field operations and, later, to overall administration. The staff disapproved, feeling
that Pat should have turned Christian Coalition entirely over to Randy
Tate. He was a former congressman, had been working side by side with
Don Hodel for eighteen months, and was already our public spokesman.
But Pat preferred to keep the duties divided. He had hired Randy as the
lobbyist and as the field general, and evidently wanted Roberta to participate in executive management.

I felt that I knew why. As mentioned in an earlier chapter, in the eyes
of the press, Christian Coalition had become "Ralph Reed's organization"
after the 1994 elections. Then, Ralph left and his replacement as CEO,
Hodel, resigned over philosophical differences with Pat. In retrospect, I
believe Pat brought in Roberta because he felt he needed someone there
whom he had known for a long period of time and who, therefore, he was
confident would be loyal to him at all costs.

Roberta had been a stand-out in the South Carolina Republican
Party since the 1980s, but came to politics late, after a career in interior
decorating. I had first met her in the 1988 Robertson presidential campaign, and since that time we had worked together on Coalition field matters related to South Carolina, as well as on an Alabama event in 1996. I
stayed with Roberta and her husband, Andy, in their beautiful Charleston
home while in South Carolina for a chapter leader seminar in 1995. They
even let associate Steve Jordan and me borrow their Mercedes for a golf
outing the next day. She and I had always gotten along well.

Before the Hodel-Robertson disagreement began to brew, the field
division had planned a retreat for state directors at the Founders Inn;
and, unfortunately, it had been scheduled to take place on a weekend that

turned out to be slightly less than two weeks after the leadership change. The state affiliates had heard nothing about Roberta's new role(s) until Pat announced during his opening speech to the group on Thursday afternoon that she would be our new national field director. The announcement came as quite a surprise to the state leaders, and certainly was an offense to Director of National Operations Chuck Cunningham, who had been elevated by Hodel and Tate the previous year over all field and voter education activities, as well as to then National Field Director Dave Welch. But Pat needed a title for Roberta, and her reputation was as a field operative—so that's probably why he chose that one.*

Considering Pat's vocal displeasure in 1996 over our lack of identifying precinct activists,† long before either Chuck or Dave had anything to do with the field operation, he likely had remained dissatisfied about our precinct organization and may have believed that Roberta could get the job done. It was an uninformed decision on Pat's part, however, as even in South Carolina our computer database was devoid of his goal of ten pro-life activists per precinct.

Over the years Roberta had done a very effective job of turning out people to precinct meetings and county conventions in her state, but she did it mainly by staying on the phone, personally encouraging them to attend a political meeting, and there just are not enough hours in the day to enact that method nationally. Further, she had no administrative experience in running such a large organization, let alone one with affiliate offices across the country. Interestingly, years later I had a chance meeting with a woman who was the respected leader of a major Christian women's group, who asked me, "Whatever happened to [Christian Coalition]?" As we discussed the demise of the Coalition, she surprised me by adding, "*That's* not an organization a *woman* can run."

The result of Pat's choice of Roberta was a bad situation for all involved: Roberta instantly was in way over her head; Pat did not realize that he'd made a mistake; the field staff was unjustly blamed for years of unorganized precincts even though those particular individuals had

---

* Ralph Reed told me that he considered asking Roberta to be interim national field director after Guy Rodgers left the Coalition in late 1993 and several weeks passed without a replacement being located; and in both 1996 and 1998 national headquarters paid Roberta a consulting fee for purposes of recruiting new state directors in a few states.

† See Chapter 9.

taken over the reins only several months earlier; and the rest of the staff were caught in the crossfire.

Chuck was aware of Pat's plan to give Roberta control of field operations. A few days earlier he, Roberta, and Randy met over lunch, and Randy explained Pat's desire for Roberta to take over, with Chuck returning to his former role, focusing only on political matters and voter guide preparation. "How do you feel about that?" Randy asked. Chuck's response was brief and to the point: "I think it stinks," he said.[2] Chuck knew well that neither he nor his staff would want any part of it. Chuck, thus, faced a new attitude from Coalition leadership, which was a turnaround since the time of the 1997 lay-offs when Pat instructed Don and Randy to "keep Chuck at all costs."[3]

Chuck's political reputation, especially among Beltway conservatives, was prodigious. Later in the year, he was ranked, along with Ralph Reed, on Roll Call's list of the fifty most influential politicos who worked to elect congressional candidates.[4] In 1998, when the Conservative Political Action Conference gave its first annual Ronald Reagan Award to the movement conservative who had done the most for the agenda, Chuck was their choice as the inaugural recipient. Chuck could have named his price at virtually any Republican or conservative operation and, soon after the state directors retreat, both he and Dave Welch left for other job offers. The loss of Cunningham and Welch (and their staff) was a major blow to the Coalition's political reputation and precipitated an onslaught of negative reports in the media, as well as many alarmed calls from state directors and activists.

The next morning, Pat spoke to the state leaders again, where he further explained his choice of Roberta to head up field operations, stressing his opinion of her success in politics and business, including, oddly, that she was "a millionaire in her own right." The state directors were still woozy from the alacrity of the changes, including Don Hodel's departure, thus Pat's "sell" of Roberta was not effective.

Missouri Executive Director Jim Berberich stood up to ask Pat a question. "With all due respect to you and Roberta," he began, "we don't understand why Chuck and Dave are being cast aside." There was no question that he was speaking for the group. What may have been alarming to Roberta and certainly was surprising to Pat—as he was not accustomed to being questioned so pointedly by a friendly audience, in his own hotel—was satisfying to the state leaders and staff present in the room.

Pat explained that she was just there to help them do their jobs even better, but no one was convinced.

Roberta assuredly felt uncomfortable, for years having been an equal to the others in the room whom she now was supposed to lead. Although, as they say, some people are more equal than others. Roberta had been named to the Coalition's national board in 1998, and prior to that had enjoyed far more access to Pat than other state directors,[‡] often even more than the other two who preceded her on the board. Likely, this had a good deal to do with her brief history as Pat's 1988 campaign chairman in South Carolina and to the fact that she always turned out a huge crowd whenever he was in her state to speak on behalf of the Coalition.

Roberta also had more access to the national headquarters staff, which was due in small part to her pull with Pat, and in greater measure to her effectiveness—over the years when I was deputy field director, any time I was asked to name our best state affiliates, South Carolina was always at or near the top—but mostly due to the force of her personality. For instance, South Carolina was the only state to be given the national organization's donor file;[§] and Roberta got it at least twice that I remember—with Ralph's approval—for organizing purposes.

The events of the weekend left a Christian Coalition that was somewhat asunder. Most of the state directors felt stunned by the changes at national, with a handful of recent additions coalescing around Roberta and others wondering what they had gotten themselves into. For both old and new, the weekend must have been shocking, recently learning of Don Hodel's departure, continuing with the changes in the national field office, and the discomfort that enshrouded the entire weekend. In spite of what had happened, however, most simply wanted to go back home, away from the turmoil and confusion, and get back to working on behalf of family values. There was no doubt, however, that dire straits were in store for the Coalition. We all knew what Jesus said happens to a house divided.[¶]

The departure of Don Hodel and the arrival of Roberta Combs, coupled with the circumstances under which the leadership changes occurred, precipitated an exodus by many on our staff. Several were released and others resigned out of their desire not to work for Roberta. She made

‡ She was one of only four or five who knew his home telephone number.
§ Any state affiliate was allowed to have the list of non-donors.
¶ See Luke 11:17.

no secret about whom *she* wanted to leave first: those likely to be the most loyal to Don Hodel or Chuck Cunningham. Even though I was a close aide to Hodel and a good friend of Cunningham, I somehow managed to remain for several months, likely due to the board's appreciation for my length of time with the organization.

Roberta was in a somewhat difficult position. She exhibited a strong desire to fulfill Pat's wishes but, even though she was a likeable person under other circumstances, as she began asserting her authority at the Coalition it seemed that "tumult" was her middle name. And to make matters worse, she faced a staff that did not want her there. This led to her having a good deal of insecurity, which manifested itself in her questioning people's loyalty—to her and to Pat.

The doubts, which were obvious, caused resentment among the employees and further alienated many from her, which she surely could feel. At the same time, however, she had come there to do a job at Pat's request. She needed to make things happen, and quickly. And any activity was better than allowing an impression to exist that the group had no direction. Although, as Richard John Neuhaus once observed, "Action divorced from theory has a way of getting you where you never wanted to go,"[5] and that was the case with the Coalition, as things steadily got worse.

Most of the energy was focused within the office, rather than projected outside the organization to the grassroots. Changes came with a flurry, and no department was immune. Assignments were rerouted, new titles were assigned, and offices were relocated. Neither seniority nor job positions were given much credence. No one was outside the scope of upheaval, and it caused a great deal of resentment, rubbing salt into wounds that were far from being healed.

The changes came so quickly it was as if people and sentiment did not matter, that anyone or anything was expendable. And Roberta was not acting alone. As one board member told me after they had released a senior staff member: "If we didn't hesitate to make the big decisions, we sure won't to make the little ones," a warning I was supposed to convey to lower level staffers.

Our resistance made things somewhat worse. As once stated on the NBC drama *ER*, "Change is like a locomotive. You're either on board or you're gravel on the tracks." In other words, you either assist in bringing the change about, or you're standing in its way. The board of directors had the legal and biblical authority over the organization, and our responsibility as staff was to either comply or leave. Most, however, felt Roberta would not be there long and were eager to outlast her. We all wanted to work to make the Coalition succeed, but we assumed that Roberta's days there would be few.

The changes instituted in early 1999 were so abrupt and abrasive that many employees were quite bitter, and some who left chose to share their feelings in the media. The more seasoned former staffers stated only the facts as they saw them, but others chose to make personal attacks on Pat and Roberta, which was unfortunate. The result of the public infighting was the tarnishing of the entire organization, name and all.

As example of the power held by the name Christian Coalition, in early 2002 radio host Rush Limbaugh announced that White House strategist Karl Rove had recently met with "the Christian Coalition" at Washington's Willard Hotel. The meeting actually was the annual leadership briefing sponsored by the Family Research Council.

In early 2000, one former staffer told *The Virginian-Pilot* that "internal power-grabbing . . . completely ruined the organization,"[6] while a board member, in turn, alleged that many employees were fired because "they were so inept," adding, "I don't know of a single one that left of his own accord."[7] From those descriptions the reporter erroneously concluded that "all of the employees who left—save Hodel—were sacked,"[8] which was not true. Several followed Don Hodel's candid example, while others were indeed fired or eventually laid off.

In retrospect, if the transition had been handled differently by Roberta, by our staff (including this author), and by Pat—meaning more of a specific description by him to the staff of the expansive nature of Roberta's role—things might have faired better for Christian Coalition, at least in the short run. Although it would not have aided the organization's long-term success, as the financial support kept eroding and the organization's sense of mission became further confused.

State directors also began to resign on the heels of the field employees. While some may have left because of dissatisfaction with events at headquarters, the reasons were due more so to the fact that presidential campaigns were gearing up and hiring than to internal happenings with the organization, although the turmoil may have made the decisions easier for some. Actually, it was quite an honor for the Coalition to have our people being sought after and taking positions in campaigns for national office.

And it was good for them and their families, too. Financially and professionally, an offer to work on a presidential campaign usually is quite attractive as the campaigns must hire the best people they can find and, at the same time, must pay them well considering the short duration of most campaigns.

Steve Forbes hired the most, with one state director going with the Pat Buchanan campaign, and two going to work for Gary Bauer. None of our leaders officially went to work for George W. Bush, although, his advisors may have felt they had the market cornered, since Ralph Reed was one of his consultants.

State leaders who chose to stay quickly lost touch with the national office, and the infrastructure of state affiliates and local chapters never recovered. At first, it was only that their phone calls went unanswered, but by the end of the year, they hardly ever heard from headquarters and, according to those with whom I spoke, totally lost confidence in national's ability (and desire) to assist them in any way. Roberta recruited new leaders in several of the states where there were vacancies; however, due to the lack of a seasoned field staff at national, those well-intentioned people were never trained or shown what was expected of them, which left them—and their state organizations—as little more than names on sheets of paper.

The ensuing couple of months were uneasy ones as the staff and Roberta adjusted to each other, as well as to our ever-increasing number of empty offices. During this time Randy Tate and Ken Hill had to keep the rest of the Coalition running while Roberta concentrated (ostensibly) on field operations. But, again, she was there with a larger mandate. In fact, she did not take an office with the field staff but chose one near Randy Tate's executive director's office on the other side of the building. She told me this was due to Pat's desire that she help with administrative duties as well as with field. And in the letter Pat wrote to Don Hodel accepting his resignation, he included words to that effect.

Pat embraced a renewed personal involvement in the organization and the return to its presidency by launching a new initiative. He personally wrote a fund-raising letter (and fronted $81,000 for the postage) appealing to our donors to help with a new action plan geared toward the 2000 elections. The letter announced the "21 Victory Club," a plan to raise $21 million dollars for get-out-the-vote activities over the next twenty-one months. Pat stopped by one day and sat alone in Don Hodel's old office, writing the follow-up letter by hand on a yellow legal pad.

Unfortunately, the 21 Victory Club was a disaster. The letter was mailed in the midst of other direct mail appeals, which hurt the success of each. Barely enough funds were raised in order to cover costs of the mailing. The follow-up letter produced similar results. I was quite surprised at the lack of success the mailings actually produced. The donors may have still been stinging from Pat's comments over Clinton's impeachment. In the end, most never returned and Christian Coalition's income dropped to only about $3 million for the entire year.

A lavish Washington, D.C. press conference announcing the initiative brought as much negative news as it did positive, as Pat was forced to answer questions about the Hodel departure, as well as those of several members of the field staff. A subsequent appearance on *Larry King Live* found similar questions for Pat.[9]

The days and weeks after the press conference brought more changes to headquarters, most notably the added decoration in the field "war room" of an expensive banner used at the recent 21 Victory press conference, as well as whatever flashy, eye-catching posters could be located from our storage room. Roberta was doing whatever she could to jump-start the organization's batteries, but it was not working.

Roberta felt the best way to keep excitement high in the office, as well as to make it "look like" lots of things were going on in the field, was to hold "God and Country Rallies" across the country at which Pat would fly in and speak. Pat, too, liked the events, enjoying the opportunity to get out with the people and motivate the troops. I had seen that first-hand with similar events held in 1996 in Texas and Alabama, which were replicated into several more events in 1998. They seemed like good ideas at first, and were billed as "tribute dinners" to Pat's 1988 campaign. At each, the respective state director where the event was held would present Pat with a large crystal bowl in appreciation of his run for the presidency. "Just keep giving me the same bowl," Pat said, so we would not keep buying new ones for each city. By 1999, the events became commonplace, with rallies, dinners or lunches being held in cities like Chicago, Shreveport (Louisiana), Kansas City (Missouri), Columbus (Ohio), and Columbia (South Carolina).

Unfortunately, fund-raising dinners and lunches with low ticket prices do not raise any money. While a dinner costing participants $1,000 or even $100 a plate reaps financial profits, one where tickets are only $25 (which we were charging) barely covers expenses; and when, as often happened, in order to fill the room lots of complimentary tickets were given away, the economic loss could be substantial. For example, at Road to Victory each year, we charged participants about $49 to attend the Saturday evening gala banquet; however, we paid the hotel about $45 per plate, which meant virtually no profit was left. This was acceptable at our national conference, which was not intended to be a fund-raising event, and where a high level of enthusiasm was the objective. Actually, at Road to Victory in later years we gave away many free tickets also. However, those were to the general conference seating—which cost us nothing— rather than to a meal event.

Furthermore, these "Pat events," as the staff affectionately—at first— referred to them, necessitated being held in locations where we already had a strong activist base in order to guarantee a large turnout. A much better allocation of funds would have been dinners or rallies held in states where our affiliates had been struggling. This would have been a boon for local organizers, assuming we were willing to settle for 250 or 300 people in the audience, rather than a thousand.

There was criticism of the events both from outside and from within. *National Review* reported that they were "complex and costly events, with balloons, light shows, and a video presentation ... [that] some say Combs is merely using ... to stroke Robertson's ego."[10] And whether accurate or not, that sentiment was echoed by the majority of our staff. These dinners and lunches were not an adequate substitute for our traditional field or- ganizing activities of voter identification, voter registration, and training seminars, and were unpopular with staff members who had been with the Coalition for several years. We felt they usurped vital resources of time and money, as well as kept the focus off building state affiliates.

From its founding, the Christian Coalition had eschewed a focus on events over grassroots organizing—although by 1995 an overemphasis on events had begun to take hold. Ralph Reed reiterated that original feeling in a 1999 newspaper interview: "It was a strategy that the Moral Majority followed. They'd fly Dr. [Jerry] Falwell in on a Learjet. They raised a little money and got people excited, but there was nothing permanent. In the end there were no precinct captains to carry out the nuts-and-bolts work of grassroots activism,"[11] he told the *St. Petersburg (FL) Times.*

Randy Tate felt strongly that Pat should know how much the events were costing, as well as what the organization was spending on travel—with Roberta flying home to South Carolina on weekends and board members coming and going repeatedly. So, he had me conduct an audit of the expenses related to the Pat events and of the travel costs for himself, Roberta, Ken Hill, and the board members. I spent a couple of days putting the information together and provided Randy with a report.

Someone, however, told Roberta what I was doing and evidently made it sound like I was investigating only her expenses. Other than Randy and myself, only two other people** knew about the project and both agreed that the events were costing too much, so I did not suspect either of them of maliciously spilling the beans. One of them shared an apartment with two members of the field staff, however, and she probably told them, not thinking it would get back to Roberta.††

A couple of days after my audit had begun, I walked past one of the accounting offices and saw Roberta poring over a stack of expense folders with the same file drawer open that I had been though the previous day. I was pretty sure that she knew what I had been doing, and *certain* that, if she did, she had the wrong idea as to why. The investigation was not an attempt by Randy or by me to single-out Roberta's expenses, both knowing full-well that she had Pat's seal of approval and that, therefore, a coup attempt would be futile.

Randy had gone up to Washington for meetings on Capitol Hill that day and I called him on his cell phone. I told him that Roberta had learned what we were doing and that she probably had the wrong idea. "We both have to tell her the truth," I said. He agreed and called her immediately. I followed up with a visit to Roberta's office, where I explained the situation, to which she was very gracious, and even offered me a hug.

My audit of the travel expenses did not exactly come at the best time. Mutual distrust was rampant in the office, with people lurking in dark rooms, eavesdropping around corners, rifling through desks, and employing amateur intimidation and espionage.[12] For example, I arrived at work one morning and could see that my computer had been tampered with overnight.

** Members of the accounting staff.
†† The person who told Roberta later apologized to me.

In the end, the plan to supply Pat with the expense audit I had prepared was overcome by other events and he saw only the part dealing with the fund-raising dinners. After the scenario was played out, however, I knew my stock would not exactly be on the rise at the *new* Christian Coalition.

# 17

## Getting Sicker

A FTER A LONG HISTORY of impediments from the Internal Revenue
Service and the agency's deliberate attitude toward Christian
Coalition it became clear that they were determined to deny our tax ex-
empt 501(c)(4) status. Therefore, in mid-Spring, 1999, the Coalition gave
up the nine and a half year battle and announced the withdrawal of its
application. A letter from the IRS officially denying our status arrived
shortly thereafter.

Approximately one year earlier, Don Hodel had met with the IRS
in an attempt convince them of their duplicitous mind-set regarding our
tax exemption, as they had granted such status to the overtly partisan
Democratic Leadership Council and to other liberal Democrat allies,
including the Sierra Club and the National Abortion and Reproductive
Rights Action League (NARAL), to name only a few. That effort was unfruitful, however. As an IRS representative haughtily told Don, "We're not
talking about *them*. We're talking about *you*."

Likewise, Randy Tate met with House Ways and Means Chairman
Bill Archer of Texas in mid-1998, hoping to get help with our IRS woes.
Archer soon spoke with the head of the IRS as well as with (Clinton)
Treasury Secretary Robert Rubin,* but had no success in ameliorating
our situation.

Along with pulling the tax-exempt application, Pat Robertson and
the board, on the advice attorneys, decided to reorganize the Coalition
into two distinct organizations: the Coalition was renamed "Christian
Coalition International" and a new, totally separate "Christian Coalition
of America" was created by national headquarters in a friendly take over

---

* What Christian Coalition considered a confidential matter was leaked to the media
by a congressional staffer.

of the Texas Christian Coalition, which already had received its 501(c)(4) status approval from the IRS.

The fact that Texas and several of our state affiliates had been granted their tax exemptions by the IRS was bemusing, considering that the agency held such an intractable position regarding the national organization. I attributed it to staff in IRS field offices either not paying attention or being new in their jobs, being "asleep at the switch," to borrow a term from Ralph Reed.

Christian Coalition of America would carry on the same non-profit, non-taxable mission originally designed in 1989. Employees and payroll were transferred to the new organization.

Christian Coalition International soon filed suit against the IRS over the matter of its rejected tax status. The IRS case was so flimsy that they immediately began to back down for most of the years in dispute, holding out only for 1992, the year of the Bush-Quayle re-election campaign. A final settlement was reached in 2006, with Christian Coalition caving in to egregious demands by the IRS in restricting its voter guides. But the Coalition was in such poor shape by that time that it was akin to the NBA ruling that the Chicago Bulls (post-Michael Jordan) no longer were allowed to dunk the basketball.[1]

Meanwhile, at headquarters, week by week, Roberta Combs's authority became increasingly evident, as did dissatisfaction among the staff, with most being uncomfortable relating to both Randy Tate and her, no one knowing who was "the boss." The power-sharing arrangement simply was not working and in early June Randy and the board agreed that he would return to Washington to run the Capitol Hill office. He eventually accepted a vice presidency with a new Internet voter education service. Ken Hill also moved back to the capital, although not with the Coalition, eventually returning to government service,[†] and ultimately accepting a post at the Department of Homeland Security. Roberta stayed in Chesapeake under the new title of executive vice president.

On the same day we learned that Randy and Ken were leaving, Dr. Billy McCormack—in town for a board meeting—walked into my office with instructions for me: "You're the cheerleader," he said, explaining that a new job responsibility of mine was to keep everyone on the staff motivated and assure them that all would be okay. Fulfilling my task would

---

† Including being inside the Pentagon on September 11, 2001, but fortunately away from the crash site.

not be easy, as I was not convinced either. And, I had lost my two closest associates only minutes earlier. Who was going to cheer me up?

I was no more excited about working for Roberta than was anyone else. And she was wary of me in spite of our having worked together on various projects since 1988. As with any individual taking over a new operation, she was unsure as to whom to bring into her inner circle. In my case, I really could not blame her. I was very close with Hodel, Tate, and Hill, the three people she had replaced, and she likely realized that my loyalties lay with them, to say nothing of the doubts she certainly still had about my role in the expense investigation. She removed most of my managerial duties, preferring that the various department managers, who until that time had reported to me as director of administration, instead work directly with her, which left me with very little to do until it came time to get ready for Road to Victory in September, a conference so encompassing annually that virtually no one lacked duties to perform.

There was some *good* news in 1999. In August, Christian Coalition's victory in the FEC lawsuit was announced. The judge, while acknowledging that our preference for certain Republicans was obvious to her, ruled that except for two minor missteps the Coalition had violated no election laws. As Coalition lawyer Jim Bopp told ABC's Cokie Roberts during an earlier episode of *Nightline*, "Christian Coalition has to be judged on what it does, not on what its hopes are . . . I've never known coziness [with a political party] to suddenly become illegal,"[2] he continued.

The winning decision provided a bright spot in an otherwise abysmal year for the Coalition. As newspaper headlines around the country portrayed our win, we celebrated. Of course, the case had taken its toll on the Coalition, costing us millions of dollars in legal fees and in manhours—researching, photocopying, and shipping documents—as well as travel and salary costs for the employees who had to testify. The entire case was an enormous distraction and the FEC was quite aware of the negative effect it had on the Coalition even though it lost in court. FEC commissioner Bradley Smith told *World* magazine in 2002, "You could trace the real decline of the Christian Coalition through the 1990s right through the period the FEC was investigating, even though the investigation failed."[3]

Road to Victory '99, held the first weekend in October, went quite well considering all the turmoil the Coalition had been through. The enthusiastic crowd was down only by about 25 percent from the 4,000 people we had the previous year. Much credit went to major donor and event specialist Sharon Helton, who produced her sixth Road to Victory in as many years.

Our keynote speaker was NFL great Reggie White, who gave a poignant message about Christ-likeness and caring for the less fortunate. I particularly remember his regret that, while many ministers rightfully rushed to aide families and students after tragedies like the one at Columbine High School in Colorado, few were as eager to minister in violent situations in *inner city* high schools across America. His point, in addition to chastising a suburban provincialism among American Christians, was that maybe the latest incidents could have been prevented if we had reached out and dealt with the earlier ones. It was not the usual speech to a mostly white, mostly Republican audience, and our people loved it.

Road to Victory was a watershed as far as many staff were concerned, having set the completion of the conference as a target date to begin their job searches. Office computers and fax machines, both in Chesapeake and Washington, began to purr with the sound of résumés being updated and sent out. The entire Washington office was looking, as was most of the staff at headquarters. Personally, while I still was not actively looking for a new job, I updated my résumé for the first time since joining the Coalition over eight years earlier.

It just seemed that the Coalition didn't *do* anything anymore, Road to Victory being the exception. The state affiliates received no attention from headquarters, mostly because of the disorientation at the national office and because in running the entire operation virtually alone, Roberta just did not have the time. This left them to their own devices regarding keeping the state affiliate afloat,‡ as national wavered.

Roberta was a hands-on manager, to say the least. Several years earlier, upon learning that she had hired a young man from another state office to be executive director of her South Carolina operation, Ralph Reed affectionately remarked to another staffer and me that she was not looking for someone actually to *run* the state affiliate. "She just wants someone, who'll, you know, get the boxes out of the car," he said, referring to how most of our state chapters transported training materials.

‡ Which some did well.

A *St. Petersburg Times* investigative article that came out the day after Road to Victory went into detail concerning the staff departures since
Roberta had assumed leadership of the Coalition. Dee Benedict, a friend
of Roberta's from South Carolina, told the reporter that the staff changes
were by design from the beginning: "I know on a national level she had
to really go up there and clean house at the invitation of Pat Robertson,"[4]
she said.

Ralph Reed also defended Roberta in the piece. "Roberta's getting a
bum rap because she is taking the steps that Robertson wanted taken, and
in some cases that involved asking people to leave. They blame Roberta
when she's only loyally serving Pat,"[5] Ralph told the reporter.[§] Both he
and Benedict were correct. Whether Roberta merely followed Pat's orders,
as they said, or whether she actually influenced his decisions in the first
place, it is hard to imagine her taking an action at that point in time without being certain of his support.

In early 2000, Roberta told *The Virginian-Pilot* that she was not worried about staff depletions,[6] and at about the same time, was quoted in
*Congressional Quarterly's Daily Monitor* as further downplaying the matter: "No one is irreplaceable ... We had senior people that we didn't need,"[7]
she said.

"Irreplaceable" was an interesting word for Roberta to use, I thought,
considering that, other than deputy Chris Freund taking over communications after press secretary Molly Clatworthy left to get married, not
one member of the senior staff *had been* replaced. Whenever one of the
division heads left the organization Roberta just took on his or her responsibilities. Her stamina was impressive, to say the least.

On October 22, Randy Tate (no longer with the Coalition) called
me to see if I had heard anything about a decision to move the national
office to the Washington, D.C. metro area. He had gotten wind of a rumor
from more than one source and wondered what I knew. I had not heard
the rumor; however, a few days earlier, that possibility had crossed my
mind. Christian Coalition International, the renamed, original Christian
Coalition with its rejected tax status, was about $3 million in debt and
was nothing more than a weight around the neck of Christian Coalition
of America, the new, tax-exempt organization. And our $20,000-a-month
Chesapeake lease was in the name of CCI. Nothing would prevent the

§ Even though, as stated in the previous chapter, he criticized her "Pat event" strategy
in the same article.

relocation of CCA; and, if CCI went under, only its creditors would care. Plus, the move was a perfect opportunity to slash payroll, as people with families in the area would certainly not pull up stakes and move to Washington for an hourly wage job. In the end, only one employee made the move.

The decision to relocate the organization's headquarters most likely had been made at a board meeting held in conjunction with Road to Victory a few weeks earlier. Two additional members had been added to the board. Both were lawyers and I suspected the board's purpose in adding them was to handle much of the Coalition's soon-to-increase legal duties, alleviating a great deal of the need to pay outside attorneys.

Each year after the November elections, the pace became really slow around headquarters, lasting through the holidays, but picking up quickly in the New Year. This November was slower than ever and to fill the time I decided to embrace Billy McCormack's prescribed role for me as motivator to the staff. I spent significant time each day talking with employees. I would check in on them, tell a joke, read a Scripture or in some way try to be encouraging. Although it may have made me seem unproductive to some, it was a board-ordered responsibility.

During this time, I kept up to date on various employees' job searches and offered assistance where I could. Many were exchanging e-mails back and forth with former employees who had gone to other positions, hoping for referrals and other job search assistance. As the size of our staff continued to shrink, I drew solace from the Prophet Jeremiah, whom God left behind to minister to the small number of Israelites left in Jerusalem while the masses had been taken to Babylonian captivity under King Nebuchadnezzar. One day late in the year my devotional Scripture reading included Jeremiah's book of Lamentations, where I noticed similarities between Israel's plight and that of Christian Coalition over the previous year. "How lonely sits the city [t]hat was full of people!"[§]

Morale around the office was dismal and the organization's health continued to decline. One former senior staff member told me that the group's spiraling downfall was, to him, like learning that a beloved relative had come down with a fatal illness, and having to watch that loved one just get sicker, day by day.

§ Lamentations 1:1.

On a Friday afternoon just after the elections, the Coalition's move to Washington, D.C. was finally announced to the staff after a reporter from *The Virginian-Pilot* got wind of the rumor and began calling in search of confirmation. That was the signal for the staff members in Chesapeake, who had not already been doing so, to begin looking for new jobs. One by one they left, and soon our staff had dwindled to about twenty, in the incoming mail and data processing operations. A little money still was coming in from our most loyal (but uninformed) donors. As I told one of the Coalition's fund-raising consultants: "We have a great file. They love America, they love God, and they love Pat."

Many supporters were still smarting over Pat's words during the impeachment of President Clinton, however, and the organization was never able to entice the majority to return. Only the most loyal—or those least aware of the group's downfall—continued to give, and even they, not for long.

Another blow to Christian Coalition's national reputation occurred in December when *FORTUNE* magazine released the results of its 1999 *Power 25* poll. After having occupied seventh place on their list for each of the last two years, we had fallen to thirty-fifth place. Writer Jeff Birnbaum summed up our decline: "The Christian Coalition experienced the biggest fall from grace ... The drop probably resulted from a shakeup in top management ... "[8] The *FORTUNE* poll results, along with a soon-to-follow lawsuit filed by a direct mail vendor whom we owed almost $400,000,** looked like they might be the final nails in the Coalition's coffin.

*Roll Call* soon reported that the National Republican Congressional Committee (NRCC) had contributed $500,000 to a new grassroots group known as the U.S. Family Network, which had ties to House Majority Whip Tom DeLay. Republican "insiders" told *Roll Call* that the purpose of the new group was "to revive organized Christian support for GOP issues" because of the financial woes and staff turmoil within Christian Coalition. "GOP insiders believe the Coalition is largely a spent political force, and Republicans are eager to have something to take its place in time for the 2000 elections and beyond" they concluded.[9]

---

** Over the next few years, other suits were filed by a direct mail shop and an additional fund-raising consultant, as well as at least one law firm, movers, additional mail shops, and consultants, according to reporter Bill Sizemore in an October 8, 2005 article in *The Virginian-Pilot*, entitled "Once-powerful group teeters on insolvency."

A few days later *The Washington Post* retold the story under a headline that read, "GOP Looking Beyond Christian Coalition in 2000."[10] This all followed on the heels of pundits questioning 2000 GOP presidential hopeful Gary Bauer's legitimacy as a candidate, postulating that he probably was running in order to establish himself as the new national spokesman for the Christian Right.[11] Party leaders already were carving up our territory and reporters were choosing our successor.

Roberta called my home the Saturday after the Coalition's relocation was announced but I was not there, getting her voice mail later in the day. For several weeks I had realized I did not want to remain with the Coalition and, further, that if management had wanted me to stay we would have talked about the possibility by that time. Finally, Roberta asked to meet with me on Friday, December 17, when she informed me that I was being laid off because the Coalition "no longer could afford my salary" as I was the highest paid staff member at the time. Of course, that was only because those who made more money had either resigned or been fired.

It was a solemn occasion to learn that my time at Christian Coalition had come to an end. On the other hand, I was delighted to be released from the turmoil of the organization, so different from the one that I had served for nine years. I soon said farewell to the remaining employees, and then left the office en route to southwest Virginia where I customarily spent the Christmas holidays. Only for the first time since 1991, I knew I would not be returning to Christian Coalition in the New Year.

# 18

## Toto, We're Not in Chesapeake Anymore

A HISTORY OF THE Christian Coalition could actually have ended with the preceding chapter. The organization that was founded in 1989 ceased operations in mid 1999—continuing to exist only on paper, if even that—and its mission was transferred to the new, Christian Coalition of America, which bore no resemblance to its predecessor and did very little of the same activity. Yet the leadership—and the media—continued to equate the two, therefore I will do so as well, accepting the synonymous nature of both groups with this chapter, before we go on to look at the legacy left by the Coalition over the decade of the 1990s.

The first weeks of the new millennium found Christian Coalition of America preparing to relocate to Washington, D.C. with most all of the employees in Chesapeake laid off and looking for jobs. Moreover, the possibilities of the fulfillment of the Coalition's ten-year plan for the 2000 election cycle appeared impossible. The presidential primary season was in gear, but rather than swinging a heavy bat, due to dire financial problems and the obfuscation of its sense of purpose, Christian Coalition, instead, was struggling for its very survival.

As the presidential election approached, the big prize still waited. A member of our movement had not yet been elected president, and we had experienced eight years of the Clinton presidency, the very antithesis to almost everything we stood for. In 2000 there was hope, however, and in November, George W. Bush carried the banner, becoming the forty-third President of the United States.

After taking office in January, 2001, President Bush, through his key initiatives and Cabinet appointments, promised to be the type of president that conservatives had waited for since Ronald Reagan left office in 1989. Even before his first hundred days had passed, *The Washington Post* reported, "President Bush is quietly building the most conservative administration in modern times, surpassing even Ronald Reagan in the ideological commitment of his appointments . . ."[1]

In October, 2001, *The 700 Club* featured a segment with political commentator Fred Barnes, where the discussion centered on President Bush's feeling that he had been called by God to lead the country through the crisis of September 11.[2] At the same time, there were numerous reports of the place that prayer and daily Bible reading played in Bush's life, including (the same day Barnes was on *The 700 Club*) a *USA Today* account of his kneeling in prayer beside a foreign head of state in the White House. The piece quoted Bush, describing his faith: "That doesn't make me better than anybody, it just adds perspective . . . The rock on which I stand is something other than the moment, the emotion of the day,"[3] he said.

In a Christmas Eve article, *The Washington Post* focused on the president's role as *the* leader of religious conservatives in America:

> For the first time since religious conservatives became a modern political movement, the [P]resident of the United States has become the movement's de facto leader—a status even Ronald Reagan, though admired by religious conservatives, never earned. Christian publications, radio and television shower Bush with praise, while preachers from the pulpit treat his leadership as an act of providence.[4]

Pat Robertson had supported Bush virtually from the outset—after Senator John Ashcroft of Missouri, Pat's first choice, and the choice of a majority of Christian Coalition state directors according to a 1998 straw poll—announced that he would not run. Pat defended Bush's pro-life credentials, noting Bush's choice of pro-life justices for the Texas Supreme Court while governor as proof that he would do likewise as president.

Pat was not happy, however, when Bush decided to skip the Coalition's annual Road to Victory conference two months before the 2000 election. Bush had a debate with Al Gore a few days later and needed that time to prepare, rather than to fly to Washington to speak to a group that already was going to vote for him. Pat showed such public displeasure with Bush's absence, at one point even being quoted by *The New York Times* as calling Bush's chances of being elected "very iffy,"[5] that Bush finally acquiesced and issued a videotaped greeting that was shown on the second day of the event. And Pat felt Bush needed the Coalition, telling a reporter with the Associated Press that his organization could "be the margin of victory and it's just unwise to take it for granted."⁶

There weren't all that many conference attendees for Bush to take for granted, however. In fact, the 2000 event was the Coalition's lowest turn-out for Road to Victory since before the Republican takeover of Congress in 1994. *U.S. News and World Report* counted just over 1,500 attendees at the conference that year, causing the Coalition, as an unnamed state leader told the magazine, to arrange tables in the Washington Hilton's cavernous ballroom in order to take up space and make the room appear to be full.⁷*

Pat Robertson was right, however, about the Coalition's *potential* role in the margin of victory in the election that rocked the country and caused pundits to dust off their copies of the Constitution. Unfortunately, aside from announcing it would distribute 70 million voter guides, an amount that would have been impossible even in 1996 at the height of its power and organizational strength, the Christian Coalition was virtually unheard of leading up to Election Day.

Christian Coalition's contribution to Bush's victory was minimal if at all. After spending the previous decade building a sophisticated grass-roots infrastructure geared toward the 2000 election, the year's arrival found the Coalition in shambles and the GOP scrambling to coordinate get-out-the-vote efforts in the pro-family community, efforts they could have counted on the Coalition to take care of just four years earlier. In the absence of an organized Christian Coalition at the national level, the Bush campaign relied on consultant Ralph Reed to work with the active Coalition state chapters across the country in their get-out-the-vote pro-gram, and likely consulted him about the fallout from skipping Road to Victory.

According to *The Washington Times*, exit poll analysis showed that six million religious conservatives did not vote in the 2000 election.⁸ In a *USA Today* article contrasting the stronger evangelical turnout for Bob Dole in 1996 with the millions who went AWOL in 2000, George Mason University's Mark Rozell gave the following analysis:

---

* A strategy we had considered as a potential necessity for the 1997 event before it was moved to Atlanta. The Washington Hilton ballroom had been filled to capacity in both 1995 and 1996, which made reaching a higher number of attendees in 1997 im-possible. Although, the pre-1997 discussion included inviting only the top activists, for specialized training.

The answer is that Dole did not deliver the religious right vote in 1996 so much as the Christian Coalition did. The religious right's leading organization was at the height of its power in the mid-1990s . . . It was organized to the precinct level throughout the country, was flush with cash and produced about 40 million voter guides for the general election . . . [By the 2000 election cycle] the Christian Coalition was barely a shell of its former self . . . overcome by multiple lawsuits, high-level-staff infighting . . . The Christian Coalition just wasn't much of a player in 2000, and the loss for Bush was real. The percentage of the electorate identified as "religious right" declined from 17% in 1996 to 14% in 2000. The turnout among white evangelicals fell 6% from 1996 to 2000.[9]

While Rozell may have given too much credit to the effect Christian Coalition had on the overall evangelical voter turnout in 1996, statistics show that if more evangelicals had voted in 2000 Bush would have gotten the lion's share of them. As *The Washington Post* reported, those religious conservatives who did vote in 2000 preferred Bush over Gore by 61 to 38 percent,[10†] and a post-election survey led by University of Akron Professor John C. Green found that those who *did* vote among regular church-going, white evangelicals—the Coalition's core constituency—voted in far larger percentages for Bush in 2000 (84 percent) than they had for Dole in 1996 (70 percent).[11]

A higher evangelical turnout in 2000 would have given Bush a greater margin of victory and spared the country the Florida recount debacle.[12] And a healthy Christian Coalition could have helped a great deal. While the scores of thousands of core activists the group had trained and motivated over the years undoubtedly engaged themselves in 2000, millions of average church-going voters stayed home, possibly due in part to their not receiving a Christian Coalition voter guide on the Sunday prior to Election Day.

Had the Coalition been in a position to conduct its usual pre-election voter education and get-out-the-vote activities, it could be argued that Bush would have won the nationwide popular vote, which would have prevented the Democrats from using Gore's popular vote margin to cast aspersions on Bush's genuine victory. And the Electoral College may have turned out differently also.

---

†. The *Almanac of American Politics* gave an even higher percentage.

Bush would have surely won more votes in bellwether states, not the least being Florida. He would have done much better in Michigan, where organized labor showed amazingly strong support for Gore after having been given the day off from work to vote and politic for the Democrats. In Pennsylvania, a strong state for the Coalition, an organized Christian Coalition get-out-the-vote campaign may have pushed him past Gore's slim margin of victory there. Bush may also have won in smaller states like Iowa, Wisconsin, and New Mexico, all of which had close margins of victory for Gore.

Christian Coalition of America was based in a plush Capitol Hill suite of offices at 499 South Capitol Street and its Internet Web site looked better than ever. Looks can be deceiving, however, and even though a host of entertainers and pro-family leaders attended an Inauguration bash it held, there appeared to be little else going on at headquarters at the time.

In further embarrassment to the Coalition, it became obvious that political insiders were more than aware that the group had lost its prowess. When *FORTUNE* magazine released its 2000 list of the *Power 25*, the Coalition had fallen to an irrelevant sixty-fifth place.[13] In only two years, the group had gone from number seven to number sixty-five.

Possibly most serious of all, the headquarters itself was in disarray. Shortly after the Bush Inauguration, ten African American employees filed a racial discrimination suit against the organization. The plaintiffs contended they were forced to enter the office through a back door and had to eat in a different break room than the white employees. They also charged that they were not allowed to attend the events in conjunction with Bush's Inaugural. And later, a white employee joined the suit, contending he had been fired due to his refusing to spy on the plaintiffs. The ordeal was even played out on the Washington, D.C. local television news complete with an undercover camera that had been smuggled into Coalition headquarters.[14]

The suit appeared to be dubious in its origin, facts, and spirit, however. First, according to a staff member who worked in the Capitol Hill office during the time in question, *every* employee was required to use the rear entrance prior to nine o'clock when the front door to the building became electronically accessible. He himself had done so on occasion. The plaintiffs, however, began their shifts before that time, which required entering through the back door.[15] Second, I recall from the Chesapeake office that hourly workers needed to unwind when on break, and often became somewhat loud. The D.C. break room's close proximity to the waiting area for visitors may have been a factor. Finally, most data processing and other hourly employees rarely attended Coalition events due to their jobs requiring them to remain at headquarters.

What may have been an otherwise workable situation, however, likely was exacerbated by the plaintiffs' awareness of an unofficial but quite evident class system that began in 1999 and undoubtedly followed the group from Chesapeake to Washington. From the outset, membership in Roberta Combs's inner circle had been obvious but volatile, dynamics far less likely to be tolerated in cosmopolitan Washington, D.C. After the group moved to Washington, Roberta staffed the office with her daughter and son-in-law, in addition to others from South Carolina, likely due to the sense of support those people provided, but which left little room in the "circle" for the rest of the staff, most of whom were African American.

If any favoritism existed in the Coalition's office in 2000, and if earlier experiences in Chesapeake were any indication, those offended were left out not so much because of what they were as because of what they were not. Roberta probably never made the connection in her mind that those employees required to enter through the back door were black, while those who used the front were white.

A January, 2002, article in *The Washington Times* announcing that the racism suit had been settled out of court for $325,000 included new information that the Coalition had come under FBI investigation for fraud in relation to the Inaugural gala held the previous January. It had been overbooked, forcing approximately 400 formally-clad attendees who had paid for the event to watch on closed-circuit television, rather than attend the actual dinner.[16] Ironically, the *Times* reporter with the byline on the piece, and who had broken the story a year earlier, also was a journalism professor at Regent University's Alexandria, Virginia, campus, meaning he was on Pat Robertson's payroll at the time he authored the article.

And where did the FBI receive at least part of its information? From individuals who were Coalition employees at the time, including, as I understood, a Caucasian woman who was not involved in the racism suit.[17] Even though Roberta's management style was no more popular at the group's previous headquarters, such retribution against her would have been unlikely there. The move to Washington made the organization more susceptible to scrutiny—from without and from within. To paraphrase Dorothy from *The Wizard of Oz*: "Toto, we're not in Chesapeake any more."

Perhaps the biggest indication that the sun had set on Christian Coalition came on December 5, 2001, when Pat Robertson formally announced his resignation as the group's president and chairman. "My active participation as a member of the Christian Coalition has come to an end,"[18] he said. On the next morning's *The 700 Club*, he shared his decision with his viewers, and announced that CBN's ministry would see its 200 millionth profession of faith in Jesus Christ by the end of the year. "That to me is paramount,"[19] he concluded. A CBN news release quoted Pat's resignation letter to the Coalition's board: "With the few years left to me of active service, I must focus on those things that will bring forth the greatest spiritual benefit."[20]

As we saw in Chapter 2, to Pat Robertson the gospel of Jesus Christ is preeminent. And Pat strongly believes that America has a special place in world evangelization, considering its role as a beacon for freedom and protection to the rest of the world, as well as the fact that American Christians fund the majority of the world-wide missions, which is one reason he has always been almost as dedicated to saving America as he has been to saving souls.[‡]

There had been at least one earlier sign that Pat may have been planning to call it quits with the Coalition. As quoted by a reporter from the *(Newark, NJ) Star-Ledger* just prior to the 2000 elections, Pat said, "I could hand it off and say we've had a good run . . . Assuming that Mr. Bush wins, with his testimony of faith, I think we can say we've done what we set out to do."[21] Pat sounded remarkably similar to Jerry Falwell's eulogy upon shutting down the Moral Majority after President George H. W. Bush was elected in 1988. "[W]e've come here to announce—mission accomplished," Falwell told the Religion Newswriters Association. "While the work of Moral Majority will go on forever, the Moral Majority organization is no longer needed."[22]

But was there more? Did Pat have additional reasons for walking away? Surely the group's slide into obscurity since Ralph Reed and, later, Don Hodel resigned was an embarrassment to Pat. And the charges of

‡ Pat had a personal link to America's spiritual and political history. His ancestor Bishop Robert Hunt was among the first English settlers in Virginia in April, 1607—*thirteen years prior to the Pilgrims in Massachusetts*—who planted a cross at Cape Henry and dedicated the new land to the glory of God.

racism and fraud that had been alleged against the group threatened to damage his public image. "[O]nce I'm involved, I'm responsible," Pat told *The Virginian-Pilot* shortly after he resigned, noting that the incumbent responsibility would divert his attention away from Regent University and CBN.[23]

According to Roberta, however, Pat simply beat her to the punch. In her speech at a rejuvenated Road to Victory in 2002, which was held after a one-year moratorium, Roberta said that late in the previous year she told Pat that she wanted to leave the organization and return to South Carolina. She said Pat replied that he was about to go on a prayer retreat and that she should wait until he returned before making her final decision. Once back from his time of prayer, he evidently told her that she could not leave because *he* was going to resign and she, therefore, needed to be the group's new president.[24]

Actually, it was unclear as to from what exactly Pat had resigned. The CBN news release read simply "Christian Coalition," but again, by that time, there was no organization of that name due to the 1999 reorganization into Christian Coalition of America. So, from which did Pat resign? Most likely, it was both, but there were no clarifications. I saw nothing making an official explanation and, oddly, no reporters seemed to inquire.

As mentioned earlier, in his January, 1999, letter accepting Don Hodel's resignation, Pat rebuffed his own suggestion that he himself step aside from the organization, stressing that if he did so the Coalition would not likely be able to survive. By late 2001, however, he had changed his mind, telling his *700 Club* audience on the morning after he resigned: "[T]he Coalition will go on with out me."[25] During the intervening two years, however, the organization's troubles had only grown worse.

Still, however, Pat had a degree of influence. His name and photo remained on the Coalition Web site; he spoke at the 2002 Road to Victory conference; and Roberta continued to consult Pat on matters. "We still talk," she told me when I inquired about Pat's resignation during a call she made to my suburban Washington, D.C. office in 2002.

The relationship must have taken a turn afterward, however, as some months later Pat's photo suddenly disappeared from the Coalition's Web site, as did the narrative regarding his role in the organization's founding. All vestiges of Pat Robertson had been wiped out of the Christian Coalition's history and public image.

Less than ever was happening at Christian Coalition by the time of the 2002 mid-term congressional elections. Voter guides were produced, but rather than being printed and distributed, were available only on the Coalition's Web site. I communicated with a few friends among the group's state directors, who were quite displeased. One (former) state director told me that he personally coordinated the production and distribution of Christian Coalition voter guides in his state in lieu of the national headquarters having done so.

An e-mail was sent from headquarters, instructing activists to "download and print [voter guides] out on your desktop printer. We strongly encourage you to print them out and make copies to distribute in your churches,"[26] read the alert. "A number of our chapters are downloading the voter guides and distributing them,"[27] the Coalition's media director told *The Washington Times*. In reality, only the most dedicated of activists would undertake such an encumbering a task.

"[T]he group does not strike fear into Democrats as it once did," wrote a reporter for *The Hill*, adding, "GOP lawmakers say the organization has both a different focus and a much smaller role to play now." The article quoted one unnamed Republican aide: "[Christian Coalition] does not have impact ... they don't have the juice."[28] Nevertheless, Roberta was undaunted, telling the Associated Press at Road to Victory, "I think that as long as we're here, we'll also have influence."[29]

The Coalition struck little fear into Republicans either. Throughout the 1990s, lack of Coalition support for an item on the GOP agenda was considered a serious blow to Party leaders in Congress. But in the fight against passage of the *Bipartisan Campaign Reform Act of 2002* (aka McCain-Feingold), which conservative groups felt was unconstitutional due to its limits on political expression, a bedrock liberty this country was founded upon, the Coalition's opposition was relegated to e-mails. In its heyday, Christian Coalition would have fought such legislation in the trenches with every fiber of its being, with chapters and activists organizing around the issue and putting pressure on their representatives in Congress, and with Ralph Reed or Randy Tate on television thundering away at Republican proponents of the legislation, promising primary opposition in their next election cycle. In 2002, however, that activity was not possible.

By 2002, the name Christian Coalition was mentioned in Washington only by conservatives who lamented the group's demise and the vacuum that left for Republican candidates needing its help. "Republicans decided they could not simply count on . . . the Christian Coalition to mobilize social and religious conservatives,"[30] wrote *The Washington Post*. As I heard a senior official at the Republican National Committee lament in the months leading up to the 2004 elections: "We don't have an organization like the Christian Coalition that we can rely on [to turn out pro-family voters this year]."[31]

Of course, the Coalition did not have the funds to work with as it had enjoyed during its heyday. With a friendly White House and Republican control of Congress, most conservative political organizations experienced a serious dip in fund-raising, just as, inversely, they had huge swells of support during the "dark ages," aka the Clinton years, when money seemed to grow on trees at times.

Although, Christian Coalition's financial problems were far worse than other groups, as evidenced by their eviction from their Capitol Hill office suite late in the year for reasons of nonpayment of rent, a fact I learned by chance through a prospective tenant of their space. The Coalition had to rely on a series of third-party fund-raising practices, such as cell phone, online shopping, and other consumer sales rebate programs, finally reporting only $5.2 million in income for the year 2002, while it had $5.6 million in expenses.[32]

About the only things of note that did happen at the Coalition in 2002–2003 were an alliance with extreme liberal Democrat Senator Charles Schumer of New York in an attempt to curtail spam e-mail[33] and a meeting between Roberta and New York's *other* extreme liberal Democrat Senator, Hillary Clinton, about a prescription drug benefit addition to Medicare.[34]

Something may have rubbed off from talking with those two liberal senators, as in mid-2003 the national Christian Coalition surprised many, and most notably its state affiliate in Alabama, by coming out in support of a referendum for a huge tax increase for social services championed by Alabama's Republican governor. Christian Coalition State Director John Giles helped lead the opposition and the eventual, resounding defeat of the tax increase, but he learned that his national headquarters was actively working against him only when a reporter notified him that Roberta had been in the state holding news conferences in support of the tax.

Giles later told the *Los Angeles Times* that his state affiliate had been victim of "a total bushwhack"[35] from its parent office.[§]

The years 2004 and 2005 were quieter than ever at the Coalition, while occurrences both expected and bizarre surfaced in 2006. First, the Coalition state affiliates began to break off from the national Coalition, when the Iowa, Maryland, and Ohio chapters announced their formal separation. In an August, 2006, article in *Legal Times*, the respective state directors from Iowa and Ohio were quoted as giving particularly poignant reasons for their state affiliates' secession: "We operated despite the noose around our neck . . . Over the last six years there was a complete lack of (national) leadership. We used to be in constant contact with D.C. lobbyists. Now nothing,"[36] said Iowa's long-time leader Steve Scheffler. And as if speaking from the same set of talking points, Ohio's director added: "This is a culmination of a diminished presence on Capitol Hill. It is about a lack of leadership at the top. It's the straying away from the original mission."[37]

When the Alabama affiliate, perhaps the most effective state chapter in the Coalition's history, announced its separation a couple of weeks later, Giles was quoted in an Associated Press article as saying there were at least a dozen reasons states were leaving, one of which being a perception that the group had diverted from its traditional concerns, such as abortion, in favor of addressing fringe issues, including access to the Internet. As Roberta Combs told the AP: "We're going to have a new mission, a new vision—much more broad-focused. [The breakaway state chapters] don't like some of the comments I've made about the environment and some of these other issues."[38]

In the *Legal Times* article, Furman University professor James Guth sounded like an undertaker poised to inject the embalming fluid: "There's no reason to pay attention to [the Coalition]. They're dead. They may continue for a while in name only . . ."[39] And as one county chapter leader in South Carolina told *The (Columbia) State* newspaper, "The [C]oalition as we knew it doesn't exist."[40] But Roberta Combs was incredulous: "I don't know why people think we've gone away," she said. "We're here every day."[41]

Finally, rumors began to circulate that Roberta Combs was searching for someone to take Christian Coalition of America off her hands,

[§] Over 30 organizations opposed the Alabama tax increase, as reported by gopusa.com on August 22, 2003.

with one prospect being former presidential candidate Alan Keyes—who declined. The term caveat emptor applied with an exclamation point, if for no other reasons than the Coalition's lingering debt, law suits from former vendors, even a suit from a law firm that formerly represented the organization, and other baggage still attached to the national group.

When Orlando pastor Joel Hunter finally was chosen as the new president of the Coalition, he either backed out or was jettisoned before his scheduled January, 2007, start because he wanted to add issues to the Coalition's portfolio, *including the environment*. Evidently, Roberta and the board had since learned that "greening" the Coalition would be a nonstarter with their remaining supporters. "When we really got down to it, they said: 'This just isn't for us. It won't speak to our base, so we just can't go there,'"[42] Pastor Hunter told *The New York Times*.

The only conceivable hope for the original spirit and mission of the Christian Coalition to revive would have been for the state chapters to have banded together, as the Colonies did over 200 years ago, assert their legal independence from the national corporation, and create a new national group to coalesce around, perhaps an informal association of Christian Coalition state affiliates. The leadership could have been one of the states' own choosing, a national Coalition that would truly serve the states, rather than ignore, detract from, and actively work against them. As we saw earlier, however, the strongest state affiliates (including Georgia) decided simply to break off and change their names, although still continuing the same mission they had been working on since the early 1990s.

Many serious blows were inflicted on Christian Coalition—some from without and others from within. Those from outside were not as devastating, but with so many blows dealt from within, opponents were hardly needed. As one who in a small way helped build the organization, I tremendously regretted its embarrassing and irrelevant status, but that made it no less real.

# Epilogue

# The Legacy

$\mathbf{R}$ALPH WALDO EMERSON WROTE, "An institution is the lengthened shadow of one man." While Christian Coalition as an organization failed to find longevity, the question nonetheless arises as to whose shadow will loom largest over the memory the Coalition leaves in American politics. Will it be that of its entrepreneurial founder, Pat Robertson? Or the talented, shrewd architect, Ralph Reed? Or perhaps the widely-respected, self-sacrificing stabilizer, Don Hodel? Or will it be the final caretaker, Roberta Combs?

Pat Robertson will weigh most heavily in a philosophical discussion—not only regarding the Coalition but also the other entities he founded, primarily CBN and Regent University. As stated by Richard John Neuhaus, founder of the Institute for Religion and Public Life: "[I]n terms of cultural and political change, [Robertson] certainly was a catalyst of historic importance."[1]

One would be hard-pressed to argue, however, that any other than Ralph Reed's name and persona will be more closely linked to that of Christian Coalition as historians ponder the organization's legacy. And we can only wonder what would have come of the group had he—or Don Hodel—remained for the long-term. Finally, Roberta Combs, still at the helm as this page was written, will have her rightful place, as well.

One evening in 1992, Ralph, National Field Director Guy Rodgers, and I were talking in Ralph's office when he indicated that a key signal of the success of the organization would be if members of Christian Coalition's staff moved on to work in significant and influential political jobs. In other words, Christian Coalition should be a training ground and a launching point for future conservative campaign managers, congressional staffers, and candidates for office.

Many among the Coalition staff graduated to such positions. Among others, members of the senior staff went on to direct communications for the Republican Party's senatorial campaign committee; to coordinate activities for a House of Representatives majority leader; to head up grassroots coalitions for the George W. Bush re-election campaign; and to assist in policy formulation for the governor of Virginia. Others have been hired by national and state public policy and political organizations, and in key positions with conservative personalities, with several working for conservative elected officials, while yet others founded new groups of their own. Wherever they are now, however, they each are stronger and better at what they do for benefit of having worked together as part of the cohesive unit that was the Christian Coalition from 1989 through 1999.

Likewise, many Coalition leaders at the state and county level were elected, appointed, and promoted to positions of influence, including a Florida congressman, at least three Republican Party state chairmen around the country, several Republican National Committee members, and at least one executive director of a state party. There are numerous state senators and state representatives from among our ranks, including no fewer than five* (four Republicans and one Democrat) who are Regent University graduates, two of whom are African American women.[2] And two Regent alumnae have been chosen as district court judges in their respective states.[3] Finally, Regent alumnus Bob McDonnell of the landmark Virginia Beach state legislative class of 1991 went on to be elected attorney general of Virginia. Their successes are even more crucial to fulfillment of Christian Coalition's motto: *giving Christians a voice in their government again.*

I was reminded of Ralph's earlier statement to Guy and me as I watched ABC's *This Week* in late 1999 when commentator Bill Kristol described Ralph as being part of the old guard support enjoyed by George W. Bush in the upcoming 2000 presidential primaries.[4] I enjoyed the oddity of Kristol's statement. Ralph Reed, youthful former leader of the Christian Coalition, *old guard*? Could it be? Old guard, at thirty-eight?

I thought of Kristol's comment a few months later as I flipped through an issue of *Newsweek* during an airport layover. Amidst a story of the Bush campaign was large photo of Bush and Ralph standing together backstage at an event.[5] "Ralph's gotta love this," I thought. After years of

* Some of these people I know personally; and some I read about in news articles, as noted.

seeking a place at the table in American politics for Christian Coalition, he not only had earned *himself* a place at that table but was discussing strategy with the man who would soon plan the menus.

Ralph had arrived. He was in a position of influence in Republican circles as an advisor to presidential candidate Bush and, later, as a member of the Republican National Committee as Georgia's state party chairman, where in 2002 he led the virtual overthrow of Democrat rule in the Peach State, helping knock-off both a sitting U.S. senator and the incumbent governor, as well as the well-entrenched leaders of both houses of the Georgia legislature.

For the first few years after leaving Christian Coalition, however, Ralph appeared to be less effective than as the executive director of the Coalition, losing early prominent elections for which he was a consultant. He seemed to be out of sight for the next couple of years, far less noticeable than in his former role, even announcing a potential shift from political consulting to advising corporate clients.[6] Often when I spoke with former Coalition staff members and state directors they asked, "What's Ralph up to these days?"

As Georgia GOP chairman, however, he worked behind the scenes, telling the *Atlanta Journal Constitution* there were three keys to the Party's future success: a strong precinct organization, an agenda to attract voters, and better quality candidates.[7] He also chose a representative to the Latino community,[8] which helped Georgia Republicans, as Ralph told *Investor's Business Daily*, garner 40 percent of the Hispanic vote in 2002.[9] And on Election Day, Ralph came back with a huge bang. It was like 1991 in Virginia Beach all over again, only to much greater heights. Georgia Democrats did not even know what was happening until election night when it was too late and they found themselves—you might say—in body bags.

Finally, in 2004 Ralph announced plans to seek the lieutenant governorship of Georgia two years later, with reporter Ralph Hallow of *The Washington Times* asserting that Ralph would use the post as a stepping-stone to later run for governor and, ultimately, for president.[10] At first it appeared that Ralph would easily win the Republican primary against his lesser-known GOP state senator opponent; however, Ralph's campaign stumbled due to a lavish and lucrative former association with disgraced Washington lobbyist Jack Abramoff, which caused Ralph to lose the Republican primary—by a whopping twelve percentage points.

A series of e-mails back and forth with his political mentor, Abramoff, full of frat-boy braggadocio, piqued the interest of the media and brought about Ralph's defeat.

And in proof that irony exists in politics, none other than Senator John McCain chaired the U.S. Senate committee investigating Ralph's relationship with Abramoff. As a consultant for the 2000 George W. Bush presidential campaign, Ralph had participated in get-out-the-vote activities for Bush against McCain in Southern states.[†] In politics, what goes around often truly does come around. Ralph was merely implicated, however, not formally accused, in the Abramoff scandal.

Ralph therefore found himself somewhat between two worlds. Christian activism saw him rise to the pinnacle of its ranks, only to return to the secular politics of his youth, an arena in which he was also very successful, yet far below the status as the central, leading figure he had been in the Christian Right. He, of course, has plenty of time to make a political comeback, as well as to play a role with Christian campaigns and causes, as Catholic leader Deal Hudson proclaimed to the *The New York Times* after the Georgia primary loss: "We forget that there is nobody who is able to craft a message for religious conservatives better than Ralph Reed . . ."[11] And Ralph may have been thinking similar thoughts himself, telling the *Times*, "First bids for elected office are always tough, and I am not the first person to lose a first campaign."[12]

Christian conservatives might be somewhat wary of Ralph for a bit, however, even with the Abramoff-related accusations being unfounded, due to the association between the two, the brush with casino gambling,[‡] the egotistical tone of their e-mails, and the few millions of dollars Ralph's firm made in the process. *World* magazine editor Marvin Olasky, for one, loudly trumpeted the connection to Abramoff as his periodical printed as many as ten investigative and strongly critical articles around Ralph's bid for lieutenant governor.[13] "[W]e keep trying to be salt not sugar," wrote Olasky, describing his publication's desire to "ask tough questions."[14]

As Christian Coalition executive director, Ralph often said that his long-term goal for the Coalition was that it be institutionalized in American culture, staying strong and prosperous over the decades, much like others, including the National Rifle Association. As he told reporters

† See Chapter 1.

‡ The focal point of the Abramoff affair.

Dan Balz and Ron Brownstein: "The 1994 election signaled our political arrival. Now we have to institutionalize . . . not [just] reach the voters and turn them out. We've already done that. Now we want to make ourselves permanent . . . It's what the social historians call professionalization [sic]."[15] But when Ralph left in 1997 experts wondered whether the organization could survive. When Don Hodel resigned two years later, they wondered again. Just shy of three years after that, Pat Robertson resigned and, by that time, there was no reason to wonder any longer, and only the most faithful even cared.

Part of the maturation for any group is that the organization must grow larger than its leader(s), a problem Christian Coalition faced, and failed, on two occasions. First, in 1997, after Ralph's resignation, the Coalition could not keep up the pace he had set for it due to the financial, legal, and regulatory problems inherited by his successors, as well as the loss of his talents before a television camera. Revenue fell drastically after his impending departure was announced and continued to decline in the first months after his replacements had signed on. Second, in 1999, almost two years later, during the impeachment of President Clinton, the Coalition was divided when its members wanted one course of action and its founder chose another.

Pat Robertson was right in a way that none of us could have imagined in January, 1999, when he said on *The 700 Club*, "Clinton's won!" While Bill Clinton kept his job after the impeachment proceedings, his "victory" over the process started a domino effect that brought on the self-destruction of Christian Coalition.[§]

While Christian Coalition failed to endure as an organization, the question arises as to what its legacy will be. How is American political life different due to the Coalition's decade-long prominence in leading religious conservatives?

A Republican presidential debate in December, 1999, showcased the huge impact Christian Coalition had made on the public discourse in America when George W. Bush was asked which philosopher had made

§ However, just as Pat's own "loss" in 1988 resulted in the beginning of Christian Coalition, which made its mark on American politics for a decade, so also with Clinton's "win" there was more than met the eye. Voters in both parties were motivated—at least temporarily—to denounce immoral behavior among their elected officials, as well as those whom they associated with them, as it may be argued was exemplified by Clinton Vice President Al Gore's loss of both their home states, Arkansas and Tennessee, as well as the quadrennial Democratic stronghold state of West Virginia, in the 2000 election.

the greatest impact on his life. The soon-to-be president responded without hesitating: "Christ. Because He changed my heart." When also asked, others in the debate followed suit, either naming Jesus or including Him among their favorite philosophers. According to *Newsweek's* Howard Fineman: "George Bush's statement that Christ was his favorite philosopher will turn out to be the most memorable sound bite of the early season ... [I]t was an extraordinary moment where secular politics and religious faith intersected."[16]

The "philosopher" question would have still been asked that night, and one or more candidates might have named Jesus as their answer. But one thing is for certain, had there not been a Christian Coalition active in America over the preceding decade (and to a lesser extent the Moral Majority before it), Bush's answer to the question would not have been a major news story for days to come. The impact of Christian Coalition's very existence, its having been active, had left an indelible impression on American politics.

Those who will write tomorrow's history books have already begun to express their opinions about the influence of religious conservatives in general and Christian Coalition in particular. Catholic University's Mark Rozell* told *The Virginian-Pilot* in late 2001 when Pat Robertson resigned as the Coalition's chairman: "Christian Coalition, without a doubt, has been the most successful social conservative organization in this country."[17]

And few could argue. Innumerable family-friendly laws are on the books at the local, state, and national levels due in part to the Coalition's support; numerous pro-family candidates were elected by voters having access to the Coalition's voter guides; and millions of new conservative voters have been trained and empowered to exercise their citizenship as never before. That is the real legacy of Christian Coalition—not merely in elections or in legislation, but in people, in the sleeping giant that was awakened by Ronald Reagan in 1980, powered by the Robertson campaign in 1988, and trained, energized, and formed into an electoral and legislative force by Christian Coalition throughout the 1990s.

As the University of Akron's John C. Green** told *The (Bergen County, NJ) Record* in 2005: "Evangelicals have become three things since 1980:

¶ Now at George Mason University.
** Later with the Pew Forum.

200

more organized politically, more Republican and more active participants in politics."[18] And Green similarly told *National Review* in early 2001: "[W]hen Republicans think about their base, they think about evangelical voters. This wasn't true twenty-five years ago."[19]

The change is not only one in terms of Christian voters, but also of Party leaders and elected officials, as listed earlier. "They're on the inside now,"[20] Furman University's James Guth told the *Greenville (SC) News* in 2001, referring to the Coalition's influence in his state, a characterization which certainly applied in most of the other states. And United Press International[††] reported that December:

> [Christian Coalition's] more active and politically skilled members outgrew the organization, making the jump into party politics. In several states, Republican Party leadership was pushed aside in favor of a more activist breed of organizers and managers, many of whom either had the support, or were themselves members, of the [C]oalition ... [W]ith the [P]resident of the United States self-identifying with their values and much of their political agenda made law, the movement may be stronger than ever even as its most well-known organization may be about to disappear.[21]

Likewise, Rozell told *The Virginian-Pilot* at the 2000 Republican National Convention in Philadelphia: "The Christian [R]ight is stronger today than ever before. Many evangelicals who once spurned political involvement have become active members of the Republican Party."[22] And the University of Virginia's Larry Sabato said in the A&E network's 2000 *Biography* on Pat Robertson: "He himself failed as a politician. And yet he went on to influence politics more than many people who are elected president or speaker of the House."[23]

Pat Robertson's words from *The Plan*, his 1989 retrospective on his own presidential campaign, therefore approach the prophetic:

> Could it be that the reason for my candidacy has been fulfilled in the activation of tens of thousands of evangelical Christians into government? This campaign taught them that they were citizens with as much right to express their beliefs as any of the strident activists who have been so vocal in support of their own radical agenda at every level of our government. For the first time in recent history, patriotic, pro-family Christians learned the simple techniques of effective party-organizing and successful campaign-

†† A news service Pat Robertson once considered buying.

ing. Their presence as an active force in American politics may result ultimately in at least one of America's major political parties taking on a profoundly Christian outlook in its platforms and party structure.[24]

The above conclusions may only be temporal, however. Religious conservatives continue to need organizations to rally around. While experts agree that the movement is a fighting force, it must continue to be coalesced and invigorated. Professor Green's opinion is too simplistic. The movement may be more astute than ever before, but without further training, the motivation of seeing its leaders on television, and the lack of an opponent in the White House, its enthusiasm has already waned. As Ralph Reed often quoted Dr. Jerry Falwell, "When (American) Christians win, they quit. When they lose, they quit. They just quit."

Christian voters must be motivated, and they must be educated with accurate voting records so that they are not outwitted by moderate Republicans masquerading as pro-family candidates—to say nothing of the well-meaning Christians who continue to vote for liberal, pro-abortion, anti-American sovereignty Democrats, who continue to mortgage the financial security of future generations of Americans through economic profligacy.

Influencing legislation requires even more sagacity and effort, requiring effective organization, so that the grassroots remain engaged in the process. Also, there is political party organizing and intra-party clout, which are impossible to attain if Christians just wait until Election Day and then go out and vote. They must get involved in local party politics and do their part in helping to choose the candidates that are on the ballot, the very influence Christian Coalition wanted its activists to achieve.

Finally, conservative Christians must continue to become candidates for public office, themselves. No matter how astute and organized Christians are, they will not heartily support moderate Republican candidates who are not "one of them" based on their core issues, and those candidates, therefore, will lose. Only the worst imaginable Democrat candidates will motivate religious conservatives to enthusiastically support Republicans who do not represent them fully.

Christian Coalition has faded into memory while the culture and the government still wait. There remains a role in American politics that can be filled only by millions of Christians and other pro-family voters. A (small "c") coalition described in *First Things* by Richard John Neuhaus as "What may be the most important sociopolitical movement of our time."[25]

Christian Coalition abdicated its leadership role, but its supporters (and millions more like them) must go on. They still are Christians and they still are Americans. They continue to love their God and their country, and they want to preserve America for their children and grandchildren.

Further, conservative Christians continue to have definite opinions about the values that America should represent. Michael Barone, in the 2002 edition of *The Almanac of American Politics*, wrote that religious issues divide the American electorate like no other, including race. "The difference in voting behavior between the Religious Right and non-Christians is bigger than the difference between blacks and whites."[26] Just as conservative Christians voted in overwhelming numbers for George W. Bush in 2000, Barone observed that non-Christians turned out in similar majorities for Al Gore.[27] In what *The American Spectator* called the "God gap,"[28] partisan voting differences between Christians and non-believers continues to widen, with "one of the most reliable predictors of a voter's behavior on Election Day [being] his behavior on Sunday morning."[29]

David Frost once asked Ralph Reed about the Coalition's ultimate success. "All we need is a culture and a government that reflect the values of middle-America, and our agenda will be realized,"[30] Ralph said. While the culture and government have gone the opposite direction in recent years, Christian Coalition's legacy is nonetheless in place. And many dedicated servants will continue to personify it.

Homemakers will distribute voter education literature throughout their Congressional District and hold their congressman's feet to the fire on family issues. Teachers will work with pro-family candidates. Business owners will provide quality services to Christian organizations. And fathers and daughters will leave successful careers to become involved in the public debate.

Grassroots leaders will run for local office. Former elected officials will roll up their sleeves to become active in the political process again. And seniors will come out of private life in order to provide seasoned, principled leadership.

Thousands upon thousands of dedicated and motivated activists will answer the Apostle Paul's call to citizenship, George Washington's call to public service, Dr. Martin Luther King's call to speak out in non-violent opposition on behalf of the oppressed, and certainly not least, the millions of silent calls from unborn children in America and around the world.

But each Christian, whether politically conservative or liberal, also answers an earlier call, a call to discipleship, to love others, and to proclaim truth, made by a Jewish carpenter almost 2,000 years ago. And He gave the marching orders: "Go ye, therefore . . ."

# Notes

## Introduction

1. Conversation with Christian Coalition staff member, ca. 1998.

## Chapter 1: A Presidential Campaign Story

1. William Neikirk, "Resurrected Robertson Regains Stage," *Chicago Tribune*, February 27, 2000.

2. Warren Fisk, "McCain Attacks Christian Right Leaders," *(Norfolk) Virginian-Pilot*, February 29, 2000.

3. John McCain, interviewed by Larry King, *Larry King Live*, March 23, 2000.

4. David Nyhan, "McCain's History-Making Speech," *Boston Globe*, March 1, 2000.

5. William Neikirk, "Resurrected Robertson Regains Stage," *Chicago Tribune*, February 27, 2000.

6. Tucker Carlson, "On the Road," *Weekly Standard*, March 27, 2000, 31.

7. Pat Robertson, interviewed by Larry King, *Larry King Live*, CNN, September 13, 1999.

8. Tucker Carlson, interviewed by Bernard Shaw and Judy Woodruff, *Inside Politics*, CNN, February 16, 2000.

9. Gary Bauer, interviewed on MSNBC, February 16, 2000.

10. Conversation with Christian Coalition staff member Barbara Ray, February 17, 2000.

11. Bill Schneider, CNN Super Tuesday wrap-up, March 7, 2000.

12. Jeff Greenfield, CNN Super Tuesday wrap-up, March 7, 2000.

13. Bob Jones IV, "Straight Talk Veers Left," *World*, March 11, 2000, 32.

14. Candy Crowley, CNN Super Tuesday wrap-up, March 7, 2000.

15. William Bennett, Op-Ed, *Wall Street Journal*, March, 2000.

16. Ibid.

17. Tucker Carlson, "On the Road," *Weekly Standard*, March 27, 2000, 28.

18. Charles Krauthammer, "McCain in 2004," *Washington Post*, March 10, 2000.

19. Pat Robertson, interviewed by Bernard Shaw, Judy Woodruff and Jeff Greenfield, CNN's Super Tuesday wrap-up, March 7, 2000.

20 Ibid.

21 Ibid.

22 Nina Easton, *Gang of Five: Leaders at the Center of the Conservative Crusade* (New York: Simon & Schuster, 2000), 403.

23 Pat Robertson, interviewed by Robert Novak and Al Hunt, *Evans and Novak*, CNN, August 5, 2000.

24 Ibid.

25 Pat Robertson, interviewed by Bernard Shaw, Judy Woodruff, and Jeff Greenfield, CNN's Super Tuesday wrap-up, March 7, 2000.

26 Judy Woodruff, CNN's Super Tuesday wrap-up, March 7, 2000.

27 William Neikirk, "Resurrected Robertson Regains Stage," *Chicago Tribune*, February 27, 2000.

28 Kris Mayes, "Bush Attempting to Lure Christians From McCain," *(Phoenix) Arizona Republic*, February 11, 2000.

29 Nina Easton, *Gang of Five: Leaders at the Center of the Conservative Crusade* (New York: Simon & Schuster, 2000), 346–47.

30 Mary Jacoby, "What Has She Done to Christian Coalition?" *St. Petersburg (FL) Times*, October 3, 1999.

31 Ibid.

32 Hanna Rosin, "Christian Right's Fervor Has Fizzled," *Washington Post*, February 16, 2000.

## Chapter 2: A New Face in Town

1 Tom Scott, Road to Victory II, Virginia Beach, VA, September 12, 1992.

2 Jonathan Freedland, "Angel Face," *(London) Guardian*, August 24, 1995.

3 Ralph Reed, CBN employee chapel service, Virginia Beach, VA, ca. 1995.

4 Conversation with Americans for Robertson staff member Randy Estes, March, 1988.

5 Pat Robertson, letter to pastors, October 20, 1989.

## Chapter 3: Never Say Never

1 *Christian Coalition Ten Year Plan 1991–2000*, January 25, 1991, 1.

2 Ralph Reed, speech to Christian Coalition mid-Atlantic state chairman and executive directors, Annapolis, MD, 1996.

3 Cal Thomas and Ed Dobson, *Blinded By Might* (Grand Rapids, MI: Zondervan, 1999), 87.

4 Pat Robertson, CBN employee chapel service, Virginia Beach, VA, 1989.

5 Christian Coalition, *American at a Crossroads* videotape, 1990.

6 Don Hodel, interviewed by Steve Scully, *Washington Journal*, CSPAN, August, 17 1997.

7   Ibid.

8   *Senate Roll Call on (Clarence) Thomas, Washington Post,* October 16, 1991.

9   Statement occurred either at a staff meeting or in a hallway discussion.

10  Ralph Reed, Road to Victory Conference and Strategy Briefing, Virginia Beach, VA, November 15, 1991.

11  Mark O'Keefe, "Robertson's Phone Corps Boosted GOP," *(Norfolk)Virginian-Pilot,* November 9, 1991.

12  Ralph Reed, interviewed by David Frost, *Talking with David Frost,* PBS, May 19, 1995.

13  Ralph Reed, interviewed on *Crossfire,* CNN, mid-1990s.

14  Ralph Reed., interviewed by Judy Woodruff, *Inside Politics,* CNN, January 25, 2002.

15  This statement occurred in a Road to Victory staff planning meeting, Chesapeake, VA, 1991.

## Chapter 4: Who Do You Trust?

1   Dan Casey, "Pat Robertson's Hideaway," *Roanoke (VA) Times & World News,* January 8, 1995.

2   Bill Clinton, letter on behalf of Democratic National Committee supporter, August 19, 1992.

3   *Christian Coalition ACTION GRAM,* March 3, 1993.

4   Conversation with Ralph Reed, October, 1992.

5   Pat Robertson, letter on behalf of Iowa Committee to Stop ERA, undated, 1992.

6   Pat Robertson, interviewed by Larry King, *Larry King Live,* CNN, 1993.

7   Statement either from a hallway conversation or a Road to Victory planning meeting.

8   I remember this statement well but do not recall whether Ralph said it in a speech or in a television interview.

9   Ann Devroy, "Baker's Fix-It Campaign Becoming More Visible," *Washington Post,* September 14, 1992.

10  Mark O'Keefe, "Bush Plans Family Values Speech Here," *(Norfolk) Virginian-Pilot,* September 3, 1992.

11  Rob Eure, "Bush Talks Jobs, Not Values," *(Norfolk) Virginian-Pilot,* September 12, 1992.

12  Jerry Alley, "A 'God-solid' Ollie Preaches to the Choir," *(Norfolk) Virginian-Pilot,* September 20, 1992.

13  Joseph Coccaro, "If Bush Fails, Fingers Will Point Toward Christian Right," *(Norfolk) Virginian-Pilot,* October 4, 1992.

14  E. J. Dionne, Jr., "Taking Credit and Placing Blame," *Washington Post,* November 5, 1992.

15  Margaret Edds and Mark O'Keefe, "Bush Loss Opens Debate On Role of Religious Right," *(Norfolk) Virginian-Pilot,* November 6, 1992.

16   Pat Robertson, *The 700 Club*, CBN, November 5, 1992.

17   Joseph Coccaro, "Robertson Despondent Over Bush Loss," *(Norfolk) Virginian-Pilot*, November 4, 1992.

18   Ralph Reed, "Hold the Obituary: Republicans are Poised for Dramatic Comeback," *(Norfolk) Virginian-Pilot*, January 29, 1993.

## Chapter 5: 10,000 New Members a Week

1   Ralph Reed, "Priorities," *Christian American*, May-June, 1997, 54.

2   Ibid.

3   Hallway conversation with Judy Liebert.

4   Michael Weisskopf, "Energized by Pulpit or Passion, the Public Is Calling," *Washington Post*, February 1, 1993.

5   Tom Coburn, *Breach of Trust* (Nashville: WND Books, 2003), 11–12.

## Chapter 6: The File's for Ollie

1   Christian Coalition, *Statement by Ralph Reed*, February 15, 1994.

2   Conversation with Ralph Reed and other staff members, 1994.

3   Charles Krauthammer, "Demonizing the Religious Right," *Washington Post*, July 8, 1994.

4   Grover Norquist, "Hate Trick, and How It's Being Used," *Washington Times*, August 16, 1994.

5   Comments about South Carolina gubernatorial candidate David Beasley. Ralph used this line often, although, I am not certain of its origin.

6   Mike Russell memo to members of the media, "Christian Coalition Survey Results from Election Night," November 11, 1994.

7   Larry Sabato, "Pat Robertson," *Biography*, A&E, July 29, 2000.

8   Century Strategies, Web news article, http://www.censtrat.com, February 12, 2001.

9   Ralph Reed, interviewed by David Frost, *Talking with David Frost*, PBS, May 19, 1995.

## Chapter 7: A Place at the Table

1   Laurie Goodstein, "Gingrich Vows to Pursue Christian Coalition Agenda," *Washington Post*, May 18, 1995.

2   Dan Balz and Ron Brownstein, "God's Fixer," *Washington Post Magazine*, January 28, 1996, 28.

3   Ralph Reed, "A Wider Net," *Policy Review*, Summer, 1993, 31.

4   Christian Coalition, *Statement by Ralph Reed, Jr.*, May 17, 1995.

5   Christian Coalition news release, "Christian Coalition's Contract with the American Family Continues String of Victories," August 7, 1995.

6    Christian Coalition *Fact Sheet*, "Contract with the American Family—An Implementation Progress Report," May 7, 1998.

7    Judie Brown, "Rhetoric Against Reality—The Christian Coalition's Failure," *Celebrate Life*, September–October, 1995, 24–25.

8    Ibid.

9    Ralph Reed, interviewed by David Frost, *Talking with David Frost*, PBS, May 19, 1995.

10   Gloria Borger, "The Ralph Reed Primary," *U.S. News & World Report* online, December 29, 1997.

11   Ralph Reed, interviewed by David Frost, *Talking with David Frost*, PBS, May 19, 1995.

12   Richard John Neuhaus, "Ralph Reed's Real Agenda," *First Things*, October, 1996.

13   Mike Russell, Christian Coalition news release, October 6, 1994.

14   Walter Cronkite, letter on behalf of The Interfaith Alliance, undated, ca. 1996.

15   William F. Buckley, "The Cronkite Crusade vs. the Christian Right," *New York Post*, May 26, 1997.

16   Craig Donegan, "Christian Coalition Subverts Democracy," *(San Antonio) Express-News*, August 29, 1993.

17   Ralph Reed, Road to Victory Conference, Washington, D.C., ca. 1995.

18   Jill Zegeer, "Young's Spiritual Message Becomes Pointed," *Charleston (WV) Daily Mail*, May 23, 1995.

19   William Edelen, "Robertson's Rantings Recall Words of Third Reich," *Pueblo (CO) Chieftain*, January 20, 1993.

20   Rod Dreher, "Jesse Jackson Hit for Slurs on 'Religious Right,'" *Washington Times*, December 8, 1994.

21   Gerry Braun, Copley News Service, "Christian Coalition Blistered as Nazi-Like By ex-GOP Official," *Washington Times*, February 1, 1993.

22   Don Moseley, letter to Virginia local Republican chairmen, October 24, 1992.

23   Don Feder, "The Left's 'Dominionist' Demons," *FrontPageMagazine.com*, May 5, 2005.

24   Anthony Lewis, "Merchants of Hate," *New York Times*, July 15, 1994.

25   "Prejudice on Parade," editorial, *New York Times*, November 11, 1992.

26   Ibid.

27   Ibid.

28   Joan E. Rigdon, "Overcoming a Deep-Rooted Reluctance, More Firms Advertise to Gay Community," *Wall Street Journal*, July 18, 1991.

29   Beth J. Harpaz, Associated Press, "Controversial New York Cardinal Nearing Retirement as Health Fails," *(Norfolk) Virginian-Pilot*, November 21, 1999.

## Chapter 8: The Right Hand of God

1    Jeffrey H. Birnbaum, "The Gospel According to Ralph," *Time*, May 15, 1995, 28–35.

2  David Van Biema, "50 for the Future," *Time*, December 5, 1994, 48–65.

3  John Sedwick, "The GOP's Three Amigos," *Newsweek*, January 9, 1995.

4  Rob Lowe, interviewed by Jay Leno, *The Tonight Show*, NBC, 1997.

5  Ralph Reed, interviewed by David Frost, *Talking with David Frost*, PBS, May 19, 1995.

6  Ibid.

7  Jeffrey H. Birnbaum, "The Gospel According to Ralph," *Time*, May 15, 1995, 30.

8  Tim Russert, *Meet the Press*, NBC, November 29, 1992.

9  Ralph Reed, interviewed by David Frost, *Talking with David Frost*, PBS, May 19, 1995.

10  Ibid.

11  Ralph Reed, interviewed by John F. Kennedy, Jr., "Ralph Reed's Second Coming," *George*, July, 1997, 90–94.

12  I do not have notes on this interview but believe it was a mid-1990s episode of NBC's *Meet the Press*.

13  Bill Sizemore, "Fired Official is a Key Player in Christian Coalition's Troubles," *(Norfolk) Virginian-Pilot*, July 27, 1997.

14  Ibid.

15  Sheryl Henderson, "Hart Ache," *Mother Jones*, July-August, 1997, 13 – 14.

16  Bill Sizemore, "Fired Official is a Key Player in Christian Coalition's Troubles," *(Norfolk) Virginian-Pilot*, July 27, 1997.

17  Nina Easton, *Gang of Five: Leaders at the Center of the Conservative Crusade* (New York: Simon & Schuster, 2000), 386.

18  Bill Sizemore, "Fired Official is a Key Player in Christian Coalition's Troubles," *(Norfolk) Virginian-Pilot*, July 27, 1997.

19  Ibid.

20  Ibid.

21  Cokie Roberts and Brian Ross, *Nightline*, ABC, October 1, 1997.

22  Bill Sizemore, "Fired Official is a Key Player in Christian Coalition's Troubles," *(Norfolk) Virginian-Pilot*, July 27, 1997.

23  Alex Marshall, "Protesters of All Kinds Bring Messages," *(Norfolk) Virginian-Pilot*, September 12, 1992.

24  Ibid.

25  Bill Sizemore, "Fired Official is a Key Player in Christian Coalition's Troubles," *(Norfolk) Virginian-Pilot*, July 27, 1997.

26  Conversation with Christian Coalition staff member, ca. 1997.

27  Bill Sizemore, "Fired Official is a Key Player in Christian Coalition's Troubles," *(Norfolk) Virginian-Pilot*, July 27, 1997.

28  Nina Easton, *Gang of Five: Leaders at the Center of the Conservative Crusade* (New York: Simon & Schuster, 2000), 388.

29  Ibid, 387.

# Notes

30  Bill Sizemore, "Fired Official is a Key Player in Christian Coalition's Troubles," *(Norfolk) Virginian-Pilot*, July 27, 1997.

31  Nina Easton, *Gang of Five: Leaders at the Center of the Conservative Crusade* (New York: Simon & Schuster, 2000), 387.

## Chapter 9: For Such a Time as This

1  George Stephanopoulos, *All Too Human: A Political Education*, (New York: Little Brown, 1999), 336.

2  Howard Fineman, "Just the Ticket?" Newsweek, August 19, 1996.

3  Conversation with former RNC and Christian Coalition staff member, ca. 1997.

4  Dan Balz and Ron Brownstein, "God's Fixer," *Washington Post Magazine*, January 28, 1996, 25.

## Chapter 10: Transition

1  Ralph Reed, Christian Coalition news release, August 29, 1996.

2  Nina Easton, *Gang of Five: Leaders at the Center of the Conservative Crusade* (New York: Simon & Schuster, 2000), 388.

3  Ibid, 386.

4  Paul Kiel, "Interview with Nina Easton," *TPMmuckracker.com* April 6, 2006.

5  Conversation with senior Christian Coalition staff member, ca. 1997.

6  E. J. Dionne, "The Religious Right Loses Its Most Skilled Tactician," *(Norfolk) Virginian Pilot*, April 25, 1997.

7  Ralph Z. Hallow, "Is There Life After Reed for Christian Coalition?" *Washington Times*, May 2, 1997.

8  People for the American Way news release, "Reed Returns to Political Roots: Pat Robertson Loses Talented Front Man, April 23, 1997.

9  Esther Diskin, "The Christian Coalition Transition," *(Norfolk) Virginian-Pilot*, April 26, 1997.

10  Richard Berke, "Associates of Bush Aide Say He Helped Win Contract," *New York Times*, January 25, 2002.

11  Ralph Reed, interviewed by Judy Woodruff, *Inside Politics*, CNN, January 25, 2002.

12  Richard Berke, "Associates of Bush Aide Say He Helped Win Contract," *New York Times*, January 25, 2002

13  Ibid.

14  Associated Press, January 26, 2002.

15  Christian Coalition news release, "Christian Coalition Releases Samaritan Project," January 30, 1997.

16  Christian Coalition, *Statement by Ralph Reed*, January 30, 1997.

17  Nina Easton, *Gang of Five: Leaders at the Center of the Conservative Crusade* (New York: Simon & Schuster, 2000), 324.

18  Mark Silk (director of the Center for the Study of Religion in Public Life at Trinity College, Hartford, CT) as quoted in "The Rebirth of Ralph Reed," *Atlanta Jewish Times*, July 23, 1999, author not shown.

19  Ralph Reed, as quoted in "The Rebirth of Ralph Reed," *Atlanta Jewish Times*, July 23, 1999, author not shown.

## Chapter 11: Welcome to Arkansas

1  I was helping her search for the file.

2  "Let Them Speak," *(Norfolk) Virginian-Pilot*, August 4, 1998.

3  Ibid.

4  Donald Lambro, "AFL-CIO plans vast effort in '98 elections," *Washington Times*, May 10, 1998.

## Chapter 12: Washington Comes to Chesapeake

1  Conversation with Don Hodel, ca. 1999.

2  Conversation with senior Christian Coalition staff member, ca. June 1997.

3  Pat Robertson, Christian Coalition news release, "Christian Coalition Names Donald Hodel New President and Randy Tate New Executive Director," June 11, 1997.

4  Peter Baker and Laurie Goodstein, "Christian Coalition Rearranges Top Posts," *Washington Post*, June 12, 1997.

5  Ralph Z. Hallow, "Hodel to Head Christian Coalition," *Washington Times*, June 12, 1997.

## Chapter 13: Farewell

1  Pat Robertson, Christian Coalition Road to Victory '97, Atlanta, GA, October 1, 1997.

2  Ibid.

3  Warren Fiske, "Both Robertson, Beyer Claimed Too Much in Race, Analysts Say," *(Norfolk) Virginian-Pilot*, November 9, 1997.

4  Jeffrey H. Birnbaum, "Washington's Power 25" *FORTUNE*, December 8, 1997, 144–158.

5  Ibid., 154.

6  Melinda Henneberger, "Ralph Reed is His Cross to Bear," *New York Times Magazine*, August, 9, 1998, 26.

7  Ken Hill, e-mail to Christian Coalition senior staff, May 7, 1997.

8  Conversation with Don Hodel, ca. 2000.

9  Melinda Henneberger, "Ralph Reed is His Cross to Bear," *New York Times Magazine*, August, 9, 1998, 26.

10   Federal Election Commission, "In the Matter of Americans for Robertson, Inc., et al," May 3, 1996, 33–37.

## Chapter 14: Holding It All Together

1   Fred Barnes, "Bauer Power," *Weekly Standard*, December 22, 1997, 18–23.

2   Dan Balz and Ron Brownstein, "God's Fixer," *Washington Post Magazine*, January 28, 1996, 26.

3   Gary Bauer, "Washington Update," February 11, 1998.

4   Christian Coalition, *New Freedom for American's Families: A Blueprint for the 21st Century*, 1998.

5   Randy Tate, Christian Coalition news release, "Christian Coalition Grassroots Campaign Brings Marriage Tax Penalty to Forefront," July 1, 1999.

6   Don Hodel, Christian Coalition news release, "Making the 21st Century Safe for Faith," September 10, 1997.

7   Randy Tate, Christian Coalition news release, January 29, 1998.

8   Ibid.

## Chapter 15: Say It Ain't So

1   Pat Robertson, *The 700 Club*, January 20, 1999.

2   Ibid.

3   George Stephanopoulos, *All Too Human: A Political Education*, (New York: Little Brown, 1999), 442.

4   Richard L. Berke, "Robertson, Praising Speech, Suggests G.O.P. Halt Trial," *New York Times*, January 21, 1999.

5   As commonly discussed at the Christian Coalition office.

6   Pat Robertson, interviewed by Sam Donaldson and Cokie Roberts, *This Week*, ABC, January 24, 1999.

7   Ibid.

8   Ibid.

9   Ralph Z. Hallow, "Christian Coalition Simmers Over Leak," *Washington Times*, February, 1998.

10  Megan Rosenfeld, "On the Stump for The Value-Added Life," *Washington Post*, May 5, 1998.

11  Don Hodel, Christian Coalition Road to Victory '97, Atlanta, GA, September 13, 1997.

12  *Pat Robertson—His Proposals Step by Step*, Americans for Robertson cassette tape, 1987.

13  Conversation with Don Hodel, ca. 1999–2000.

14  Pat Robertson, letter to Regent University supporter, January 27, 1999.

15  Conversation with Don Hodel, 1999.

16  Ralph Reed, interviewed by David Frost, *Talking with David Frost*, PBS, May 19, 1995.

17  Pat Robertson, as interviewed by Larry King, *Larry King Live*, CNN, September 13, 1999.

18  Nina Easton, *Gang of Five: Leaders at the Center of the Conservative Crusade* (New York: Simon & Schuster, 2000), 344.

19  Pat Robertson, as interviewed by Larry King, *Larry King Live*, CNN, September 13, 1999.

20  Ralph Z. Hallow, "Christian Coalition President Resigns," *Washington Times*, February 10, 1999.

21  Stuart Rothenberg, "Has the Christian Coalition Lost Its Political Muscle?" *Roll Call*, March 8, 1999.

22  Ralph Z. Hallow, "Christian Coalition President Resigns," *Washington Times*, February 10, 1999.

23  Ibid.

24  Ron Fournier, Associated Press, "Oregon's Hodel Resigns from Christian Coalition," *(Portland) Oregonian*, February 10, 1999.

## Chapter 16: *Designing Women* Meets *The West Wing*

1  Conversation with Roberta Combs, 1999.

2  Conversation with Randy Tate, 1999.

3  Conversation with Christian Coalition senior staff member present at December 16, 1997, board meeting.

4  "Roll Call's Fabulous Fifty," *Roll Call*, 1998.

5  Richard John Neuhaus, "Ralph Reed's Real Agenda," *First Things*, October, 1996.

6  Liz Szabo, "Christian Coalition Losing Clout," *(Norfolk) Virginian-Pilot*, February 19, 2000.

7  Ibid.

8  Ibid.

9  Pat Robertson, interviewed by Larry King, *Larry King Live*, CNN, April, 1999.

10  Benjamin Domenech, "Slouching Toward Irrelevance," *National Review*, January 21, 2000.

11  Mary Jacoby, "What Has She Done to Christian Coalition?" *St. Petersburg (FL) Times*, October 3, 1999.

12  For examples see Robert Schlesinger, "Christian Coalition Struggles to Overcome Its Internal Divisions," *The Hill*, June 23, 1999.

13  Senior Christian Coalition staff member.

## Notes

## Chapter 17: Getting Sicker

1   I thought of this line when preparing for a 2001 media interview. However, when putting the finishing touches on the book, I ran across an article where an unnamed GOP strategist said something similar about the Coalition, albeit regarding a different subject and time period. Dan Balz, "Christian Coalition: A Staff to Match Its Goals?" *Washington Post*, March 12, 1999.

2   James Bopp, Jr., interviewed by Cokie Roberts, *Nightline*, ABC, October 1, 1997.

3   Tim Graham, "Courtroom Coalition," *World*, April 6, 2002.

4   Mary Jacoby, "What Has She Done to Christian Coalition?" *St. Petersburg (FL) Times*, October 3, 1999.

5   Ibid.

6   Liz Szabo, "Christian Coalition Losing Clout," *(Norfolk) Virginian-Pilot*, February 19, 2000.

7   Matthew Tully, "Christian Coalition is Moving to D.C., Months Behind Schedule," *Congressional Quarterly Daily Monitor*, March 15, 2000.

8   Jeffrey H. Birnbaum, "How to Buy Clout in the Capital," *FORTUNE*, December 6, 1999.

9   *Roll Call*, NRCC Maneuvering to Fill Christian Coalition Gap," as reported in *The White House Bulletin*, Bulletin Broadfaxing Network, December 7, 1999.

10  Juliet Eilperin, "GOP Looking Beyond Christian Coalition in 2000," *Washington Post*, December 15, 1999.

11  Including a late 1999 *Washington Times* piece.

## Chapter 18: Toto, We're Not in Chesapeake Anymore

1   Dana Milbank and Ellen Nakashima, "Bush Team Has 'Right' Credentials," *Washington Post*, March 25, 2001.

2   Fred Barnes, interviewed by Pat Robertson, *The 700 Club*, CBN, October 9, 2001.

3   Judy Keen, "President Bush's Faith," *USA Today*, October 9, 2001.

4   Dana Milbank, "Religious Right Finds Its Center in Oval Office," *Washington Post*, December 24, 2001.

5   Richard L. Berke, "Some Quiet Support on Stigmatic Topics," *New York Times*, September 27, 2000.

6   Eun-Kyung Kim, "Pat Robertson: Coalition Important," Associated Press, September 29, 2000.

7   Michael Shaffer, "Say a Prayer for the Christian Coalition," *U.S. News & World Report*, May 21, 2001.

8   Ralph Z. Hallow, "Religious Right Loses Its Political Potency," *Washington Times*, May 20, 2001.

9   Mark J. Rozell, "Bush's Wild Card: The Religious Vote," *USA Today*, September 21, 2004.

10    Thomas B. Edsall, "Census a Clarion Call for Democrats, GOP," *Washington Post*, July 8, 2001.

11    Associated Press, "Voters Differ on Religion and Presidential Politics," January 27, 2001.

12    A similar thought was expressed by Bush pollster Fred Steeper, interviewed by Ralph Z. Hallow, "Christian, But No Longer a Powerful Coalition," *Washington Times*, March 14, 2001. "We probably could have won the popular vote and not have had a tie in Florida," he said.

13    Jeffrey H. Birnbaum, "Fat & Happy in D.C." *FORTUNE*, May 28, 2001, 94 – 100.

14    Del Walters, "Suing the Christian Coalition," I-Team Exclusive, WJLA-TV, July 31, 2001.

15    Conversation with former Christian Coalition staff member, ca 2002.

16    George Archibald, "Christian Coalition Settles Workers' Race-Bias Lawsuits," *Washington Times*, January 3, 2002.

17    Conversation with former Christian Coalition staff member, ca. 2002.

18    Pat Robertson, interviewed by Associated Press, December 5, 2001.

19    Pat Robertson, *The 700 Club*, CBN, December 6, 2001.

20    Pat Robertson, CBN news release, "Pat Robertson Resigns From Christian Coalition," December 5, 2001.

21    David Gibson, "A Politicized Robertson Leaves Right in the Lurch," *(Newark, NJ) Star-Ledger*, October 29, 2000.

22    Marjorie Mayfield, "'Mission Accomplished': Moral Majority To Disband," *(Norfolk) Virginian-Pilot*, June 12, 1989.

23    Steven G. Vegh and Bill Sizemore, "Robertson Departs Christian Coalition," *(Norfolk) Virginian-Pilot*, December 6, 2001.

24    Roberta Combs, Christian Coalition Road to Victory '02, Washington, D.C., October 11, 2002.

25    Pat Robertson, *The 700 Club*, CBN, December 6, 2001.

26    "Christian Coalition Voter Guides Are Now Available," Christian Coalition of America e-mail, November 4, 2002.

27    Larry Witham, "Religious Activists Spar Over Voters Guides: Churches Weigh Biennial Political Roles," *Washington Times*, November 2, 2002.

28    Michael S. Gerber, "Can Christian Coalition Rise Anew?" *The Hill*, October 9, 2002.

29    Associated Press, "Christian Coalition Pitches Its Power," October 12, 2002.

30    Dan Balz and David S. Broder, "Close Election Turns On Voter Turnout," *Washington Post*, November 1, 2002.

31    Republican National Committee conference call with pro-family leaders, 2004.

32    Christian Coalition of America financial report for fiscal year ending December 31, 2002.

33    Devlin Barrett, "Spam Fight Unites Liberal, Conservatives," Associated Press, June 11, 2003.

## Notes

34  Jennifer Berry Hawes, "Charleston Native Leads Christian Coalition of America Down New Paths," *(Charleston, SC) Post and Courier*, August 25, 2003.

35  Jenny Jarvie, "Christian Coalition is Splintering," *Los Angeles Times*, September 5, 2006.

36  Nathan Carlile, "Christian Coalition Struggles for Viability," *Legal Times*, August 7, 2006, 10.

37  Ibid.

38  David Crary, "Christian Coalition Losing Chapters," Associated Press, August 23, 2006.

39  Nathan Carlile, "Christian Coalition Struggles for Viability," *Legal Times*, August 7, 2006, 10.

40  Lee Bandy, "Christian Coalition Fading Fast," *(Columbia, SC) State*, September 18, 2005.

41  Nathan Carlile, "Christian Coalition Struggles for Viability," *Legal Times*, August 7, 2006.

42  Neela Banerjee, "Pastor Chosen to Lead Christian Coalition Steps Down in Dispute Over Agenda," *New York Times*, November 28, 2006.

## Epilogue: The Legacy

1  Steven G. Vegh, "Robertson Building His Legacy on Religion, Politics," *(Norfolk) Virginian-Pilot*, March 22, 2005.

2  Jon W. Glass, "Political Aspirants Have Regent Roots," *(Norfolk) Virginian-Pilot*, April 8, 2004.

   Joe Miracle, Regent University news release, "Regent Alum Serves as Speaker Pro Tempore in Louisiana," April 28, 2004.

3  Jon W. Glass, "Political Aspirants Have Regent Roots," *(Norfolk) Virginian-Pilot*, April 8, 2004.

   Devorah Williams, "Regent Alumna Elected NC District Court Judge," January 8, 2002.

4  William Kristol, *This Week*, ABC, 1999.

5  Unfortunately, I did not purchase the magazine, therefore I cannot reference it here.

6  Jim Galloway, "Wunderkind Image Shed as Reed Takes Helm of GOP," *Atlanta Journal Constitution*, May 13, 2001.

7  Ibid.

8  Tinah Saunders, "Reed Goal is Ending Fighting in Party," *Atlanta Journal Constitution*, May 13, 2001.

9  Sean Higgins, "Georgia GOP's Reed Expects Big Gains for Party In South," *Investor's Business Daily*, December 10, 2002.

10  Ralph Z. Hallow, "Reed Said to See Georgia As Path to the White House," *Washington Times*, January 18, 2005.

11  David Kirkpatrick, "Rejected by Evangelical Base, Politician Ponders Next Role," *New York Times*, July 22, 2006.

12 Ibid.

13 Thomas B. Edsall and Dan Balz, "From a Conservative, a Lack of Compassion for Ralph Reed," *Washington Post*, March 26, 2006.

14 Marvin Olasky, "Tough Questions," *World*, March 4, 2006.

15 Dan Balz and Ron Brownstein, "God's Fixer," *Washington Post Magazine*, January 28, 1996, 27.

16 I took notes on the 1999 interview where Howard Fineman uttered these words, however, I neglected to record the specific network, program and date.

17 Steven G. Vegh, "Robertson Departs Christian Coalition," *(Norfolk) Virginian-Pilot*, December 5, 2001.

18 John Chadwick, "Preaching Politics," *(Bergen County, NJ) Record*, April 2, 2005.

19 John J. Miller, "Out of the Arena: Pat Robertson, Past and Present," *National Review*, May 28, 2001.

20 Dan Hoover, "Christian Coalition Fraying at the Edges," *Greenville (SC) News*, June 4, 2001.

21 Peter Roff, "Analysis: Faded Robertson Fades," UPI, December 6, 2001.

22 Warren Fiske, "Christian Coalition Still a Force at Convention," *(Norfolk) Virginian-Pilot*, August 2, 2000.

23 Larry Sabato, "Pat Robertson," *Biography*, A&E, July 29, 2000.

24 Pat Robertson, *The Plan*, (Nashville: Thomas Nelson, 1989), 177.

25 Richard John Neuhaus, "Ralph Reed's Real Agenda," *First Things*, October, 1996.

26 Michael Barone, "The 49% Nation," *Almanac of American Politics* (Washington, DC: National Journal, 2002), 27.

27 Ibid.

28 Patrick Hynes, "Keeping the Faith," *American Spectator*, February 6, 2007.

29 Ibid.

30 Ralph Reed, interviewed by David Frost, *Talking with David Frost*, PBS, May 19, 1995.

# Acknowledgments

Always foremost, the **Lord Jesus Christ**, Son of God and Creator of the universe—the only name under heaven by which we may be saved (Acts 4:12).

**Kellie**, my darling wife—a publishing and marketing expert, who always believed in this project.

**Mom and Dad**—who instilled in me the values of faith, honesty, and hard work.

## CHRISTIAN COALITION LEADERS AND STAFF

**Ann Ballard**—for her tireless dedication to Christian Coalition, its cause, and its activists. Christian Coalition's longest-serving employee.

**Chuck Cunningham, Chris Freund, Ken Hill, Steve Jordan, Lisa Pesquera, Guy Rodgers, Molly Shepherd, The Honorable Randy Tate, Paula Wells,** and **SteveWolkomir**—co-workers who provided friendship in good times as well as (for those who remained) during troubled months.

**Barbara S. Hodel**—my favorite person who has a building named after them; and one with whom I look forward to running in the streets of heaven . . . or sooner.

**The Honorable Donald Paul Hodel**—a true Christian, mentor, and friend; a patriot and consummate Reaganite; who taught me that "servant" begins with "I."

**Ralph E. Reed, Jr.**—a brilliant strategist who showed me that "cannot" should exist in no one's vocabulary.

**The Rev. M. G. "Pat" Robertson**—whose vision and commitment to our Lord have paved the way for countless advancements against the gates of hell.

**Christian Coalition State Directors** across America—for their supreme service and sacrifice to the movement, and for their friendship; to name a few, **Jeff Baran, Sara Hardman, Clay Mankamyer,** and **Bob and June Russell.**

**RESOURCE** *Publications*, for all their help and support for *this* publication. I especially thank Christian Amondson and his editorial staff for all their advice and service.

# About the Author

Joel D. Vaughan is special assistant to the president with a multi-national Christian ministry. He served with the Christian Coalition from 1989–1999 in positions ranging from volunteer, to deputy national field director, to director of administration and assistant to the president. Vaughan was vice president of a political advertising firm, and served in political campaigns and organizations. A native of the Commonwealth of Virginia, he holds a bachelors degree in economics and business, and a masters degree in biblical studies. He and his wife, Kellie, reside in Colorado, along with their kitten, Virginia.

Joel Vaughan may be contacted at ccRiseandFall@live.com

# Index of Names

# Index

# Index

# Index

Reed, Ralph (cont.)
and 1996 Republican National
Convention, 97–101; 102, 104, 106;
resignation of, 107–10; and Karl
Rove, 111–12; 113, 116, 117, 118,
119, 120, 123, 125, 128; and 1997
Road to Victory farewell, 133–36;
and Christian Coalition financial
crisis, 139–41; 144, 145, 149, 157,
160, 161, 162, 164, 165, 166, 170, 172,
176, 178, 179, 185, 191, 195, 196; and
lt. governor race, 197–98; 199, 202,
203, 220
Reese, Pee Wee, 136
Richards, Ann, 73–74
Ripken, Cal, 126
Robb, Charles, 27, 71
Roberts, Cokie, 153–54, 177
Robertson, Dede, 129, 134, 136
Robertson, Gordon, 14, 28
Robertson, Pat, ix, xi; and 2000 primaries,
3–10; and Christian Coalition
founding, 11–15, 23; and 1988 presidential campaign, 16–17, 202; 18, 20,
21, 22, 28, 30, 31, 32, 34, 35, 36, 38,
40, 42, 44, 46, 48, 49, 53, 55, 58, 60,
62, 64, 66, 67, 69, 71, 72, 73, 74, 79,
81, 82, 86, 87, 89, 92, 93; and 1996
Republican National Convention,
98; 102, 103, 104, 105; and Reed resignation, 110–11; 113, 114, 115, 119,
120, 123, 125, 126, 129, 134, 135, 136,
137, 138; and Christian Coalition
financial crisis, 139–42; 143, 145,
146, 147; and Clinton impeachment,
151–60; and Hodel resignation,
161–62; hiring Roberta Combs,
163–70; 171, 172, 173, 174, 175, 179,
181, 184, 185, 188; resignation of,
189–90; 195, 199, 200, 201, 220
Robinson, Jackie, 136
Rodgers, Guy, 20–21, 26, 34, 39, 40, 41, 42,
46, 62, 63, 64, 67, 165, 195–96, 219
Ross, Brian, 129–31, 134
Rothfeld, Mike, 38
Rove, Karl, 111–12, 169
Rozell, Mark, 185–86, 201, 200–201
Rubin, Robert, 175
Rudman, Warren, 4, 8

Russell, Bob and June, 47, 220
Russell, Mike, 56, 81, 87, 103, 132
Russert, Tim, 87

Sabato, Larry, 74, 201
Santorum, Rick, 73
Sasser, Jim, 73
Scanlan, Fr. Michael, 21
Scanlon, Heidi, 54, 67
Scheffler, Steve, 193
Schlafly, Phyllis, 2, 42, 99, 101, 126, 149, 162
Schumer, Charles, 192
Schwartz, Rhonda, 129
Scott, Tom, 11–12
Seinfeld, Jerry, 56
Shafer, Fred, 11
Shelby, Richard, 27
Shepherd, Molly Clatworthy, 179, 219
Smith, Bradley, 177
Sorkin, Aaron, 152
Specter, Arlen, 147
Stallings, Moody, 29, 92
Stanley, Charles, 21, 47
Stephanopoulos, George, x, 88, 96, 151
Stolle, Ken, 29, 31
Sutherlin, Allan, 12
Synar, Mike, 63

Tate, Randy, 28, 74, 125–27, 132, 137, 138,
139, 140, 142, 143–45, 146, 147, 149,
150, 153–57, 162, 164, 165, 166, 170,
173, 175, 176, 177, 179, 191, 219
Testrake, John, 56
Thomas, Cal, 22
Thomas, Clarence, 26–27
Tucker, Jim Guy, 100
Tucker, Karla Faye, 157
Twain, Mark, 36

Vaughan, Kellie, 219, 221
Vaughan, Ralph and Mary K., 219
Ventker, Dave, 92
Volle, Paul, 154

Wallace, George, 44
Warner, John, 64, 70, 71
Washington, George, 203
Watts, J. C., 98
Weinhold, Dick, 28, 141

# Index